CHILDREN OF BABYLON

CHILDREN

of

BABYLON

Suzanne Chandler

LONGMEADOW
PRESS

Copyright © 1993 by Suzanne Chandler

Published by Longmeadow Press, 201 High Ridge Road, Stamford, CT 06904. All rights reserved. No part of this book may be reproduced or utilized in any form or by any means, electronic or mechanical, including photocopying, recording or by any information storage and retrieval system, without permission in writing from the Publisher.

Cover design by Mike Stromberg

Interior design by Richard Oriolo

Library of Congress Cataloging-in-Publication Data

Chandler, Suzanne, 1962–
    Children of Babylon / by Suzanne Chandler.—1st ed.
    p.   cm.
    Includes bibliographical references.
    ISBN (invalid) 0-681-41624-4
    1. Motion picture actors and actresses—United States—Biography. 2. Children as actors.   I. Title.
PN1998.2.C43 1992
791.43′028′092273—dc20
[B]   92-35655
                                                                CIP

ISBN: 0-681-41642-4

Printed in United States of America

First Edition

0 9 8 7 6 5 4 3 2 1

ACKNOWLEDGMENTS

The author would like to express her gratitude to the people who helped make this book possible:

Madeleine Morel and Daniel Bial for their guidance and professionalism.

David Adler and Tim Ryerson for their encouragement.

To my parents, Lawrence and Eileen Chandler, for their belief in me and this project.

And special thanks to Ray Whalen, Sr. and the staff of Globe Photos whose assistance on this project were immeasurable.

CONTENTS

Introduction   xi

PART I   AFTER CANCELLATION

Lauren Chapin Didn't Know Best	7
Tommy Rettig: Life Without *Lassie*	15
Patty Duke: From Miracle Child to Manic-Depressive	18
Butch Patrick: Demon Child	28
Kristy McNichol: From Family to Empty Nest	30
The Curse of Diff'rent Strokes	37
Enough Is Enough	50
The Life and Loves of Danny Bonaduce	55

PART II   ALL IN THE FAMILY

Drew Barrymore: Little Girl Stoned	65
Carrie Fisher: Princess Leia Lands in Rehab	73
Jamie Lee Curtis: An Imperfect Life	80
Desi Arnaz, Jr.: Little Ricky Grows Up	88
At the Wheel with Griffin O'Neal	94

Part III   The Rise and Fall of the Brat Pack

Whatever Happened to Emilio Estevez?	107
Good Time Charlie Sheen	116
Moore or Less	124
Ally Sheedy: Poetry from the Edge	133
Born Again Christian Slater	140
The Poison Penns	147

Part IV   Sex, Photos, and Videotape

Lisa Bonet's Double Image	165
The Taming of Melanie Griffith	171
Traci Lords: A Test of Character	180
How Low Is Lowe?	185
Julia Roberts: A Pretty Available Woman	193
Brooke Shields: Mother's Little Girl	203

Part V   The Comeback Kids

Jodie Foster: Running from Her Past	216
Matthew Broderick: The Road Back	227
Anjelica Huston: Out of the Shadows	233

Part VI Fade to Black

Brandon de Wilde	246
Dominique Dunne	250
Heather O'Rourke	254
Rusty Hamer	258
Rebecca Schaeffer	261

Part VII From Here to Obscurity

Conclusion	279
Bibliography	283

INTRODUCTION

Hollywood history is filled with the shocking accounts of former child stars whose lives have gone awry. Mickey Rooney, Elizabeth Taylor, Judy Garland, and James Dean are just a few of the former child actors whose lives have been closely linked to tales of substance abuse, sexual promiscuity, and in some cases tragic endings.

Despite this fact, each year hordes of overly ambitious parents flock to Hollywood with tots in tow in the desperate belief that they have sired the next Jodie Foster or Ron Howard. They send these youngsters to voice, acting, and singing lessons. They drag them from one cattle call to the next in the hope that their child will be discovered, become famous, and make tons of money. What many of them fail to realize is that for the most part talent is secondary. Probably the most important requirement that one really needs to make it in show business is, namely, a connection.

More than other industries, Hollywood is awash in nepotism. Would young **Macaulay Culkin** be where he is without encouragement from his aunt Bonnie (*Die Hard*) Bedelia? Would a rather effete-looking **Jason Gould** have won the role of an aspiring football player in *The Prince of Tides* had not the star and director been his mother Barbra Streisand? Would a tough-looking babe named **Tori Spelling** be a featured cast member of "Beverly Hills 90210" if the executive producer of the show were other than her father, Aaron Spelling, creator of such hits as "Dynasty" and "Charlie's Angels"?

Would **Sophia Coppola** have been given the opportunity to replace an ailing Winona Ryder and thereby contribute to the critical and commercial failure of *The Godfather, Part III* had not the director been her father, Francis Ford Coppola? During the storm of controversy that surrounded her casting, Sofia defended her suitability for the role: "Instead of casting some pretty model, I look like I could be Al Pacino's daughter. Like, I have a nose." Mr. Coppola, it should be noted, is the man responsible for launching the career of his homely nephew Nicholas Cage.

Although critics cried foul over the casting of **Jenny Lumet** in the Timothy Hutton starrer *Q & A,* directed by her dad, Sidney Lumet, the aspiring actress remained undisturbed: "First of all, I think nepotism is great. Second of all, f __ k them! I'm not too worried about what other people think. I think that in one of the truly nastiest industries, anything to get a leg up is a good idea. . . . I mean, if I'm bad, I'll find out." Indeed, she was terrible, and has watched her career fizzle out.

The list of young actors who have risen to prominence with the helping hand of a friend or relative is an extensive one. In fairness, nepotism is not confined to the film and TV industries, but what makes Hollywood different from the more mundane fields of business is the astronomical rewards that can be achieved by those who do succeed.

In 1990, **Macaulay Culkin** received $100,000 to star in the John Hughes comedy *Home Alone.* After the film grossed over $300 million at the box office, the young star was paid $1 million to co-star in the Jamie Lee Curtis film *My Girl.* In 1991, Mack demanded and received a contract in excess of $5 million to star in the sequel to *Home Alone.* Along the way, young Macaulay has earned the reputation of a spoiled brat and the nickname MacMonster.

Another factor that differentiates the offspring of Hollywood is the impact, often negative, of their financial success and celebrity status on their character development and personality.

SOPHIA COPPOLA'S LACK OF BEAUTY AND TALENT DIDN'T STOP HER FATHER FROM CASTING HER IN *THE GODFATHER, PART III*, REPLACING AN "EXHAUSTED" WINONA RYDER. *RALPH DOMINGUEZ/GLOBE PHOTOS*

*E*DDIE FURLONG (*TERMINATOR 2*), SEEN HERE WITH GIRLFRIEND SOLIEL MOON FREY (OF "PUNKY BREWSTER" FAME), HAS BECOME A TEENAGE SEXUAL THRILL-SEEKER. *T. RODRIGUEZ/GLOBE PHOTOS*

When casting directors chose **Eddie Furlong** to portray Linda Hamilton's son in *Terminator 2,* they probably did not realize the impact it would have on his life. Since the film's tremendous success, Eddie has become a fourteen-year-old walking hormone—a "sperminator" so to speak. Additionally, Eddie's mom wound up in court battling her sister for his custody and control of his new wealth. Jeff Bridges, who co–starred with Eddie in a father-son drama, *American Heart,* told *US* magazine in 1992: "He's had a tough life with everything that's happened to him since *Terminator 2.* Balancing it all—all the accolades, and smoke up your ass, and chicks . . . He's a celebrity and I have a lot of concern about what it's doing to him."

Success for many young actors can often become a fatal attraction from which they never recover. In most instances, they plant the seeds of their own destruction during the lush days of their good fortune. They experiment with the "toys" of success—drugs, booze, and varied sexual misconduct. They consider themselves above the rules and regulations set by parents, elders, and the moral codes of society. After all, stars have special talents, special needs, and special license, don't they?

The one thing they often fail to do is nurture or improve the talents they lay claim to. Those who do study acting, music, or dance and maintain their star status rarely learn life's most valuable lessons until it's too late. Inevitably the fast life catches up with them. In many cases, they wind up in rehab or, worse still, stamping license plates.

Does this happen to all child actors caught up in the Hollywood maelstrom of publicity, perks, and worldwide fame? The answer is an obvious no. There are many former child stars who have not only survived their exciting youth but have gone on to become important players in the industry. Sarah Jessica Parker is a notable example of a child actress who has bridged Broadway (*Annie*), television ("Equal Justice") and film (*L.A. Story* and *Honeymoon in Vegas*). Jennifer Jason Leigh (daughter of the late actor Vic Morrow) has also eschewed the self-destructive ways of many of her contemporaries and has matured into a fine actress in her own right.

On television, former child actresses Valerie ("One Day at a Time") Bertinelli, Nancy ("The Facts of Life") McKeon and Melissa ("Little House on the Prairie") Gilbert-Brinkman have each carved out their own place on network series, miniseries, and made-for-television movies.

There are many more young actors who have quietly left Hollywood and gone on to have normal lives and successful careers far away from the spotlight.

In recent years, many young actors have fallen from grace only, like the legendary phoenix, to rise from the ashes of their fallen careers. Some do public acts of contrition while telling their tales of woe in print and on TV. Others pen tell-all autobiographies that detail the seamiest activities in their past. They ask for forgiveness and, most importantly, a second chance—a chance to recapture the youth, the innocence, the glory, and the money they have thrown away. Some are given that chance and continue forward without looking back. Those who do not learn from their mistakes fade away into well deserved obscurity.

How can one characterize the young stars of Hollywood today? They

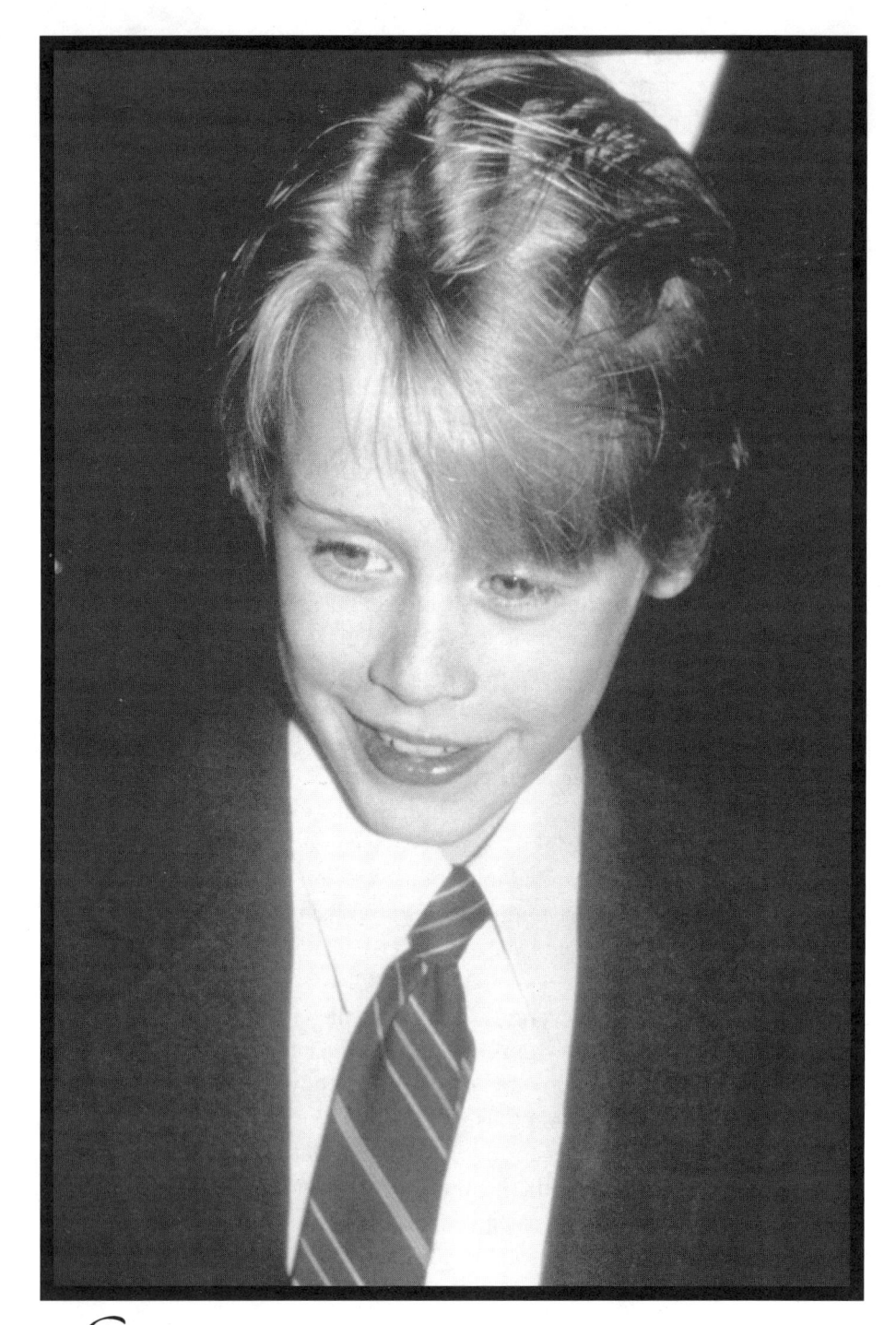

Since the enormous success of *Home Alone,* stage parent Kit Culkin now demands $10 million per movie for the "acting" services of his son Macaulay. Along the way Mack has earned the reputation of a brat and the nickname MacMonster. *John Barrett/Globe Photos*

are gifted and untalented, arrogant and humble, mean spirited and generous, dull and brilliant. They are many things to many people, but they share one common attribute. They are celebrities created by the magic wand of Hollywood. They were, are, and always will be the Children of Babylon.

PART I

AFTER CANCELLATION

What happens to television child actors after their series are cancelled? Recent events suggest that these young stars, who once earned large salaries and the adulation of loving fans, sink into depression, drugs, alcohol, and a life of crime. But contrary to popular opinion, former child stars have been getting into trouble for quite some time.

Tommy Rettig left "Lassie" to find himself years later arrested for illegally growing marijuana and smuggling cocaine. Paul Petersen of "The Donna Reed Show" spent years using drugs before returning to a second career as a writer and counselor of young actors.

Across the Atlantic, Jack Wild was another casualty of early fame. Jack, who received an Oscar nomination for his spirited performance of the Artful Dodger in *Oliver* (1968) and who later had his own Saturday morning TV series, "H. R. Puff 'n Stuff," spent ten years on the bottle. In 1991, Jack returned to the big screen in *Robin Hood: Prince of Thieves*. Of his small role

M ISSY GOLD, (LEFT) PLAYED A NEAR-PERFECT CHILD ON "BENSON" AS DID YOUNGER SISTER TRACEY ON "GROWING PAINS."
RICHARD HEWETT/GLOBE PHOTOS

he says, "It was the first job I actually got to do sober." Jack credits his renewed belief in God for helping him conquer his addiction.

A born-again Christian, Lauren Chapin is another person who straightened out her rather messy life. After "Father Knows Best" was cancelled in 1960, little "Kitten" Anderson became a prostitute in order to earn drug money. Working today as an evangelist, Lauren says, "I'm tickled pink to be a Christian, so I'm real proud of it. Jesus Christ has helped me a lot." Hallelujah!

Patty Duke, who starred on Broadway in *The Miracle Worker* and later in her own television series, has explained her years of wildly erratic behavior as a result of a medical condition known as manic depression.

AFTER CANCELLATION

*T*RACEY GOLD BECAME A COVER GIRL FOR *PEOPLE* MAGAZINE AFTER HER HOSPITAL STAY FOR ANOREXIA IN 1992. *LISA ROSE/GLOBE PHOTOS*

Kristy McNichol, however, says that her troubles in the early eighties were due to a "female hormonal thing."

With the arrests of Dana ("Diff'rent Strokes") Plato, Danny ("The Partridge Family") Bonaduce, and Adam ("Eight Is Enough") Rich during the early nineties, a new cottage industry materialized in which a former child actor emerges to tell his or her story of the "dark years" to the rapt viewers of Oprah, Phil, Geraldo, or Sally. They bare their souls to newspapers and magazines. They write books and become guest lecturers. They claim their intent is to "help others," but their words and actions reek of self-promotion.

Tracey Gold, who spent seven years on the ABC sitcom "Growing Pains," is one young actress who has turned her various illnesses into publicity events. In 1989, she disclosed to the press that she suffered from a learning disability. In 1992, Tracey took a much publicized leave of absence from her show to enter a hospital to treat her anorexia nervosa. After two weeks of treatment, however, she checked out of the hospital and onto the cover of *People* magazine.

The uppermost desire for most of the Hollywood has-beens is to recapture the days when the world lay at their feet. Those who are unwilling or unable to accept the inevitable, lash out wildly at a world they feel has unfairly shunted them. Hollywood, they say, has used them, abused them, and then discarded them aside. In their minds Hollywood owes them and now they have come to collect. But what does Hollywood really owe them? In August of 1991, Danny Bonaduce penned his own thoughts on this subject for *Esquire* magazine.

> Most child actors were lucky enough to get the part in the first place. They cry and complain that now they are no longer little and cute, Hollywood has no use for them. What we often fail to appreciate is that being little and cute may have been our only skill. Now that we are not so little anymore, and certainly not cute, some of us may have to face reality, stop whining and get real jobs.

Lauren Chapin Didn't Know Best

The unhappy child of a broken home, Lauren Chapin found the family environment she so desperately needed in 1954 when she was cast in the role of little Kathy "Kitten" Anderson on the popular family series "Father Knows Best." But after the show ended six years later, Lauren suffered a drug-related identity crisis, which spanned almost twenty years. During postsitcom years, Lauren wandered through several failed marriages, heroin addiction, prostitution, suicide attempts, and prison time.

Lauren's maternal grandmother had once been a studio teacher whose class lists had included Mickey Rooney, Judy Garland, and Elizabeth Taylor. Marguerite Chapin, Lauren's mother, was a socially ambitious woman who used her own mother's connections with casting agents and directors to get auditions for her three children: Michael, Billy, and later, Lauren.

By the time Lauren was born (May 23, 1945), both her brothers were professional actors. Before he had reached his teens, Michael had appeared

CHILDREN
OF
BABYLON

8

Lauren Chapin (*CENTER*) with her "Father Knows Best" co-stars (*LEFT TO RIGHT*) Jane Wyatt, Elinor Donahue, Billy Gray, and Robert Young. *GLOBE PHOTOS*

in scores of films, including the Roy Rogers western *Under California Stars* (1948). Billy made his motion picture debut when he was only twenty-two days old, playing the "daughter" of Gary Cooper in *Casanova Brown* (1944). His impressive list of film credits includes *The Kid from Left Field* (1953), *There's No Business Like Show Business* (1954), *Naked Alibi* (1954), and *The Night of the Hunter* (1955).

The nature of the television business meant that Marguerite was constantly on the move, seeking work for her sons. When Lauren was only four, Marguerite and Billy moved to New York while he spent two years on Broadway in *Three Wishes for Jamie*. His work in the play would earn the eight-year-old the New York Drama Critics Award as the most promising actor of the year.

During their absence, Michael was sent off to military school and Lauren was enrolled in a Catholic boarding school. Lauren claims that her father sexually abused her on weekends. Although this abuse stopped when Marguerite and Billy returned from New York, her home life was far from normal. After several violent arguments, the Chapins separated and eventually divorced.

In 1954, Hazel McMillian, a family friend who happened to be a talent agent, took an interest in Lauren. Recognizing her daughter's money-making potential, Marguerite enrolled her daughter in acting, voice, and diction lessons.

"Father Knows Best," which began as a radio series on NBC in 1949, starred Robert Young as the patriarch of an idealized American family. In 1954, CBS transferred this popular show to television. Young continued his role as Jim Anderson, while the other roles were eventually filled by Jane Wyatt (as Margaret), Elinor Donahue (as seventeen-year-old Betty), and Billy Gray (as fourteen-year-old James Jr.). Lauren was selected over two hundred other girls for the role of nine-year-old Kathy Anderson.

The show, which made its debut on CBS on October 3, 1954, was not particularly successful, and CBS decided to cancel it after its first season. After a flood of viewer protests, NBC revived the series and put it on its fall schedule, where it would remain for the next five years.

Marguerite used her children's earnings to live an elegant lifestyle, but in the course of her very social life she developed a severe drinking habit. To Lauren, "My mother was not one of those loving alcoholics; she was one of those mean witches. It created a lot of hassles. I thought she was just mean and terrible and she hated me and I hated her." Marguerite was once arrested while driving under the influence, and thrown in the drunk tank.

During her years on the show, Lauren received her education at the studio school. "In all honesty, our school was hardly one that emphasized scholarship," she later wrote in her own autobiography. "Learning our lines was far more important than learning how to spell the words on our spelling list or how to do our latest math homework. If something was going to suffer, it wasn't going to be the show."

Initially, Lauren enjoyed her television family, but just as she was having problems at home, so did her series co-stars. According to Lauren, "On the screen, we may have looked like the ideal family, but on the set we resembled men and women living on the edge and looking for a place to jump." There was no exaggeration in her statement.

Robert Young was suffering bouts of severe depression that accompanied his alcoholism. Elinor Donahue, who was married and pregnant, was having marital problems that would eventually be settled in divorce court. In 1962, a public relations nightmare erupted when Billy Gray was arrested and charged with possession of a controlled substance after being stopped by police for drunk driving. No excuse could make up for the fact that the all-American son had been caught with pot. He was sentenced to three months in jail and three years probation.

As for Lauren, her situation at home had deteriorated to the extent that she was constantly running away. She would often go to her father's home and refuse to return to work. The show's producers eventually went to court to force her to live with her mother until the series ended or she had reached age eighteen.

The series abruptly came to a halt in 1960 after Robert Young decided he wanted out. He had spent a total of eleven years, on radio and television, playing Jim Anderson and was bored to death with the role. Given the strained relationships among the cast, not to mention the expense and difficulty of actually filming the series, the studio readily obliged.

Of the five principal cast members, Robert Young, Jane Wyatt, and Elinor Donahue continued to enjoy successful careers. Young went on to other television series, including "Window on Main Street" (1961–1962) and "Marcus Welby, M.D." (1969–1976). After overcoming his own alcohol addiction, he became the spokesman for Sanka decaffeinated coffee. Despite winning three Emmy awards for her role as ever faithful Margaret Anderson, Jane Wyatt earned "star" status for her role as Spock's mother on one episode of "Star Trek"—a part she brought to the screen in *Star Trek IV: The Voyage Home* (1986). Elinor Donahue hopped from one series to the next: "The Andy Griffith Show" (1960–1961), "Many Happy Returns" (1964–1965), "The Odd Couple" (1972–1974), "Mulligan's Stew" (1977), "Please Stand By" (1978–1979), and "Days of Our Lives" (1984–1985).

As for Billy Gray, his well-publicized arrest cut short his acting career.

Before she became an evangelical minister, Lauren spent years selling her body for drug money. *ADAM SCULL/GLOBE PHOTOS*

LAUREN CHAPIN
DIDN'T KNOW BEST

His attempts to remain an actor went unnoticed and after two marriages Billy found work as a motorcycle racer.

Lauren, who was just turning thirteen, was entering that awkward, unmarketable phase for child actors. This combined with a general lack of interest on her part effectively ended her career. After Marguerite enrolled her in an exclusive prep school, it became immediately evident that her daughter was not ready for the structured class world. A poor student when she actually went to school, Lauren became a troublemaker.

At Lauren's request, her father went to court and won custody of his fourteen-year-old daughter. Her joy at living with her father's new family was short-lived when, according to Lauren, he began to sexually abuse her just a few months after she moved in.

At age sixteen, Lauren dropped out of high school and married her eighteen-year-old car mechanic boyfriend. As Mrs. Jerry Jones, Lauren's new-found happiness at being away from her troubled parents was short-lived. Still basically children, the young couple was not prepared for the responsibilities of marriage. The financial difficulties were exacerbated when Lauren's mother filed suit against Lauren for all of her residual money.

Lauren desperately wanted to have a child, but during the five years of her marriage she miscarried eight times before separating from her husband. (They were divorced in 1965.) A fixation in reducing her weight led Lauren to an addiction to diet pills that eventually began a sixty-pill-a-day habit.

At age eighteen, Lauren came into a trust fund worth $18,970 and immediately went on a seven-month spending spree. After the money dried up, she wandered through a series of low-paying jobs, including carhop, waitress, dog groomer, insurance claims examiner, and airline stewardess. Lauren says, "You name it and I did it." With respect to the drugs, you name it and she took it.

Totally dependent on pills, nineteen-year-old Lauren eventually became a prostitute in order to earn money for the drugs she desperately craved. She later stated, "No one had ever told me about prostitution, that it was immoral or illegal." She stretched her credibility even further when she said, "I was valuable because I could help men unwind and forget about their troubles. I saw myself as a kind of psychologist."

On a drug run with her pimp, twenty-year-old Lauren was arrested in Mexico and would later receive probation. After she returned to L.A., she married a drug dealer. The most memorable thing about that experience was that she, her new husband, and her brother Billy got high on acid before the ceremony. Later, when she discovered that her husband had never divorced his first wife, she filed for and received an annulment.

In order to feed her increasing appetite for drugs, Lauren would occasionally shoplift. After being arrested in L.A. for check forgery, Lauren was sentenced to seven years in the California Rehabilitation Center for narcotic addicts.

In prison, she earned her high school diploma and attended AA meetings. She served sixteen months before being paroled at the ripe old age of twenty-three. With no place to call home, Lauren wound up living on the streets and eventually ended up in a psychiatric ward. It was there that she met her third husband, a Mexican drug dealer. (Because the papers from their Mexican wedding were never filed in the U.S., the marriage was technically invalid.)

Despondent by her all-consuming addiction, Lauren attempted suicide by using a meat cleaver to sever her left hand. After being found unconscious on the street, Lauren was taken to a local hospital, where doctors managed to save her hand, although she has no feeling in it.

After becoming pregnant by another drug-dealing boyfriend, Lauren decided to quit the drug scene once and for all. With no money to return home, Lauren, two months pregnant at the time, made $50 turning her last trick. The first of her children, Matthew Edward Chapin, was born on January 1, 1973. Her second child, a daughter, Summer Ryann Elizabeth, was fathered six years later by a man who came to install a phone in her apartment.

In the mid seventies, Lauren faced severe health problems, including hepatitis and viral encephalitis (an inflammation of the brain). After narrowly avoiding death, Lauren moved in with her brother Michael and his wife. While attending a nondenominational church with Michael's family, Lauren had a religious experience and became a born-again Christian.

For a short period, Lauren, along with her two children, lived across the street from her brother. She earned a living by working in a brokerage house and giving lessons in natural childbirth. In 1981, at the age of thirty-five, Lauren was ordained as an evangelist in the Full Gospel Church. Three years later, she moved to Killeen, Texas. Since then, she has travelled across the country, working as an evangelist.

In 1988, Lauren met and married her fourth husband, a firefighter, and together they have been working to counsel teens and preteens who are addicted to drugs and alcohol. Lauren and her husband are also strong advocates for tighter controls for television programming "In an effort to stop the images of blood and gore and easy sex that are flooding our homes." (For anyone looking for images of blood and gore and easy sex, one can purchase Lauren's tell-all autobiography, *The Lauren Chapin Story: Father Does Know Best*.) Lauren's most recent acting credits include the 1979 reunion special "Father Knows Best Christmas Reunion" and a cameo role in the Gary Coleman TV movie *Scout's Honor* (1980).

Looking back on her television years, Lauren told writer Lynn Woods, "I have nothing but admiration for the message of 'Father Knows Best.' I'm trying to raise my family like the Andersons. I believe the husband should be the head of the household, and the mom should be home nurturing the kids and the whole family should attend church. After all, if I didn't have 'Father Knows Best' to pattern myself after, what else would I have?"

Tommy Rettig:
Life Without Lassie

Tommy Rettig began his career at age five, touring alongside Mary Martin in the road company production of *Annie, Get Your Gun*. After the show's run, Tommy became one of the most successful child actors of his day, working in radio, television, and film (*Panic in the Streets, River of No Return,* among others). By 1954, twelve-year-old Tommy was earning $2,500 a week as Jeff Miller, the original master of a loyal collie named Lassie. The grueling schedule of the show (six days a week, thirty-nine weeks a year) proved to be too much for the young star ("It was a nightmare—just hit your mark and say your lines."). Tommy was relieved to have outgrown the role in 1957, when he was replaced by Jon Provost. After "Lassie," he decided to retire from acting and finish high school. "I wanted to be normal; you know, chase girls, race cars, and party," he says.

After an early marriage at age eighteen, which produced two sons, Tommy decided to return to acting. Unable to make a comeback, Tommy

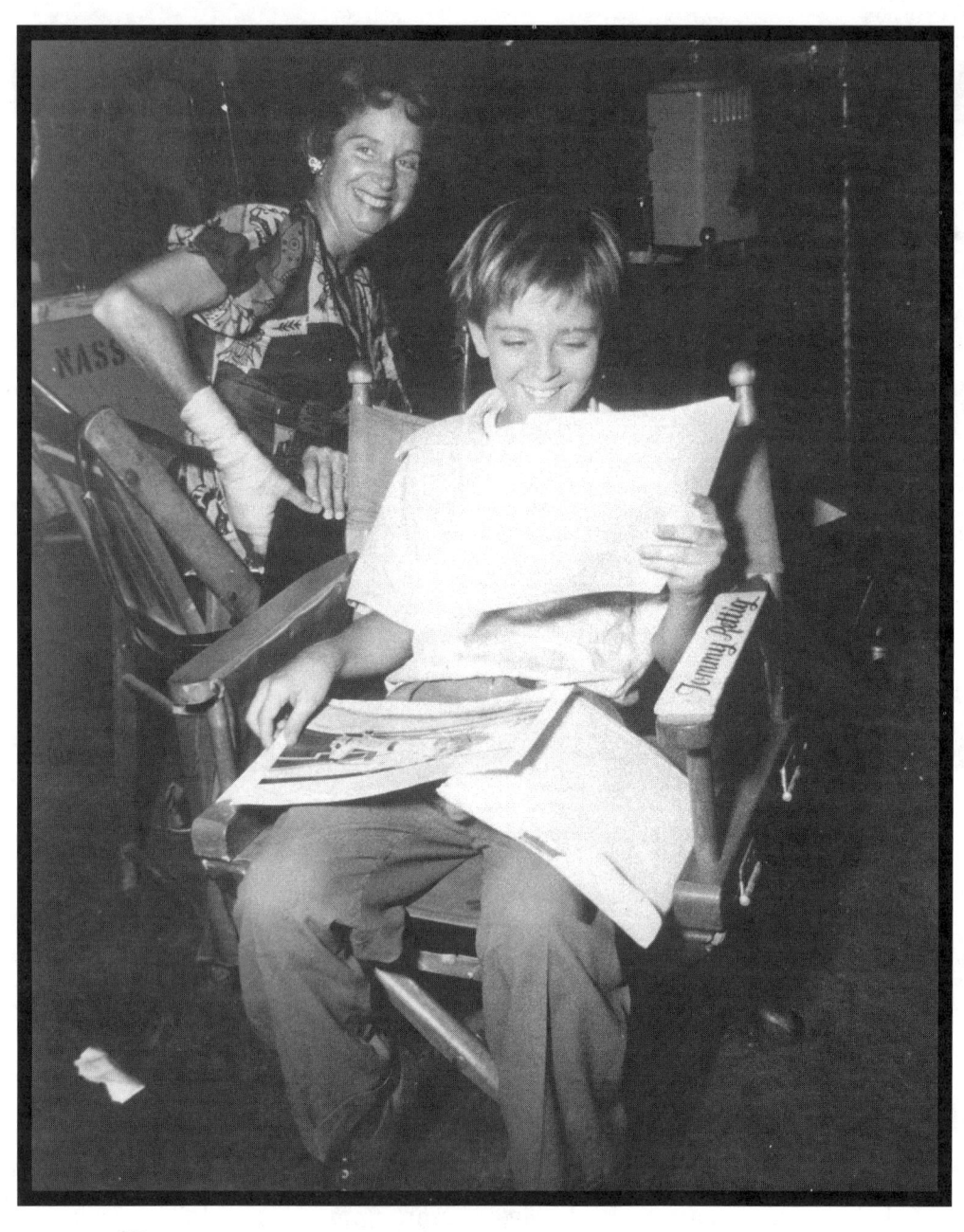

During his post-"Lassie" years, Tommy Rettig was arrested several times on charges ranging from marijuana possession to cocaine smuggling. *Globe Photos*

became a flower child and moved to central California to become an organic farmer. In 1972, Tommy was arrested for growing marijuana plants between rows of corn on his farm. After spending one night in jail he received a suspended sentence.

In 1975, he was arrested again, this time for smuggling cocaine into the country from Peru. Tommy explained that the liquid cocaine discovered in his possession was actually just part of the research he was doing for a book he planned to write. The jury didn't buy that explanation and found him guilty. He was initially sentenced to five and a half years in jail—a conviction that was eventually overturned.

In 1980, Tommy was arrested at a cocaine lab, but because his complicity could not be proven, the charges were dropped. After his divorce, he took a variety of odd jobs, including photographer and insurance broker. In 1983, he became a computer programmer and coauthored a best-selling reference manual. He told *People* magazine in 1988, "I'm at the happiest place I've ever been. I'm happy with myself, my career, and my life."

Patty Duke: From Miracle Child to Manic-Depressive

When Patty Duke assessed her behavior as "crazy as a bedbug," this was no slight exaggeration. Patty, whose family history gives new meaning to the word dysfunctional, was the youngest child of an alcoholic father and an emotionally unstable mother. Her time at home was brief, however, and she was eventually turned over to John and Ethel Ross, her ambitious managers. A victim of the Rosses' alleged emotional and sexual abuse, Patty survived a turbulent adolescence only to wind up as a self-destructive young adult. In 1982, Patty was diagnosed with manic depression, putting an end to the rumors of drug abuse that had circulated throughout years of her erratic behavior. Her life has been a roller coaster ride that has included suicide attempts, anorexia, and three failed marriages, including one that lasted all of thirteen days.

Patty Duke was born on December 14, 1946, at Bellevue Hospital in New York and christened Anna Marie. The youngest child of John Patrick and Frances Duke, little Anna was raised on the lower East Side with older siblings Carol and Raymond.

Patty Duke: From
Miracle Child to
Manic-Depressive

19

T HE STAR OF HER OWN TELEVISION SHOW AT AGE SIXTEEN, PATTY DUKE WAS AFFECTIONATELY REFERRED TO BY HER CO-WORKERS AS THE LITTLE SH___ . MAX B. MILLER/GLOBE PHOTOS

Patty's father was a quiet alcoholic who drifted through a series of odd jobs that included parking lot attendant, cab driver, and handyman. Her mother was a fragile woman who went through periods of deep depression while her husband spent his paychecks down at the local bar. When Patty was six, Frances, tired of her husband's failings, asked him to leave. The children rarely saw him after that.

It was actually Anna Marie's brother Ray who was the first actor in the family, appearing in small productions sponsored by a local boys club. After a local talent scout spotted Ray, he was introduced to John and Ethel Ross, managers who worked with child actors. With their help, Ray was able to find work in commercials and on television.

Frances, who was struggling to make ends meet by working as a cashier, took her daughter to the Rosses to see if she had any talent. Reluctant at first, John and Ethel agreed to work with Anna on her appearance and speech. The first thing they did was to rename the child Patty (after another famous child star, Patty McCormack). One day Ethel bluntly stated, in words Anna would never forget, "Anna is dead. You're Patty now."

At first Patty would spend her off hours and weekends training with the Rosses, but by age thirteen she was living with them full time. Patty would only see Frances once a week, when Frances came to the Rosses to do their laundry.

Patty's first speaking part came at age nine, when she portrayed an Italian waif in the Armstrong Circle Theatre presentation of the sinking of the *Andrea Doria*. Her other early credits came in the form of television commercials and on the soap opera "The Brighter Day."

In 1958, John Ross spotted an article in *Backstage,* a theater publication, which mentioned that *The Miracle Worker* was being prepared for the Broadway stage. From that moment, the Rosses did nothing but drill Patty for the role of Helen Keller.

During her preparation period, John Ross managed to get Patty a spot on the "$64,000 Challenge." She, along with Eddie Hodges (of *The Music Man*) managed to win the full amount by displaying an incredible knowledge of popular music.

The following year, the nation would be stunned by the revelation that many of the winners of "$64,000 Challenge" were selected and given answers before appearing on the show. In 1959, the New York District Attorney began an investigation into the show and issued a subpoena to Patty. Under directions from John Ross, Patty swore under oath that she had not been given any of the questions or answers. In November, she was flown to Washington, D.C., and forced to testify before the House Special Subcommittee on Legislative Oversight. At first Patty stuck to her original story, but

PATTY DUKE: FROM
MIRACLE CHILD TO
MANIC-DEPRESSIVE

21

Patty's incoherent acceptance speech at the 1970 Emmy Awards added to the speculation that she was addicted to drugs.
BOB V. NOBLE/GLOBE PHOTOS

when Arkansas Senator Oren Harris asked, "Now, Anna Marie, are you sure you've told us the truth?," Patty broke down and replied, "No sir, I have not." The show's associate producer had coached Patty before the program.

The Miracle Worker, which opened on Broadway on October 19, 1959, won unanimous praise from critics and audiences alike. Of Patty's performance, *New York Times* theater critic Brooks Atkinson wrote: "As Helen, little Miss Duke is altogether superb—a plain, sullen, explosive, miniature monster whose destructive behavior makes sympathy for her afflictions impossible, but whose independence and vitality are nevertheless admirable." On March 7, 1960, Patty had the honor of having her name raised above the title of the play, along with Anne Bancroft's.

In the "golden age" of television, Patty was also able to gain valuable learning experiences working alongside some of Hollywood's living legends. She played opposite Helen Hayes in *One Red Rose of Christmas* (1959), Sir Laurence Olivier in *The Power and the Glory* (1961), Richard Burton and Rosemary Harris in *Wuthering Heights,* and Myrna Loy in *Meet Me in St. Louis.* These performances led to small film roles in *The Goddess,* starring Kim Stanley, and the lighthearted comedy *Happy Anniversary,* starring David Niven and Mitzi Gaynor.

After leaving *The Miracle Worker,* Patty's second role was in *Isle of Children.* Although her portrayal of a terminally ill child was praised, the show lasted only eleven performances. Her disappointment with the show's closing was short lived and in 1962 Patty, accompanied by the Rosses, flew to Hollywood to begin filming the movie version of *The Miracle Worker.*

When the awards were presented in April of 1963, Patty became the youngest performer to win an Oscar in a regular category when she was named best supporting actress. She won the award overcoming stiff competition from child actress Mary Badham for *To Kill a Mockingbird,* and the critics' favorite Angela Lansbury for her highly praised performance in *The Manchurian Candidate.*

In September of that year, "The Patty Duke Show" made its debut, and Patty became the youngest person in television history to have a prime-time series named after her. Patty starred in the dual role of Patty Lane, an outgoing teenager, and Cathy Lane, her quiet Scottish cousin who happens to be her exact double. Patty, at first excited by the opportunity to do a dual role, quickly became disenchanted. Speaking of this afterward she said, "Because of the inherent limitations of the roles, I got bored very quickly. And the longer it went on, the more I began to hate it. It felt like a trap."

Patty was simultaneously going through severe growing pains. She later complained to Rex Reed, "I was working like an adult, with none of the advantages. I couldn't go to any of the parties because nobody was supposed

AFTER YEARS OF THERAPY AND LITHIUM TREATMENT, PATTY HAS TURNED HER LIFE AROUND PERSONALLY AND PROFESSIONALLY. SHE AND HER FOURTH HUSBAND, MICHAEL PEARCE, WERE MARRIED IN 1986.
RALPH DOMINGUEZ/GLOBE PHOTOS

to see the little shrimp smoke or drink." Indeed, when interviewed by *Newsweek,* Patty sounded rather imperious when she refused to be photographed holding a cigarette. "I represent something wholesome," she said. "I have an obligation to my people."

During the first season, Patty met a man she would eventually marry, Harry Falk, who worked on the series as an assistant director. Harry, who was fourteen years older than seventeen-year-old Patty, was married, a stumbling block of little consequence to the young star.

John and Ethel, frightened of losing control of their primary breadwinner, arranged to have the show moved to L.A., in hopes of destroying the relationship. Patty became furious and completely severed her relationship with them. She stormed out of their apartment, shouting, "I'm going to Fire Island, and I'm going to sleep with Harry." During the show's third and final season, the Rosses were barred from the set.

Ill prepared to handle her sudden freedom, Patty began to enter the fast-paced L.A. lifestyle, which included late nights, drinking, and smoking. Professionally, Patty was temperamental and made excessive demands from the studio. In her own autobiography, *Call Me Anna,* Patty recalled, "The drinking got so heavy that I was called on the carpet many times for looking hung over during filming, because I was. My not-so-affectionate nickname on the show became The Little Sh __ , as in 'Get the little sh __ up here."

When Patty began to spend a lot of time with her stand-in on the show, a woman twenty years her senior, rumors circulated of a lesbian relationship. These rumors were laid to rest on November 26, 1965, when Patty and Harry were married. Harry, now divorced, was thirty-three, and Patty was one month shy of her nineteenth birthday.

Immature and ill equipped for the responsibilities of marriage, Patty went on a spending spree and did her best to indulge her new husband. Their purchases included a colonial mansion in Beverly Hills, with a 360-degree view of L.A., and a four-car garage that housed Harry's Porsche. Harry was fond of antiques, and the house was soon filled with them. Patty even used her influence on the show to force the studio to allow Harry to direct several episodes.

In 1966, after 104 episodes, the series ended and Patty fell into depression. She later explained, "If you've belonged some place all your life, unhappy though it may be, that place is home. The feeling of abandonment when it's gone is just as real as your mother giving you up to live with other people."

After making guest appearances on only a few television shows, Patty's depression led to a bout with anorexia. Her weight dropped to seventy-six pounds before she received professional help. It was during this period that Patty would begin a long period of psychoanalysis.

In order to change her image, Patty signed up, along with Barbara Parkins and Sharon Tate, for the film adaptation of Jacqueline Susann's torrid best-seller *Valley of the Dolls* (1967). The film, which cynics dubbed "VD," centers on the lives of three Hollywood women: Anne Welles (Parkins), a Grace Kelly type of beauty; Neely O'Hara (Duke), a young singer turned addict a la Judy Garland; and Jennifer North (Tate), an international sex symbol in the Marilyn Monroe mold.

The filming of the movie became the talk of tabloids as reports of temper tantrums came from the set. Judy Garland, who was cast as a fading actress, was fired after only a few days when she refused to come out of her trailer.

During the publicity tour for the film, Patty made a conscious effort to redefine her image and subsequently earned the nickname Little Miss Sewer Mouth. Speaking to *Look,* she explained, "I gotta act tough. I mean, everyone's bigger than me. Everybody's got a bigger bra size. I'm like a little man. I'll tell you one thing. I'm not doing any more Patty Lanes."

After the film opened to scathing reviews, Patty was quick to point the finger. "We got no direction," she whined. "An actor can't go out there alone and make a movie. I don't know any actor who doesn't need a director. We were flying blind, in a fog."

After infidelities by both parties, Patty and Harry filed for divorce after only three years of marriage. Reflecting on these years, Patty said, "I was looking for a father. I've been looking for a father all my life and now it's time I stood on my own two feet."

During the summer of 1968, Patty filmed *Me, Natalie,* the story of an ugly Jewish girl from Brooklyn who finds romance in New York's Greenwich Village. Her behavior on the set was erratic and reports circulated of angry outbursts, suicide threats, and promiscuity. Patty took thirty Seconal one evening in a botched suicide attempt.

According to Patty, when Fred Coe found his star drinking beer on the set, he began to reprimand her. A belligerent young woman, Patty would have none of it: "I stood up, threw the bottle into the river, and told him in front of everyone to take his movie and shove it up his ass, I quit." After a truce was arranged by her manager, Patty returned and finished the film, which was another failure on her resume.

Patty made a strong comeback in the television movie *My Sweet Charlie* (1970). The story centers on a young, pregnant Southern woman and an educated Northern black man who both take refuge in an empty house one night. Hostile toward each other at first, they later learn mutual respect.

During the film's four-week shoot, police acting on a tip found a small stash of marijuana in her closet. Patty insisted that the drugs were planted, possibly by someone offended by the racial overtones of the movie. The matter was dropped.

After a guest appearance on "The Merv Griffin Show" in March of that year, seventeen-year-old Desi Arnaz, Jr., called up Patty and invited her to dinner. This dinner would initiate a hot romance, which became the talk of Hollywood.

When Lucille Ball found out about her son's new romance, she was furious. Patty, after all, was seven years older than Desi, divorced, and wildly unpredictable. When Lucy tried to cool the relationship by taking her family to Hawaii, a stubborn Patty followed them. The relationship went through hot and cold periods. During one of their off periods, Patty had a brief affair with John Astin, a married actor best remembered for his portrayal of Gomez on "The Addams Family." When she became pregnant by Astin, Patty let the public believe the child was Desi's.

By 1970, Patty had earned a reputation as a moody, temperamental actress who was widely believed to be a drug addict. She has fervently denied these allegations, blaming her unruly behavior on manic depression. "It was declared that I was on drugs. It was declared that I said I was on drugs. I would probably be too frightened to do that, but maybe, who knows, I was manic, maybe I did. I certainly behaved badly."

One of the events that reinforced the public's perception of Patty occurred during the 1970 Emmy awards held at the Century Plaza Hotel. After winning the award for Best Actress for *My Sweet Charlie,* Patty gave a rambling, incoherent acceptance speech to a silent audience. Backstage, after learning that her co-star Al Freeman, Jr., did not win in his category, Patty tried to return the award. In a speech full of obscenities, she told the press she was leaving show business to become a doctor. Columnist Marilyn Beck reported that she had bumped into Patty before the ceremony, and that the glazed actress mumbled, "I'm stoned out of my mind."

Her emotional downslide continued and in June of 1970 Patty married Michael Tell, a man she barely knew. The marriage, which, according to Patty, was never consummated, lasted thirteen days. After a complete breakdown, Anne Bancroft came to her rescue and helped arrange a hospital stay. After their divorce, Patty never saw Michael again.

After divorcing his wife, forty-two-year-old John Astin married twenty-five-year-old Patty on August 5, 1972. Although John was an easygoing type, their years together were tumultuous. Patty's main difficulty stemmed from her bad relationship with John's three children, as well as raising their own infant sons, Sean and Mackenzie.

In the early seventies Patty agreed to let two men she met in a parking lot manage her money. Three years later, the Astins discovered that most of their money was gone and that her "accountants" had failed to file income taxes during that time. She later admitted, "We were extraordinarily in debt. We lost everything—in the six figures."

Flat broke, John and Patty went on the road, performing in various plays and appearing on TV game shows. After twelve strenuous years, Patty's marriage dissolved when John became a devout Buddhist and attempted to convert the rest of the family. They were divorced in 1985.

In 1982, after years of wildly uncontrollable mood swings, Patty was diagnosed as a manic depressive, a medical condition characterized by alternating fits of euphoria and deep depression. One treatment for manic depression is a daily dosage of lithium carbonate—an element normally present at the necessary level in the body—which corrects an imbalance in the body's biological system. Patty's treatment has virtually put an end to the screaming fits, suicide attempts, and unpredictable behavior that plagued her early years. Shortly after she began treatment, Patty served as president of the Screen Actors Guild, a post she held for six years.

Patty met her fourth husband, Michael Pearce, during the filming of the TV movie *A Time to Triumph* (1985). To prepare for her grueling role of a thirty-year-old army recruit, Patty spent several weeks training with Michael, an eleven-year career army officer. The fact that Michael was married and had two young daughters was a relatively unimportant consideration to Patty. They were married in Lake Tahoe on March 15, 1986, just six months after they met. The couple now reside in Idaho with their adopted son Kevin.

Most of Patty's adult career has been spent on television. Aside from her Emmy for *My Sweet Charlie,* Patty has been nominated on seven other occasions, taking home statues for *Captains and the Kings* (1976) and the remake of *The Miracle Worker* (1979). Her forays on network series have been less successful. "It Takes Two," co-starring Richard Crenna, lasted only two seasons, while "Hail to the Chief" was cancelled after only seven episodes in 1985.

Patty's most recent successes have come from her literary abilities. In 1987, Patty coauthored the favorably reviewed, best-selling autobiography *Call Me Anna,* which was made into a television movie. In 1992, Patty coauthored another book on the subject of manic depression, *A Brilliant Madness,* which describes the symptoms and treatment for those suffering from the illness.

Patty's two oldest children, Sean and Mackenzie, have both dabbled in acting. Mackenzie spent three years on the NBC sitcom "The Facts of Life" before retiring at age fifteen. Sean's credits include *Goonies* (1985), *Memphis Belle* (1990), *Toy Soldiers* (1991), and *Encino Man* (1992).

BUTCH PATRICK: DEMON CHILD

For Butch Patrick, who portrayed the Munster's youngest son Eddie from 1964 to 1966, life was a picnic. "I was like the mascot of Universal Studios," he recalls. "I used the back lot as my private entertainment center."

After the series ended, Butch's career began to fizzle and at age sixteen he made his first drug purchase and remained dependent for years. He later admitted to *People* magazine, "I did a lot of coke and psychedelics. Occasionally I'd be the middleman and get the stuff for free." With no marketable skills to fall back on and an expensive addiction, Butch wandered aimlessly through a series of low-paying jobs that included waxing cars and selling Christmas trees.

In 1979, twenty-five-year-old Butch spent eleven weekends in jail after being convicted of possession of two hundred Quaaludes. Despite his stint in jail, Butch remained an avid consumer of drugs until 1987, when he went cold turkey and kicked his habit.

*O*F HIS FELONY CONVICTION, BUTCH PATRICK (*LEFT*) SAYS, "I CAN'T VOTE AND I CAN'T SERVE ON A JURY. BIG DEAL." *GLOBE PHOTOS/RANGE FINDERS*

In November of 1991, Butch was arrested and charged with stealing $130 from a limo driver before beating him. He was subsequently convicted of the beating but cleared of the robbery charges. Butch has described his fame as a double-edged sword, saying, "Sure, sometimes you're in the spotlight; limousines pick you up. There's other times, because of who you are, you're put in a position to defend yourself for no reason other than being you."

BUTCH PATRICK: DEMON CHILD

Kristy McNichol: From Family to Empty Nest

Movie and television audiences have watched Kristy (Christine Anne) McNichol grow up in front of the cameras. While known to TV audiences as a regular cast member of "Empty Nest," she is best remembered as Buddy Lawrence on the dramatic series "Family." The years between these two hit shows, however, were filled with a series of personal and professional crises that almost destroyed her career.

Kristy and her brother Jimmy were raised by their mother Carolynne after she divorced her husband James McNichol, a carpenter, in 1965. Carolynne supported herself and her children by working as a part-time secretary and film extra. Kristy and Jimmy became interested in acting after watching their mother work as an extra on "Family Affair."

Kristy began her career in television commercials, and later found small parts on TV ("Love, American Style," and "The Love Boat"), which eventually led to a feature role in the short-lived family drama "Apple's Way" (1974–1975). Jimmy also found work on two television series: "The Fitz-

K RISTY MCNICHOL AND HER GOOD FRIEND INA LIBERACE, ONE OF SEVERAL WOMEN MCNICHOL HAS BEEN ROMANTICALLY LINKED WITH IN THE TABLOIDS.
RALPH DOMINGUEZ/GLOBE PHOTOS

patricks" (1977–1978) and "California Fever" (1979). With both Kristy and Jimmy earning sizeable incomes, Carolynne quit her job and became a full-time stage mother. One casualty of Carolynne's ambitions, however, was her youngest son Tommy, a nonprofessional, who was raised by his grandparents.

Following the cancellation of "Apple's Way," Kristy was cast as Letitia "Buddy" Lawrence, the tomboy daughter in ABC's "Family." The show told the story of the affluent Lawrence family, played by James Broderick, Sada Thompson, Meredith Baxter-Birney, Gary Frank, and Kristy. Superior writing and character development distinguished the series, while strong acting earned Emmy awards for most of the cast. Kristy won the award for Best

Supporting Actress in a drama series in 1977 and 1979. Sada Thompson won for Best Actress in 1978; Gary Frank won for Best Supporting Actor in 1977.

Kristy also won praise from critics for her performances in the television films *Like Mom, Like Me* (1978), *Summer of My German Soldier* (1978), and *My Old Man* (1979). In 1978, she made her motion picture debut as Burt Reynold's daughter in the dark comedy *The End*.

Kristy reportedly earned $15,000 per episode for "Family." With other television and film roles and earnings from the sale of posters, dolls, and a recording contract, Kristy's income swelled to over $1 million a year. One drawback of this new-found success was the egomania it created for both mother and daughter. A reporter with *TV Guide* found that people on the set of "Family" referred to Kristy as "snippy," while another co-worker said, "If we could, we'd like to bar mothers from the set."

As for Kristy and Jimmy's income, between 20 and 25 percent went into their trust funds, 15 percent was kept by Carolynne as a management fee, and the rest was invested in real estate. Carolynne eventually moved her family into a $170,000 home complete with swimming pool, tennis court, and hot tub. She purchased a red Scirocco for Kristy and treated herself to a white Corvette. She then proceeded to hire an entourage for the family, which included a live-in maid, a private secretary, a business manager, a public relations firm, and a separate agent to handle Jimmy's dwindling career. Carolynne said at the time, "With my kids' careers and real estate investments, I can't seem to make a wrong move."

In 1978, Kristy told *Washington Post* reporter Bill Kaufman that she was being very selective in her film and TV projects. "I'm given all kinds of movie scripts which really aren't for me. They all imply sex, drugs, and booze. It's stuff that I hate when it's presented in some ways. I can't pretend to be that sort of kid."

In 1980, at age seventeen, Kristy had her first starring role, opposite sixteen-year-old Tatum O'Neal in the R-rated teen sex comedy *Little Darlings*. The film's premise consisted of Kristy and Tatum competing as to who could lose their virginity first at a summer camp. Although most critics were more impressed with Kristy's performance, the film's crew preferred Tatum's quiet professionalism to Kristy's impatient and disdainful moods.

Soon after her eighteenth birthday, Kristy moved into her own $250,000, four-bedroom home with close personal friend Ina Liberace. When rumors began to circulate about her relationship with Liberace's niece, Kristy rebuked, "It's because I act like a tomboy in my movies. Well, I'm not into being gay." Nevertheless, national tabloids have subsequently linked Kristy romantically with female model Melisande Casey and actress Martha Allen.

*S*HORTLY AFTER *THE PIRATE MOVIE* BOMBED, CHRISTOPHER ATKINS BECAME AN ALCOHOLIC AND KRISTY MCNICHOL SUFFERED FROM A "CHEMICAL IMBALANCE." *SYLVIA NORRIS/GLOBE PHOTOS*

The following year, she moved into a $1.75 million, four-bedroom home in Beverly Hills. The house had a garage large enough for her three cars: a Jeep, a Fiat, and a Jaguar.

The cancellation of "Family" in 1980 marked a turning point in Kristy's career. With the exception of the Neil Simon comedy *Only When I Laugh,* Kristy languished in such second-rate TV fare as *Blinded by the Light* (1980), co-starring her brother, and *The Night the Lights Went Out in Georgia* (1981).

Likewise, her motion picture career never lived up to its promising start. In 1982, *The Pirate Movie,* co-starring Christopher Atkins, received abysmal reviews, while her other feature role that year was in the unreleasable *White Dog*.

KRISTY MCNICHOL: FROM FAMILY TO EMPTY NEST

Kristy (here with brother Jimmy) vehemently denied rumors that she was addicted to drugs. *JOHN BARRETT/GLOBE PHOTOS*

Kristy McNichol: From Family to Empty Nest

Unable to revive her film career, in 1988 Kristy returned to her television roots, with a regular role on NBC's "Empty Nest." John Barrett/Globe Photos

When *Esquire* magazine interviewed Kristy in 1982, they found an uptight, moody star. When asked why she almost never read any of her fan mail, she brusquely responded, "I get a lot of feedback just walking around. I hear so much from people on the street, from my family. I don't need to go home and read letters saying how great I am."

The pressures of her sliding career finally caught up to her in December of 1982 while filming the romantic comedy *Just the Way You Are*. Kristy was hired, for a reported $1.6 million, to portray a handicapped flutist who disguises her leg brace with a cast while vacationing in the French Alps.

When the production took a two-week Christmas break, Kristy returned to California and, with only seventeen days of shooting left, refused to return to work on the $16 million production. When MGM/UA issued a statement that its star had a chemical imbalance, rumors began to circulate that Kristy suffered from drug addiction and/or manic depression. Kristy later denied the rumors, stating that her breakdown was the result of years of high pressure in the business.

> It all came to a head. All the rejection, all the ups and downs of my career—not having a childhood, coming from a broken home, not going to school, all these people telling me to do this and do that and not having any say-so.

After a year of intensive therapy, Kristy returned and completed the film, which received respectable reviews but was ignored by most moviegoers. Her subsequent work included mediocre work in film (*Dream Lover, You Can't Hurry Love,* and *The Forgotten One*) and television (*Women of Valor,* and *Children of the Bride*). In response to her stagnant career, in 1985 Kristy enrolled in the California College of Hair Design, worked briefly as a hairdresser, and later studied to be a real estate appraiser.

On the set of the television movie *Love, Mary* in 1987, a reporter with *TV Guide* found an insecure, temperamental actress whose performance was being coaxed by a nail-biting director. During the interview she referred to her illness as "a female hormonal thing" and pleaded with the writer, "It's important for me to say that I wasn't on drugs, because I wasn't."

Unable to revive her film career, in 1988 Kristy returned to television as Richard Mulligan's police officer daughter on the NBC sitcom "Empty Nest." Her new found stability ended in October 1992 when Kristy was written off the hit series after being diagnosed with "bi-polar depression."

THE CURSE OF DIFF'RENT STROKES

Probably no other group of child actors in television history had generated as many lurid stories than the cast of "Diff'rent Strokes." Launched on NBC during the fall of 1978, the show told the story of two black brothers (Todd Bridges and Gary Coleman) from Harlem who, after being orphaned by their mother, are taken in by a wealthy, white millionaire (Conrad Bain) and his daughter (Dana Plato). The show ran successfully on NBC from 1978 to 1985 and moved to ABC in 1986 for its eighth and final season.

Each week, a problematic situation would arise for one or all of the children that would be resolved in a tidy lesson at the show's end. Although the series was basically a lighthearted look at the problems facing an interracial family, there were episodes devoted to very serious subjects, including child abuse, bulimia, and the dangers of hitchhiking. Former First Lady Nancy Reagan appeared on one episode to preach the evils of drug abuse (apparently to little effect).

The Drummond children may have grown up happy and well adjusted, but Gary Coleman and Todd Bridges (here with TV dad Conrad Bain) did not. *RALPH DOMINGUEZ/GLOBE PHOTOS*

BEFORE HE BEGAN SUING THEM, GARY SPENT SOME HAPPY MOMENTS WITH HIS PARENTS, SUE AND WILLIE COLEMAN. *GLOBE PHOTOS*

GARY COLEMAN

Despite the size of the cast, which at various points included Dixie Carter, Charlotte Rae, and Janet Jackson, the main attraction of "Diff'rent Strokes" turned out to be the show's child stars. Of the three child actors, Gary Coleman immediately became the audience favorite.

Born on February 8, 1968, Gary suffered from a congenital kidney problem discovered when he was eighteen months old. When he was five, his right kidney was removed, leaving only his left kidney, which functioned at only 40 percent of normal capacity. That same year, Gary had a kidney transplant and then began taking growth-inhibiting steroids and other immunosuppressive drugs to inhibit the body's rejection of his new organ.

According to Danny Bonaduce, Gary now fills his days collecting real guns and toy trains. ROBERT LANDAU/GLOBE PHOTOS

Before appearing on "Diff'rent Strokes," Gary appeared in numerous television commercials starting at age six. In 1977, he won a CLIO award for best commercial of the year, honoring a spot he had done for a Chicago bank. After a talent scout for Norman Lear saw the commercial, he was brought to Hollywood to appear in a pilot based on the Little Rascals. Although that show failed to be picked up as a regular series, Lear placed Gary under contract and gave him small roles on episodes of "America 2-Night," "Good Times," and "The Jeffersons." In 1978, NBC programmers decided to design a show around this ten-year-old, pint-size curiosity.

Gary's character, Arnold Jackson, was a mix of many elements: shy but impudent, sweet but pesky, smart but naive. This characterization was occasionally undermined by Gary's own acting style, which relied on exaggerated gestures (such as eyeball rolling), heavy delivery, and a propensity to mug for close-ups.

During the show's annual hiatus, Gary kept busy with other acting projects. Owing to his small stature, however, he found himself confined to portraying youngsters in a series of overly precious movies. He appeared with Robert ("Benson") Guillaume in three nauseating TV films: *The Kid from Left Field* (1979), *The Kid with the Broken Halo* (1981), and *The Kid with the 200 I.Q.* (1981). His other television credits include *Scout's Honor* (1980), *The Fantastic World of D.C. Collins* (1983), and *Playing with Fire* (1984).

Gary made his feature film debut in *On the Right Track* (1981), portraying an adorable shoeshine boy who lives out of a locker at a train station. This may have seemed like a cute idea on paper, but the premise was hardly worthy of a feature film. His second feature, *Jimmy the Kid* (1983), had one critic noting that, "The presence of Coleman in the lead quickly diminishes any form of sincerity, not to mention how sad it is to see some talented actors having to center their abilities around this obnoxious ball of energy."

In 1983 Gary's health took a turn for the worse when his kidney began to fail and he was forced into daily dialysis. With the pressures of an aging series, normal teenage growing pains, and an uncertain health situation, fifteen-year-old Gary began family therapy with his parents. Speaking to *People* magazine in 1983, Gary declared, "I haven't turned rebellious yet and I don't think I ever will."

During November of 1984, Gary underwent a second transplant operation. Just one year after the surgery, however, the kidney began to fail and Gary was once again placed on dialysis.

By 1986 he was working steadily, taking in as much as $1.2 million annually. At home, his bedroom was stocked with model trains, computer games, and videocassettes of his favorite movies. Although he was a millionaire several times over, this four-foot, nine-inch seventeen-year-old had become thoroughly disenchanted with Hollywood. Gary remarked to *TV Guide*, "The reason my room is so big and that I live in it most of the time is that there's nothing real about L.A." He added, "When I first started acting I thought, 'All these stars, movies, premieres—isn't it wonderful and interesting and nice!' But it's shallow. Around the fourth season of 'Diff'rent Strokes,' my spirit just kind of died. Money, money, money—that's all that's ever put into my face any more from people in the business."

In 1987, nineteen-year-old Gary took a vacation with his close friend Dion Mial, an aspiring singer whom he'd met years earlier. Upon his return he fired his parents as managers and replaced them with Dion and his mother, Terry. By February of 1989, Gary's relationship with his parents became so strained that he filed a lawsuit against them, alleging that the

No, THIS ISN'T A MUG SHOT. IT'S ONLY TODD BRIDGES AFTER HIS ACQUITTAL ON ATTEMPTED MURDER CHARGES. *BOB V. NOBLE/GLOBE PHOTOS*

Colemans had mishandled his assets and diverted $1 million to their own accounts. Gary complained to *People* magazine, "They made stupid investments. They spent too much on cars, houses, furniture." Although he also admitted, "I did my part, too—I spent thousands of dollars on model trains."

Since his estrangement from his parents, Gary has maintained a reclusive lifestyle, living in Los Angeles, Denver, and later Phoenix, Arizona. Since 1986, Gary has had three unsuccessful kidney transplants and has reportedly become lax with his dialysis treatments.

Former co-star Todd Bridges believes that most of Gary's problems stem from his height, or lack of it. In a 1992 interview, Todd stated, "When he started he was short and he knew he was going to be short. And when me and Dana Plato were growing, he was not growing. And it really emotionally damaged him . . . and Gary Coleman, I feel, is very emotionally wrecked."

Dana Plato

During the height of "Diff'rent Strokes" sucess, writer Bill Davidson predicted a bright future for Dana, which included a "promising film future that could put her in the same class with such other phenomenal teenagers as Linda Blair, Jodie Foster, and Brooke Shields." It was an interesting, if somewhat overly optimistic, prediction.

Dana, born on November 7, 1964, was the adopted child of Kay and Dean Plato, a childless couple who owned and operated a trucking company in Los Angeles. Two and a half years later they divorced and Kay received custody of Dana. "He got the trucks and I got the baby," Kay told *TV Guide*.

At age six, Dana began her career on television, plugging everything from Kentucky Fried Chicken to Hallmark cards, in over a hundred commercial appearances. Along with the commercials, Dana made guest appearances on television ("The Six Million Dollar Man") and had minor roles in films, which included *Return to Boggy Creek* (1972) and *California Suite* (1978).

Dana was cast in the role of Kimberly Drummond after luckily losing out for a part on another NBC sitcom, the short-lived "Hello Larry." During her six seasons on "Diff'rent Strokes," Dana became a very wealthy young woman, earning as much as $22,000 per episode. During the show's annual hiatus, she continued to work in such projects as *Beyond the Bermuda Triangle* and *Sweet Sixteen and Never Been Killed* (1981). "My earnings touched a million dollars at one point," says Dana. I had two homes in the

San Fernando Valley—one with a twenty-four-track studio—and two boats docked in Marina del Rey."

Dana's career abruptly ended in 1984 when, during the show's sixth season, an unexpected pregnancy forced her to leave the series. Her absence from the show was explained as Kimberly's post-high school studies in Paris. Shortly thereafter, Dana found herself facing several personal dilemmas, the first of which occurred when her estranged father unsuccessfully sued her for support.

In 1984, Dana married Lenny Lambert, a drummer—a union that lasted until the birth of their son, Tyler, in 1985. Four years later, after being swindled out of her savings by unscrupulous accountants, Dana had to sell off most of her prized possessions. Bankrupt and in debt to the I.R.S., Dana turned her son over to Lenny. "I miss him terribly," she says. "But with his father, he's got a family. It's better for him."

Dana has attributed her personal and professional fall from grace as a result of her long-term alcohol addiction. In 1992 she confessed to a national tabloid, "It was Bloody Marys for breakfast, top them up for lunch, and then, not content, I'd guzzle down a six-pack. The cocktail hour began a binge lasting all day and all of the night." The death of her adopted mother, Kay, sent Dana on a two-month bender that landed her in Cedars-Sinai Medical Center for treatment.

In an effort to restart her career, Dana posed seminude for the June 1989 issue of *Playboy*. The move, however, backfired, and only generated interest from porn film makers.

She eventually wound up in Las Vegas and shared a $550 a month apartment with a boyfriend, his best friend, and eleven cats. After a brief stint working for $5.75 an hour as a cashier/tourist attraction at a local drive-through cleaner's, she was eventually fired after a dispute with another employee.

On the morning of February 28, 1991, Dana applied for job in her apartment complex picking up trash. After being turned down, she dressed in black, donned sunglasses, and walked over to the local video store. According to police, Dana entered the store and demanded all of their money. The clerk, who immediately recognized her, asked if she was kidding. Dana reportedly pulled out a pellet gun and said, "Does this look like I'm kidding?" Before leaving the store with the $164 she had collected, she dropped her hat and sunglasses.

When Dana returned to the store fifteen minutes later to retrieve her sunglasses, the police promptly arrested her and charged her with armed robbery. Four days later, Wayne Newton posted her $13,000 bail because he knew "the trauma of being a child star."

To celebrate her "comeback," Dana happily autographed copies of the Playboy issue in which she displayed her natural assets.
JOHN BARRETT/GLOBE PHOTOS

DANA PLATO (HERE WITH CO-STAR GARY COLEMAN) WAS BOOTED FROM THE SERIES AFTER SHE BECAME PREGNANT IN 1984.
GENE TRINDL/GLOBE PHOTOS

Dana later pleaded guilty to a lesser charge of attempted robbery. The charge was reduced under a plea bargain agreement arranged by her lawyers. She eventually received five years on probation and was ordered to perform four hundred hours of community service.

In January of 1992, Dana was arrested once again, this time for forging a ... ls. Dana was charged with four co... e by fraud and four counts of b... Dana, who was in custody for th... d to falsifying the prescriptions. ... e for leniency, saying, "I need he... ges came to her defense, and in a ... s finally come to the point in life w... parently agreed and gave Dana a ... e years' probation.

... I hadn't gotten caught, it could ha... e because I could have died of a ... s, "I don't mind being watched. W... someone looking over your sh...

in ... er and has recently been seen

...ES

To... bles stemmed from a hard add... it. According to Todd, "The only ... committed was using drugs." But that is certainly not the only crime he's ever been accused of. After "Diff'rent Strokes" ended its run, Todd accumulated a list of criminal charges that included carrying a concealed weapon, assault with a deadly weapon, and attempted murder.

Born on May 27, 1965, Todd is the youngest of three children born to Betty, a drama teacher, and Jim Bridges, a theatrical agent. While Todd was still a tot, Betty and Jim began to prepare their son for a career as an actor. At age four, Todd was also a pro, modeling for magazine ads and acting in television commercials. After a guest appearance on the series "Barney Miller," eight-year-old Todd was cast as a street-smart urchin on the series spin-off "Fish" (1977–1978). His work on that show, along with appearances on other network series ("Little House on the Prairie," "Roots," "The

Waltons," and "The Love Boat"), led to his being cast as Willis Jackson on "Diff'rent Strokes."

In 1981, entertainment writer Bill Davidson described Todd Bridges as a "possible future matinee idol in the Billy Dee Williams mold." At the time, sixteen-year-old Todd certainly seemed to have that goal in sight. During the course of the show's eight-year run, audiences watched Todd mature from a awkward twelve-year-old to a charismatic twenty-year-old teen idol. Todd earned as much as $30,000 per episode.

By the time he reached eighteen, Todd began to make headlines with a series of bizarre and sometimes violent incidents. In July of 1983, he was stopped by Beverly Hills police for speeding and running a red light. A search of his car uncovered a loaded .45 pistol, for which he was promptly arrested. Todd reported to the police that he was trying to protect himself from KKK members who had shot at him at his home in Canoga Park several months earlier. Because his permit to carry the weapon had expired, Todd received a $240 fine and a year's summary probation.

On the set of "Diff'rent Strokes," his rivalry with co-star Gary Coleman was no secret to production staffers. In fact, the two young men had to be pulled apart by Conrad Bain during an on-set scuffle that same year. "Gary Coleman had a huge, gigantic dressing room," Todd later whined. "All I wanted was one half that size."

When the show was finally cancelled in 1986, his career ended and his legal troubles continued to escalate. He filed suit against his accountants, claiming that they had embezzled from his trust fund and left him owing $200,000 in back taxes. His ongoing feud with local police earned him a large number of traffic tickets.

In July of 1986, Todd pleaded no contest to making a bomb threat to an auto customizer with whom he had a dispute. In lieu of a one-year jail term he was placed on three years' probation, fined $2,500, and ordered to perform 300 hours of community service and pay $6,000 in restitution.

With encouragement from his publicist, in 1988 Todd entered a drug rehabilitation program and joined Alcoholics Anonymous. Although he managed to remain sober for six months, the death of his AA sponsor sent Todd back to his old self-destructive ways.

In February of 1989, Todd was charged with firing eight bullets from a .22 revolver into Kenneth Clay, an alleged cocaine dealer, in an L.A. ghetto. Clay managed to survive despite wounds to his right shoulder, left armpit, upper lip, and neck. Unable to raise the $2 million bail, Todd spent nine months in jail awaiting trial.

During his trial, Todd testified that in the days preceding the shooting he "was getting high around the clock," with a 14-gram-a-day cocaine habit.

At the time of the incident he was coming off a four-day high and, therefore, could not remember shooting Clay.

In November of 1990, Todd was acquitted of attempted murder and attempted voluntary manslaughter. The jury, however, deadlocked on the charge of assault with a deadly weapon and Todd was released on $25,000 bail until he could be retried. Two months later, Todd was acquitted of the assault charge.

Six months later, Todd and a companion were arrested for possession of 48 grams of cocaine with intent to sell. The charges were dropped when prosecutors were unable to prove who the drugs actually belonged to.

In recent years, Todd has met resistance from casting directors and producers in his attempts to come back into the business. "I get the auditions, but I think a lot of it is they're not sure, they don't know, they don't trust me as much," says Todd. "So I think I have to keep pounding the pavement."

Todd's most recent credits include a guest appearance on "The New Lassie" (ironically enough, playing a young cop) and a 1991 antidrug documentary. An outspoken critic of drug abuse, Todd frequently lectures in schools, halfway homes, and prisons.

ENOUGH IS ENOUGH

T he young actors of "Eight Is Enough," perhaps one of the more popular shows of the late seventies, have generated their own share of horror stories. Based on the book by Thomas Braden, "Eight Is Enough" told the sometimes comic, sometimes serious, escapades of a middle-aged couple raising eight free-spirited children. The show, which ran on ABC from 1977 to 1981, starred Dick Van Patten as mild-mannered newspaper columnist Tom Bradford and Diana Hyland as his devoted wife, Joan. (After completing only four episodes, Hyland died from cancer. Tom remained a widow, until the following season when Betty Buckley joined the cast as second wife, Abby.) While the Bradfords embodied all-American values on the TV screen, the lives of some of the young actors off the show were a far cry from the wholesome appearance viewers were accustomed to seeing.

Grant Goodeve, who portrayed the eldest son, David, struggled for years with alcoholism. (Now fully sober, Grant has switched careers and is

When he was eleven years old, Adam Rich reportedly walked around the set of "Eight is Enough" drinking rum and Coke.
STEVE SCHATZBERG/GLOBE PHOTOS

now a gospel singer.) Willie Aames, who portrayed Tommy, survived his own drug and alcohol addictions and eventually wound up on the syndicated TV series "Charles in Charge." Lani O'Grady, who portrayed the eldest daughter, Mary, claims that pressures brought on by the show led to her Valium addiction. The most bizarre story in the group involves Susan Richardson, who reported to the tabloids that she was held hostage while working on a film in South Korea. (She now resides on a Pennsylvania farm.)

If anyone's career landed with a resounding "thud" it was Adam Rich, who portrayed the youngest child on the show, adorable Nicholas Bradford.

After taking acting lessons at age four, Adam began making the rounds of casting agents and during the course of the next five years made over a hundred commercials. In 1977, nine-year-old Adam won the role of Nicholas. During the show's four-year run, however, Adam picked up more than a few bad habits. At age eleven, Adam began drinking rum and cola between takes.

After the series ended in 1981, Adam had roles in two short-lived series, "Code Red" (1981–1982) and "Gun Shy" (1983). Arrested for possession of marijuana in 1983, Adam soon began to experiment with LSD and cocaine. After dropping out of high school in 1986, Adam continued his bad habits. A five-foot, three-inch overweight actor, the only work available to Adam were the two specials that reunited the show's cast in 1987 and 1989.

Fed up with their son's excesses, Adam's parents (who had divorced) disassociated from their son. Adam had infrequent contact with his father, a retired mechanic, while his mother changed her phone number. During his later teens, Adam estimates that his drug addiction cost him a million dollars. After the money ran out, Adam took drastic and painful steps in order to satisfy his drug need. He later admitted to *People* magazine, "What I used to do was lean up against a wall and knock my shoulder out on my own to get IV morphine and prescriptions to last me a couple weeks. I did this about twelve times and after that my arm couldn't stay in the socket." Adam eventually had to have surgery to repair his damaged shoulder.

During the filming of "An Eight is Enough Wedding" (1989), a drug binge put him in a two-week coma from which he almost died. Over the next three years, Adam wandered in and out of five rehabilitation programs but was unable to kick his habits as his legal problems continued to escalate. In 1990, Adam pleaded guilty to drunk driving and was placed on five years' probation.

In March of 1991, Adam was arrested and charged with burglary. According to police, after being refused painkillers at a local hospital, Rich smashed the window of a pharmacy with a tire iron with the intention of

Adam spent his post-showbiz years throwing himself into walls and down stairs in order to get prescription drugs.
DONALD SANDERS/GLOBE PHOTOS

Enough Is Enough

53

stealing morphine. Dick Van Patten posted the $5,000 bail, saying, "I just did what anybody would do for a friend."

Less than twenty-four hours later, Adam was arrested again, this time for shoplifting a pair of sunglasses and socks valued at $29.75 from a Bullock's department store in downtown L.A. He was released to his father's custody after putting up an additional $250.

At the hearing for the burglary charges held in September of 1991, Adam fell asleep in court. The judge postponed the hearing and ordered that Adam be tested for drugs. According to Adam, those tests were inconclusive and on that day he was just "tired and nervous."

One month later, Adam was arrested yet again, after allegedly pocketing a drug-filled syringe from a hospital in Marina Del Rey, where he was being treated for yet another dislocated shoulder. He was held on $20,000 bail.

For the shoplifting charges, prosecutors allowed Adam to plead no contest to a trespassing charge and on October 31, 1991, Adam was fined $250 and placed on two years' probation. In addition, he was ordered to complete a drug rehabilitation program and ordered to do his shopping elsewhere.

In January of 1992, Adam was jailed after officials claimed that he threw himself down a flight of stairs at a drug rehab center in an attempt to get painkilling drugs. Denied bail, the judge in this case sentenced Adam to thirty days in jail.

THE LIFE AND LOVES
OF DANNY BONADUCE

"I was an obnoxious child," says Danny Bonaduce, referring to his years on the musical sitcom "The Partridge Family." "It was a grown-up world, and sometimes acting like a grown-up when you're ten years old doesn't look right." Danny's immaturity, however, carried over into his adult life, filled with cocaine addiction, spur of the moment marriages, and an arrest for an altercation involving a transvestite prostitute.

Born on August 13, 1959, Danny is the youngest of three children raised by Betty and Joe Bonaduce. The Bonaduces, television script writers who worked together on the original "Bill Cosby Show," divorced in 1974. At age two, Danny began earning his keep as a child model and later as an actor in commercials. He was a television veteran by the time he auditioned for "The Partridge Family" seven years later.

Loosely based on the experiences of a real-life recording family, the Cowsills, "The Partridge Family" depicted the comic exploits of a widowed

DANNY BONADUCE (*RIGHT*), HERE WITH DAVID CASSIDY, WAS ARRESTED FOR THE BEATING OF A TRANSVESTITE PROSTITUTE.
HERM LEWIS/GLOBE PHOTOS

mother and her hyperactive children, who take their musical act on the road in a multicolored bus. The show, which ran on ABC from 1970 to 1974, starred Oscar winner Shirley Jones as harried mother Shirley Partridge.

Although David Cassidy became a teen idol on the show, it was Danny Bonaduce who was the comic star of the series. Danny played his role of a wisecracking troublemaker to perfection. Shirley Jones remembers her former co-star as a rebellious little kid. "When I was working with him, I would swat him once in a while and make him behave," she told *People* magazine in 1992. "We got along really well, but you just had to keep him in line."

Danny thoroughly enjoyed the four years he spent wearing bell-bottoms and crushed velvet tunics. "I spent my childhood on jet planes and with mayors. I didn't play baseball, but I did ride an elephant. I missed out on football, but I flew on the Concorde. I totally lucked out."

But Danny's luck was quickly running out. By the time the series was cancelled in 1974, Danny was well into his awkward teens. Short and overweight, the unemployable actor moved away from home over the next several years and proceeded to spend all of the $350,000 he had earned from the show.

His acting credits after the show ended came in several unreleased kung-fu films and various guest appearances, including "C.H.I.P's," "California Fever," "Moonlighting," and "Spenser for Hire." He also lent his voice to several cartoon series, including "Partridge Family 2200 A.D." and "Goober and the Ghost Chasers." According to Danny, "There's a time, when things are at the bottom is when you find yourself clawing over the bodies of "My Three Sons" to get on "The Love Boat," that you realize that things aren't going as planned." Things are definitely not going as planned when you find yourself opening supermarkets and singing on cruise ships, as Danny did.

In 1985 he was arrested for possession of four grams of cocaine after running a red light in West Hollywood. The charges were later dismissed when Danny agreed to enter a drug counseling program.

Shortly thereafter, Danny met a Japanese woman in an L.A. restaurant. Three days later, they were married, so that the woman could apply for a green card. The couple separated six months later.

In 1989, Danny moved to Philadelphia where he landed a job as a raucous late-night deejay at WEGX-FM. In a 1989 interview with *People* magazine, Danny declared, "I'm one of the luckiest men alive, because I basically have no skills, and if I had to get a job and function in the regular world, I couldn't do it. I'm only qualified to be a celebrity."

Just one year later, however, Danny was arrested in Daytona Beach, Florida, after allegedly attempting to buy $20 worth of crack cocaine. After pleading no contest to the charges, he was sentenced to fifteen months' probation and community service. Deciding to make a fresh start in his life, Danny relocated to Phoenix, Arizona, where he landed another deejay slot at KKFR radio.

In 1991, Danny married his second wife, Gretchen, during their first date. According to Danny, after Gretchen declined to go to bed with him, saying, "No, no. I'm sorry I can't do that 'til I'm married," Danny went through the yellow pages and called a minister and "we were married by midnight."

The marriage did little to provide tranquility. In April of 1991, Danny was arrested in connection with the robbing and beating of a transvestite prostitute. The police report alleged that Danny picked up a prostitute and paid him/her $20 to perform oral sex. When the prostitute, who was actually a man dressed as a woman, refused an encore performance, Danny allegedly beat the transvestite, took back his money, and fled the scene by car while patrol cars and police helicopters chased him on a 90-mph sweep through central Phoenix.

Alerted by local residents, police found Danny, naked and bloodied, hiding in the bedroom closet of his apartment. After a struggle, Danny was arrested and booked with the felony charges of flight, aggravated assault, and strong-arm robbery. Facing a two-year prison sentence and a $150,000 fine, Danny pleaded guilty to endangerment and no contest to misdemeanor assault.

Danny later denied that he was seeking sex from the hooker. "That's completely untrue," he said. "The police never even considered charging me with soliciting sex for money. There was no sex involved and no attempt at soliciting sex. . . . I pleaded guilty to winning a fistfight and running home." At his sentencing in August of 1991, Danny received three years' probation and was ordered to perform 750 hours of community service. Additionally, he was ordered to pay $4,500 in restitution to the victim of his assault, who suffered a broken nose during the incident.

The incident cost Danny his job at KKFR. Said Danny, "I guess it was because I brought so much bad publicity to the station." He paused, then added, "I also tripled their ratings." Not one to let grass grow under his feet, Danny launched another career as a stand-up comic. His first gig was as opening act for "Partridge" co-star David Cassidy. According to Danny, "David's a fairly serious man. He told me it was time to start being funny and stop being a joke. He made me feel awful."

After a ten-year absence from acting, Danny returned to Hollywood to film *America's Deadliest Home Video,* in which he plays a video-cam fanatic who is forced by a gang of thieves into taping crimes.

PART II

ALL IN THE FAMILY

It would seem a natural advantage in the movie industry to be the son or daughter of a successful acting parent. Indeed, Hollywood history is filled with legendary acting dynasties. The names Fonda, Bridges, and Huston are just a few examples of families who have seemingly passed on their talent from one generation to the next. While some may question whether talent can be inherited (the Brat Pack is a case in point), it would appear that being the offspring of a famous parent is not all it's cracked up to be.

This is especially true when the child's parents pass on not only their talent (or some smattering thereof) but their propensity to indulge in such vices as booze, drugs, sexual promiscuity, or marital infidelity. Thus, it is not surprising that Mackenzie Phillips, who spent years trying to emulate her famous junkie father, would herself become a hard-core addict.

Mackenzie's parents, Baltimore socialite Susan Adams and John Phillips (founder of the original The Mamas and the Papas) were divorced

CHILDREN OF BABYLON

After years of erratic behavior and one highly publicized drug arrest, in 1980 Mackenzie Phillips was fired from the hit show "One Day at a Time." *Steve Schatzberg/Globe Photos*

FRANCIS FORD COPPOLA (*CENTER*) SPENT YEARS GROOMING HIS SONS GIO AND ROMAN FOR CAREERS IN THE FILM INDUSTRY.
RICHARD CORKERY/GLOBE PHOTOS

when she was three years old. A wild child, by age twelve Mackenzie had formed her own band and had experimented with booze and pot. Small film parts in *American Graffiti* and *Rafferty and the Gold Dust Twins* led to her being cast, alongside Bonnie Franklin and Valerie Bertinelli, in the sitcom "One Day at a Time."

Mackenzie's life from this point on dissolved into that old self-destructive pattern of sex and drugs. In 1977, she was found sprawled on a West Hollywood street and was arrested for possession of cocaine and public intoxication. In 1980, on the rebound from an affair with a married man, she wed musician Jeff Sessler, whom "even his mother described as an asshole." The union lasted all of seven months. Her erratic behavior on and off the set of "One Day at a Time" resulted in her well-publicized dismissal from the show in 1980.

Alone and hopelessly addicted, Mackenzie spent her days watching soap operas and snorting, freebasing, or shooting cocaine. "There were mirrors, razors, empty tequila bottles, and half-eaten pizzas lying all over the apartment," she later recalled. After two near-fatal overdoses, Mackenzie checked into a rehab program where her father was being treated for his cocaine and heroin addiction. Clean and sober since 1985, Mackenzie performs alongside her father with the new Mamas and the Papas. She also travels around the country giving lectures on the horrors of addiction.

Like Mackenzie, Desi Arnaz, Jr., Drew Barrymore, Carrie Fisher, Jamie Lee Curtis, and Griffin O'Neal are all offspring of major Hollywood figures whose destructive paths were followed. An astute business man but lousy father figure, Desi Arnaz's drinking, gambling, and womanizing set a poor example for his young son. Thus, the revelation that Desi Jr. had also taken a liking to wine, women, and song was not especially startling.

While the name Barrymore has become synonymous with talent and hard living, it was especially shocking to read in the tabloids that the clan's youngest member had become a twelve-year-old coke head. Other surprising details about her extensive substance abuse were revealed by fifteen-year-old Drew herself in her own tell-all autobiography *Little Girl Lost*.

Griffin O'Neal was also drawn into the seductive Hollywood lifestyle at a very early age. "Living in this town, you know, growing up with the money and the peer pressure and the bad influences that go around you . . . you tend to lose track, you tend to act stupid." One of Griffin's most reckless acts wound up costing the life of Francis Coppola's son, Gio.

Carrie Fisher found that being the child of very famous, very divorced, parents set her apart. She explained to one interviewer, "I can't run into a room and say, 'You know how you felt when you saw your dad more on TV than you did in life?' Literally, the only person I can talk to about this is Jamie Lee Curtis. Her father (Tony Curtis) was a womanizer and a drug user. So was mine." Jamie Lee Curtis agrees: "You're a child trying to develop an identity and a sense of self-worth, and all this Hollywood stuff plagues you and makes you kind of wonder who you are."

DREW BARRYMORE:
LITTLE GIRL STONED

At age six, Drew Barrymore was the youngest star of an acting dynasty. By the age of twelve, she had become a pint-size party girl with an appetite for booze, pot, cocaine, and older men. In 1992, America's sweetheart emerged as a teenage tart who in her own words is "a person without pride; someone who will do what it takes to get a film."

The name Barrymore has been associated with the theater from the early 1800s. The name is also associated with high living, alcoholism, and self-destruction. Drew's grandfather, John Barrymore, Sr., one of the finest Shakespearean and movie actors of the twenties and thirties, drank himself to death at age sixty. Drew's aunt, Diana, also an addict and alcoholic, died at age thirty-eight.

With his father's good looks, John Drew Barrymore had no difficulty finding work in Hollywood, albeit in grade-B films, the more notable of which included *The Sundowners* (1950), *While the City Sleeps* (1956), and *Never Love a Stranger* (1958). John, however, garnered more press for his

CHILDREN OF BABYLON

66

DREW BARRYMORE, HERE WITH MOTHER JAID, HAS FULLY LIVED UP TO THE FAMILY TRADITION OF FAST LIVING. *GLOBE PHOTOS*

volatile temper and bouts with alcoholism than for his acting ability. He was arrested several times on charges stemming from drunk driving, hit-and-run driving, and engaging in violent quarrels with his first two wives. John later spent time in Italy to star in a series of low-budget costume pictures before returning to the U.S. Shortly thereafter, he was arrested for possession of marijuana.

When Drew's mother, Ildyko Jaid Mako, an aspiring actress, met John Jr., he was twice divorced and hopelessly addicted to women, booze, and drugs. During their brief and stormy marriage, Jaid repeatedly tried to reform John, but to no avail. By the time Drew was born on February 22, 1975, Jaid had separated from her husband.

Jaid managed to raise Drew in West Hollywood, by supplementing her meager acting wages with a waitress job at a trendy L.A. nightclub. After a friend submitted Drew's photo to a talent agent, Jaid let her daughter audition for commercial work. An eleven-month-old Drew won her first commercial for Gainsburgers dogfood. The assignment was a memorable one for Drew in more ways than one; during the shooting, she was bit by the ad agency's puppy.

In 1980, Drew made her motion picture debut with a bit role in Ken Russell's *Altered States* (which also marked the motion picture debut of William Hurt), and followed up in the made-for-TV flick *Bogie*.

Drew's biggest break came after being spotted by director Steven Spielberg. Although she lost out to Heather O'Rourke for a featured role in *Poltergeist,* Drew won the role of Gertie, the younger sister, in the heart warming family drama *E.T., The Extra-terrestrial*.

Released in 1982, the enormous success of *E.T.* astounded its makers and made celebrities of the film's child actors, Henry Thomas, Robert McNaughton, and Drew. Drew later admitted to entertainment reporter John Tesh in 1992 that this instant fame was scary: "I was just, you know, some little kid and, you know, going into every place in the world and having no one bat an eye at me and all of a sudden I couldn't walk out of my front door. And being six years old, you know, I couldn't go to the movies; you know, my mom couldn't let me because I would just get mobbed and that was really hard to deal with."

With the $75,000 that Drew earned from *E.T.*, Jaid stopped waitressing to manage Drew's blossoming career while pursuing her own auditions. (Jaid, who had only moderate success as a stage actress, can be seen on film in the role of a prostitute in the 1982 film *Night Shift*, starring Henry Winkler.) Jaid eventually shelved her own acting ambitions to handle Drew's increasing popularity. She said later, "I wanted to make sure Drew is centered, balanced, and has a valid sense of worth."

D‎REW'S FORMER STEADY, COREY FELDMAN, WAS ARRESTED IN 1990 AFTER BUYING A LARGE QUANTITY OF COCAINE AND HEROIN.
RALPH DOMINGUEZ/GLOBE PHOTOS

In 1984, Drew earned a reported $500,000 to portray a ten-year-old who sues her callous, career-oriented parents (Ryan O'Neal and Shelley Long) for divorce due to emotional neglect, in the film *Irreconcilable Differences*. Compared to the fun she had filming *E.T.*, Drew would later describe this movie's three-month production as "utter hell." During the production, which was wrought with "nonstop fighting," Drew became exhausted with the numerous retakes of virtually every scene.

Her other role that year was in Stephen King's *Firestarter*, starring George C. Scott and Martin Sheen. The film's premise consisted of a young girl's ability to set things on fire at will. Although critics and audiences were largely unimpressed with the film, Drew managed to catch the eye of

DREW BARRYMORE:

LITTLE GIRL STONED

69

Drew's first addiction was to nightclubs. By age twelve, she was hooked on cocaine. *Sylvia Sutton/Globe Photos*

Stephen King, who offered her a featured role in his next project, *Cat's Eye*.

In the course of such heady experiences, both Drew and her mother succumbed to the L.A. nightlife. Drew had a hard time adjusting to her normal responsibilities at school. A below-average student, Drew believed that the students and teachers were jealous of her. Of course, her weekend nightlife did little to help her with her studies. Later, Jaid said, "I just felt that if we were together, somehow it was all right to be out late."

Drew's first addiction was to the nightclubs that she and her mother frequented. She later recalled, "I just wanted to go out and have a good time and I thought that it was pretty nifty that, you know, I, eight-years-old, could go tromping past all the forty-year-olds and get in like that, you know, and get carried in there, literally. Um, I thought that that was pretty cool at the beginning and then it just sort of became very normal, a very normal lifestyle."

Her mother even held her tenth birthday party at the Limelight in New York, allowing Drew to disco until 2 a.m. By this time she was smoking cigarettes and sneaking drinks from other glasses. At a party at her agent's house, Drew once passed out after crawling behind the bar and downing several vodkas. She began smoking pot after being offered some by a friend's mother. From cigarettes, booze, and pot, it was only a short time until she made the big step into the hazy world of cocaine. She was addicted by age twelve.

Never a strict disciplinarian, Jaid later told *People* magazine's Todd Gold, "So where was I? The question is a shocker since our lives have been intertwined like braids, almost two of us against the world. But when she turned nine or ten, I felt I had to give her time and space. I began to lose perspective on what was going on with Drew." No kidding. Jaid apparently never smelled the liquor on Drew's breath or noticed all the times her daughter came home stoned.

By the time she entered sixth grade, Drew was constantly fighting with her mom and earning "piss-poor grades" in school. During the days, "I just went to school, ditched school, hung out with friends and went to movies." At night, Drew would often sneak out with a friend to go club-hopping, knowing that her celebrity status would earn her instant admission to the trendiest nightclubs.

Drew tried to balance her constant partying with a waning acting career. She spent four months in Germany filming the TV movie *Babes in Toyland,* followed by four months in New York filming *See You in the Morning* (1989), a drama about the effects of divorce on children, which starred Jeff Bridges and Farah Fawcett.

During her stay in New York, Drew became an infrequent visitor to her mom's apartment, dropping off or picking up clothes. By that time she and Jaid were having screaming matches that usually ended when Drew fled to a friend's apartment. After Drew told her mom that she (Jaid) needed to "get laid," the angry woman threw a $100 bill at her thirteen-year-old daughter and kicked her out of the apartment.

After lifting her mother's credit card, Drew embarked on a two-day, coke-filled cross country adventure, which was cut short when two private detectives hired by Jaid intercepted her and brought her in handcuffs to a private rehab facility. At $500 per day, the ASAP Family Treatment Center in Van Nuys, California, offers counselling to drug-addicted youngsters and their families.

Jaid later said, "Like most parents, I had no idea what was going on." Both Jaid's and Drew's behavior has raised many questions, such as, Why didn't Jaid notice all the times her child was obviously drunk, or stoned, or out until early morning? Questions aside, Drew emerged from the clinic in 1989 proclaiming to be free from her dependencies. She told her tale of substance abuse to the shocked readers of *People* and *TV Guide,* while filming the ABC special "15 and Getting Straight." One network publicist, however, became increasingly concerned with the situation. "Frankly, I'm uncomfortable with this," she said. "I don't know if it's part of her therapy or what, but it smacks of exploitation."

But after only six months, Drew broke her sobriety by smoking marijuana. Slowly but surely she began to regress and once again took on her old foe, her mother. The two fought constantly until Drew and a friend moved into their own apartment. One month later, after a fight with some of her friends, Drew accidentally slashed her wrist and had to be rushed to a hospital.

From there she returned to the ASAP center for a three-month stay. ASAP convinced Jaid to check in for six weeks of separate counselling at a clinic in Phoenix. After Drew's release she moved in with David Crosby, the musician of Crosby, Stills, Nash & Young fame, and his wife, Jan. The Crosbys had lived through their own ordeals with drug and alcohol abuse. (David has been straight since his eleven-month jail sentence for a drug and weapons charge.)

Drew has had a hard time convincing producers to give her a second chance. She lost out to Winona Ryder for roles in *Heathers, Great Balls of Fire, Edward Scissorhands,* and *Bram Stoker's Dracula.* She was also passed over for a part in *Cape Fear,* a role that earned Juliette Lewis an Academy Award nomination. "I've watched other actresses take parts right out of my hands because they're older," she complained to *Movieline.* "You can't help hating your competition, and any actress who says they don't get jealous is lying. I mean, people think Julia Roberts is so wonderful because she's tall and pretty and all she does is shake her ass and smile."

Drew becomes indignant when talking about the Hollywood system: "Hollywood is a town where bullsh __ walks and money talks. . . . It's very irritating for me when I know certain actors are totally f __ ked up on drugs and are working in movies back to back, yet it gets covered up. Why the f __ k wasn't I excused for 'exhaustion' or 'the flu?'"

No longer the adorable pigtailed little girl, Drew has recently taken some startling image changing roles. In the 1992 film *Poison Ivy,* Drew stunned viewers by giving Sara ("Roseanne") Gilbert a deep tongue kiss. In promoting the movie, she boasted to one reporter, "Well, we cross so many boundaries in this little number, it's going to shock the sh __ out of America."

Equally shocking was the nude cover photo of Drew on the July 1992 issue of *Interview* magazine. In the photo essay that graced the inner pages, the seventeen-year-old was seen frolicking naked with her fiancé James ("The Heights") Walters and several female models. On "The Arsenio Hall Show," she described the essay as a "free, loving, piece on friendship, love, and the environment and so on and so forth." Arsenio noted what a "nice, little onion" she had. So much for art.

Although she has managed to generate an enormous amount of publicity, Drew's most recent acting assignments have been less than noteworthy. Despite the controversy that surrounded the film's release, *Poison Ivy* failed to ignite any box office fires. Her 1992 film *Gun Crazy* went unreleased and made its way to television via pay cable.

As for her future, Drew aspires to develop into an all-around actress. "I do want to do Lolita, but I also love to do character roles. I'd love to get a part where I'd have to shave my head. I love stuff like that, and that is how you perfect your craft." In the interim, Drew has tried her hand on network television, portraying an aspiring actress on the short—lived Aaron Spelling series "2000 Malibu Road" (1992).

Drew also has directing aspirations. "I have a complete desire to direct. I've been writing, working on a treatment, and I would really love to direct it."

Carrie Fisher: Princess Leia Lands in Rehab

The product of one of Hollywood's most famous broken homes, Carrie Fisher achieved her own fame by starring in the most successful film series of all time—the *Star Wars* trilogy. After becoming an "overnight sensation," Carrie soared into her own deep space, embarking on a ten-year drug binge. She survived her own very public divorce and emerged from rehab with a pen in hand, and has since become a successful author and screenwriter.

"I was born into something much larger than myself," says Carrie, referring to her parents, crooner Eddie Fisher and actress Debbie Reynolds. Edwin Jack Fisher staked his claim to fame in the early sixties as a teen idol with such hits as "Lady of Spain," "Fanny," and "Oh, My Papa." Early in his career, Eddie was constantly performing, whether in concert or on the radio. After Eddie lost his voice before one performance, a local musician recommended that he visit Dr. Max Jocobson, a respected doctor, who gave special "vitamin cocktails" that provided extra energy. Jacobson had a large

Carrie Fisher, seen here with Debbie Reynolds, began a singing career at age thirteen, performing with her mother in Las Vegas.
GLOBE PHOTOS

CHILDREN OF BABYLON

clientele of celebrities, which included Marilyn Monroe, Jay Lerner, and John F. Kennedy. What most of these patients did not know was that the mixture that Jacobson injected into them was only 15 percent vitamins. The rest was a mixture of amphetamines, today known as speed.

Mary Frances Reynolds was born in El Paso Texas in 1933 and was later raised in Burbank, California. From a middle-class, Baptist family, Debbie became a typical California teenager. Popular and outgoing, Debbie won the Miss Burbank Beauty Contest of 1948 and received a six-month contract at

Warner Brothers with an option that was picked up by MGM. Her first movie appearance was at age sixteen in *The Daughter of Rosie O'Grady* (1949). Two years later, she became a major player, starring alongside Gene Kelly in *Singin' in the Rain*. She had made a total of ten pictures before she met Eddie.

Born in Los Angeles on October 21, 1956, Carrie Frances Fisher was only three hours old when she was photographed for *Modern Screen* magazine, which was doing a story touting the film *Bundle of Joy,* starring Eddie and Debbie. Despite such outward appearances of happy family life, the marriage was fraught with tension and arguments over Eddie's erratic behavior.

During their marriage, the couple became close friends with Elizabeth Taylor and Michael Todd. Eddie was so close with Elizabeth's third husband that when Debbie gave birth to a baby boy in February 1958, they christened the child Todd Emmanuel Fisher in honor of Mike Todd. Three weeks after Todd was born, Mike was killed in the crash of his plane, *Lucky Liz*. When Eddie began to spend more time consoling the widow Todd than at home, a major Hollywood triangle developed.

After Eddie divorced Debbie and subsequently married Elizabeth, his reputation dived precipitously. It was well known that he was a virtual no-show father to his children, Carrie, 2, and Todd, age 1. He made only two alimony payments before claiming a lack of funds. He never sent presents to his children.

The bad publicity generated by the divorce damaged the careers of both Liz and Eddie. Many believe that the scandal cost Liz the Oscar for her performance in *Cat on a Hot Tin Roof*. In 1960, Eddie co-starred with Taylor in the film *Butterfield 8*, in which Liz's real life-and-death struggle with pneumonia helped her secure an Academy Award.

Eddie's career was more severely damaged. With the reputation of a Hollywood heel, his record sales dropped dramatically, while low ratings forced NBC to cancel his television show. Although he continued to sing in nightclubs, Liz Taylor remained the show's biggest draw, as she was conspicuously seated in the audience every night.

In 1963, Taylor began a scorching affair with Richard Burton during the lensing of *Cleopatra,* and her marriage to Eddie soon dissolved. After a brief marriage to Connie Stevens, Eddie's life dissipated into booze, drugs, and numerous women. Carrie described her father to writer Tim Appelo: "He's not very powerful—more carried along by events, and thinking with his little head. It wasn't easy to wrangle him down to speed, especially since he was always *on* speed."

Despite the divorce, Carrie and Todd were raised in a privileged

CARRIE FISHER:

PRINCESS LEIA

LANDS IN REHAB

CARRIE (HERE WITH *STAR WARS* CO-STAR MARK HAMILL) ONCE DESCRIBED HER WILD 20S AS NOT ONLY "CHANGING SEATS ON THE TITANIC . . . BUT DATING THE CREW, TOO." *NATE CUTLER/GLOBE PHOTOS*

CHILDREN OF BABYLON

environment. "We grew up on the Map of the Stars. We played games on the tourists. If they shot stills, we ran. If they shot films, we stood still." When Todd wanted a tree house, Debbie had an eighty-five-foot Monterey pine planted on her front lawn. Referring to her home as a "broken mansion," Carrie told *People* magazine, "The place was wired for security into the police. Teams of people brought us up, millions kept it clean."

Carrie began her professional career at age thirteen, performing in her mother's Las Vegas nightclub act. "When I started smoking dope with the dancers in my mother's act, I realized that the kind of music I was singing wasn't the kind of music I was listening to. I was listening to Joni Mitchell and singing 'Meantime,' 'I Got Love,' or 'Fascinating Rhythm.' . . . I was sort of being groomed for Lizahood."

Being the offspring of what she refers to as a "golden womb" had its drawbacks. As she later recalled to *Glamour* magazine in 1987, "You can't imagine what it was like growing up with my mother. I thought she was the most beautiful woman in the world. I saw other people's mothers, and I couldn't believe that she was my mother. I didn't look anything like her. I felt real ugly."

But Debbie was having problems of her own. After divorcing Fisher, she married retail footwear magnate Harry Karl, who drank and gambled his way through both their fortunes. Facing a financial crisis, Debbie returned to New York in 1972 to star in the Broadway show *Irene*. Carrie, age fifteen, dropped out of Beverly Hills High School to join the chorus of the show. That same year, she made her film debut in *Shampoo*, where she asked Warren Beatty, "Wanna f __ k?"

The following year, Carrie went to London to study acting at the Central School of Speech and Drama. Upon her return two years later, she went to a joint casting call for directors Brian DePalma and George Lucas. Although DePalma turned her down for the title role in *Carrie* (a part which made Sissy Spacek a star), George Lucas admired her tough persona and cast her as spunky Princess Leia Organa in his space saga *Star Wars*.

After the monumental success of *Star Wars*, Carrie returned to New York and became fast friends with the "Saturday Night live" cast. During the filming of *The Blues Brothers*, Carrie was briefly engaged to Dan Ackroyd, with whom she admits having discovered LSD. Carrie's drug consumption was varied and included marijuana, ecstasy, MDA, and Percodan ("It's hard to get. You have to lie to doctors.") She will readily admit, "I loved acid. Acid is like MDA with colors. I liked the colors."

In 1983, at age twenty-seven, Carried surprised her family and friends by marrying long-time steady, singer Paul Simon in a spur-of-the-moment ceremony. After seven turbulent years of dating, Carrie and Paul took their vows in Simon's Central Park duplex. The guest list included Charles Grodin, Lorne Michaels, George Lucas, Kevin Kline, Penny Marshall, Robin Williams, Teri Garr, Christie Brinkley, and Billy Joel. The marriage lasted eleven months.

She partly blames her father for her unsuccessful marriage, "Since my father went away when I was two, what I wait for with every man is when he's going to leave. I just leave first because I can't face that."

After being substance free for three months, Carrie went on a drug

*T*ODAY, WRITING KEEPS CARRIE VERY BUSY: "PERFECT KARMA FOR A HIGH SCHOOL DROPOUT," SHE QUIPS. "HOMEWORK FOR THE REST OF MY LIFE."
ADAM SCULL/GLOBE PHOTOS

binge in L.A. and wound up in the hospital after some friends found her unconscious from an accidental overdose of sleeping pills. "So they took me to the hospital and since I was unavailable for comment on what I had taken, they took it out. That scared me to death."

She immediately entered a thirty-day detox program in Century City. After outlining the incident in a humorous essay for *Esquire* magazine, Carrie decided to use her experiences as the basis for a novel. *Postcards from the Edge* was a thinly veiled roman à clef describing the stress of having a famous parent and being a drug addict—all while making fun of the shallowness of Hollywood.

The book became a best-seller and was turned into a major motion picture starring Meryl Streep and Shirley MacLaine as an addicted young actress and her famous mother. Her second book, *Surrender the Pink* (1990), is the story of a soap opera writer who stalks her ex-boyfriend and his girlfriend.

Despite her success in the *Star Wars* trilogy, Carrie's subsequent roles have been, for the most part, unmemorable: *Mr. Mike's Mondo Video* (1979), *Under the Rainbow* (1981), *The Man with One Red Shoe* (1985), *Hollywood Vice Squad* (1986), *Amazon Women on the Moon* (1987), *The Guardian* (1987), *Appointment with Death* (1988), *Loverboy* (1989), *She's Back* (1989) and *The 'Burbs* (1989).

In recent years her acting roles have been that of second banana. She was Meg Ryan's pal in *When Harry Met Sally . . .* and an oversexed casting director in *Soap Dish*. The roles may have been small, but her performance in both proved that she is a talented actress with a strong sense of comic timing.

During the summer of 1992, Carrie and her long-time steady Bryan Lourd became the proud parents of a baby girl named Billie Catherine Lourd. About the possibility of remarriage Carrie says, "My mother always worked, but between both my parents, they were married seven times. I don't have a strong role model for relationships. I know how to get the job done, but I'm not a nurturing person. I'm stimulating, but not soothing."

Jamie Lee Curtis: An Imperfect Life

Jamie Lee Curtis is another Hollywood princess born to famous parents: the daughter of Janet Leigh and Tony Curtis. By age twenty-three, she had rightfully earned the crown of Scream Queen after battling several psychotic killers in a series of highly commercial horror films.

Janet Leigh (born Jeanette Helen Morrison) was eighteen years old when actress Norma Shearer spotted a photograph of Janet on her father's desk. She brought Janet to Hollywood, where she was made a contract player for MGM. Janet came to California with no acting experience and became a steady actress. Although she was best remembered for that famous shower scene in *Psycho* (1960), her rather impressive body of work includes *Touch of Evil* (1958), *The Manchurian Candidate* (1962), and *Bye Bye Birdie* (1963).

Tony Curtis (born Bernard Schwartz) was a struggling twenty-six-year-old actor when he married the pretty twenty-four-year-old blonde in 1951.

JAMIE LEE CURTIS:
AN IMPERFECT LIFE

ℐamie (in "Perfect" form) wrote in her high school yearbook: "My bosoms aren't big, but they're mine." *GLOBE PHOTOS*

Beginning in 1957, both their careers began to soar. Curtis's role in *Sweet Smell of Success* led to more substantial parts in *The Defiant Ones* (1958) and *Some Like It Hot* (1959).

Born on November 22, 1958, Jamie, along with her older sister Kelly, were raised in a privileged environment. Their home was a fifteen-room villa across the street from Pickfair, the legendary estate built by Mary Pickford and Douglas Fairbanks. Their parents socialized with Frank Sinatra, Jerry Lewis, Kirk Douglas, Robert Wagner, and Natalie Wood.

In 1962, Curtis and Leigh divorced after eleven years of marriage. Jamie was three-and-a-half, sister Kelly, five, when Tony left. Jamie has described her father as a "ghost," a virtual stranger with whom she had no contact. She later acknowledged, "He's not a father, on any level. . . . He never meant anything to me."

Less than one year after their divorce, both Curtis and Janet had remarried. Janet found lasting love with businessman Robert Brandt, while Tony, then forty-two, married eighteen-year-old Austrian-born Christine Kaufmann, who had co-starred with him in *Taras Bulba* (1962). Four years and two children later, Tony once again divorced. In 1968, he flew to Las Vegas to marry twenty-three-year-old Leslie Allen, a model. The marriage, which took place in Buddy Hackett's hotel suite, lasted until 1981 and produced two more children.

Jamie lived a fairly normal life until her teens, despite the occasional headlines generated by her father's activities. When Jamie was in seventh grade, Tony was arrested at London's Heathrow Airport for possession of marijuana, much to the chagrin of the American Cancer Society, who had hired him as spokesman for their I Quit campaign.

Jamie's high school years, which she describes as "a f __ king killer," began at Beverly Hills High ("a designer school") before she was transferred into the ritzy Westlake School in Bel Air. When her mother accepted a role on Broadway, Jamie transferred to Choate, the preppy boarding school in Connecticut, for her senior year. Under her picture in the school's yearbook, Jamie wrote, "Weirdness is a virtue that only some can project successfully. My bosoms aren't big, but they're mine."

After graduating from Choate in 1976, Jamie returned to California, where she spent three months studying drama at the University of the Pacific in Stockton before dropping out. "I wasn't into it," she recalls, "I partied. I was a little sister at a fraternity and a member of the Martini Club."

After losing the lead part on the "Nancy Drew" television series, Jamie became a contract player for Universal Studios, earning $235 a week. Although Jamie firmly denies using her family connections to jumpstart her career, the fact that her godfather, Lew Wasserman, was head honcho at

JAMIE LEE CURTIS:

AN IMPERFECT LIFE

JAMIE LEE CURTIS IS QUICK TO DEFEND HER SCREAM QUEEN TITLE: "I WAS NEVER IN THE SWAMP THING VIII GETTING F___KED BY A BEAST FROM THE SWAMP." *JOHN PARTIPILO/GLOBE PHOTOS*

CHILDREN
OF
BABYLON

84

Jamie says that doing drugs with her father, Tony Curtis (here with wife Janet Leigh) was no big deal. "It would be like getting drunk with your parents. Only we chose to freebase."
CRAIG SKINNER/GLOBE PHOTOS

Universal certainly couldn't have hindered her progress. She began her acting career on television with appearances in series, including "Columbo," "Quincy," "Emergency!," "The Love Boat," and "Charlie's Angels," and a recurring role on the 1977 TV series "Operation Petticoat" (based on the 1959 film that starred her dad).

At age eighteen, however, she became an overnight star when John Landis cast her as Laurie, the studious babysitter, in the horror classic *Halloween* (1978). She spent the next two years earning the title of Scream Queen in a series of mediocre thrillers: *The Fog* (1980), *Prom Night* (1980), *Terror Train* (1980), *Halloween II* (1981), and *Road Games* (1981). In an interview with *Movieline*'s Lawrence Grobel, Jamie expressed no regrets for this collection of work: "In my early work, I was always holding up the morals of the young women of America. I was the smart girl; I never played the bimbo, the slut. I was never in "*The Swamp Thing VIII*" getting f __ ked by a beast from the swamp. I never had to sacrifice my own integrity."

Despite her film successes, her personal life was in disarray to put it mildly. She had already been engaged to writer Ray Hutcherson, then to production designer Michael Riva (who was also grandson of Marlene Dietrich). At this time, she began a three year odyssey of self-discovery aided by booze and cocaine. "It was this weird summer, the summer of '83, when a lot of single women did a lot of cocaine and hung out in West Hollywood." She later told reporter Eric Sherman, "I just flipped out—nothing drastic, nothing dramatic. A lot of relationships. A lot of drugs. A lot of questions, no answers." Although she says she was never addicted, she readily admits that quitting was difficult: "Luckily, I never had to check myself into any drug rehab place."

At the same time, Tony Curtis was badly addicted to cocaine. "He was in bad shape," says Jamie, "and I wasn't in great shape. I was doing drugs; he was doing drugs. We did drugs together. It's no big deal. It would be like getting drunk with your parents. Only we chose to freebase." Today, Jamie's relationship with her father, who lives in Hawaii, remains cordial but distant.

Tired of the horror genre, Jamie switched gears and transformed herself into a sex symbol of sorts. In 1981, she was seen in the television film, *Death of a Centerfold: The Dorothy Stratten Story*, based on the life of the former Playboy Playmate who was murdered by her husband the previous year. She followed up as a secretary/hooker in another TV movie, *Money on the Side*. Jamie continued to garner more attention for her exposed body parts in the 1983 films *Love Letters* and the Eddie Murphy vehicle *Trading Places*. Says Jamie, "I'm singled out because of the physical beauty of my body, period. If I didn't have as sensational a body, this part of my career would have gone unmerited."

After spotting a photograph of Christopher Guest in an issue of *Rolling Stone* magazine, Jamie called his agent. "I rambled on about how I'd never done anything like this but would like to meet Chris." He took Jamie's number and said he would relay the message, but nothing happened. Three months later, Jamie and Christopher spotted each other in a restaurant. The two were married on December 18, 1984, at the home of Rob Reiner, with both Tony and Janet in attendance. (Unable to have children of their own, the couple adopted a daughter in December of 1986).

Then came *Perfect* (1985). According to Jamie, "The way they pitched the story to me—they didn't have a script yet—it was about an Olympic athlete who gets burned by the press. Kind of interesting. But it turned into, you know, me bumping and grinding my body. The plot came down to six lines, ten seconds. The rest of it was me going "And a-one and a-two . . .'"

To get in *Perfect* physical shape, Jamie spent several months training in aerobics, weight lifting, and swimming. She also began giving lessons at the Beverly Hills Sports Connection.

After the critical carpet-bombing the film received, Jamie found herself taking supporting roles in rather obscure movies, including *A Man in Love, Amazing Grace & Chuck,* and *Dominick and Eugene.* In 1988, she portrayed a sexy con artist in *A Fish Called Wanda* (1988), a film that later earned co-star Kevin Kline an Oscar for best supporting actor. Although he liked her straightforwardness, David Denby in *New York* magazine wrote, "Jamie Lee Curtis doesn't have the technique of a comedienne; nor, apart from the famous chest, is she beautiful enough to play a devastating femme fatale convincingly."

Despite generally good reviews for *Wanda,* Jamie still was not on the "A" list for acting assignments. The need for work led her to take the role of a rookie cop hunted by an obsessed psychotic killer in Katherine Bigelow's *Blue Steel.* "This was just another one of those jobs you took because you needed a job that year and nothing else was around." The film was universally panned by the critics, including Denby, who described the film as "made by a woman about a woman, and, worse than any macho folly, it turns uniforms, violence, and guns into fetish objects."

Jamie recently enjoyed success on television portraying fledgling reporter Hannah Miller in the ABC sitcom "Anything But Love," co-starring Richard Lewis. The show, which began its limited run during the spring of 1989, received promising ratings, in part due to the strong lead-in of "Roseanne." Behind the scenes it was anything but love when, after six episodes, the original creative staff quit or was fired, depending on which version you hear. "I wasn't pleased with the writing," Jamie related to *TV Guide,* "I won't lie. The scripts weren't always funny enough, and I felt from the beginning that we had no idea what we were doing with my character and Richard's." Despite all her input, the show lasted only two seasons.

In 1991, Jamie appeared in two films: *Queens Logic,* an ensemble film that died a quick death after its release, and *My Girl,* in which she, along with Dan Ackroyd, played supporting roles to child actors Macaulay Culkin and Anna Chlumsky.

Of her life today Jamie says, "I have the life I have always wanted. I have a family I love and the kind of work I like to do. Every day I tell myself, 'I did it!'"

Desi Arnaz, Jr.: Little Ricky Grows Up

"I'm probably the only flesh and blood human being ever brought into the world by a television network," Desi Arnaz, Jr., once said. The birth of Lucille Ball's son was the media event of 1953, which was incorporated into the storyline of her hit series "I Love Lucy." Desiderio Alberto Arnaz y de Acha IV was born by cesarean section on the very night (January 19, 1953) that CBS ran the highly rated episode in which Lucy and Ricky Ricardo became proud parents. "The brass wanted me born the same night a child was delivered to my mother before fifty million people. And it was done."

Although Desi Jr. (along with sister Lucie) made only one cameo appearance on the final episode of that famous series, many people confuse him with Richard Keith, the young actor who portrayed Little Ricky. (Richard, whose real name is Keith Thibodeaux, has overcome a serious drug addiction and is now a Christian rock musician in Jackson, Mississippi.) "I can still remember watching the show when I was about three and wondering who was the baby with Mommy and Daddy. When my parents said it was me, I was confused because I knew it wasn't. So I had this identity problem, and it wasn't helped any by people calling me Little Ricky, a name I learned to despise."

The second child of Hollywood's most famous couple, Desi Jr. quickly learned that growing up with money and fame does not guarantee happiness. The marriage of Lucille Ball and Desi Arnaz was quite different from the carefree lives of their television counterparts. Desi's drinking, gambling, womanizing, and dramatic mood swings were legendary in Hollywood. In 1960, after twenty stormy years, the marriage ended.

After the divorce, Lucille moved with her children to New York, where she enrolled them in Catholic schools while she worked on the Broadway show *Wildcat*. There, she was introduced to comedian Gary Morton, whom she married in November of 1961. After the show's brief run, Lucille and her family returned to California. Desi later referred to his early years as "chaotic." An overweight and insecure child, Desi did poorly in school and opted for role of class clown.

In 1965, at age twelve, Desi Jr., along with thirteen-year-old Dean Paul Martin (son of Dean Martin) and a school friend Billy Hinsche, fourteen, formed the short-lived but successful pop trio Dino, Desi, and Billy. The group got its start by warming up audiences of *The Lucy Show* and was given a recording contract by Frank Sinatra. They were a hit among the teen set and made appearances on "The Dean Martin Show" and "The Ed Sullivan Show." Lucille soon regretted her decision to allow Desi to perform with the group. At age thirteen, while traveling across the country with the band, Desi began to drink heavily. By age fifteen, after the demise of the group, Desi was financially secure. "That's when I turned to drugs."

Lucy, who had by this time discovered her son's drinking habit, brought both her children onto her sitcom "Here's Lucy" in 1968 to keep a closer eye on them. Lucie and Desi Jr. were given three-year contracts to portray her children, Kim and Craig Carter. Their salary was $17,600 the first year, $20,400 the second, and $25,200 the third year.

Even though he was working steadily on the show and made guest appearances on other series, including "The Brady Bunch" and "The Mothers-In-Law," Desi Jr. began to immerse himself further into drug addiction. At first he experimented with marijuana; later he used amphetamines and barbiturates. At sixteen he was using LSD, mescaline, cocaine, and Quaaludes. Soon after, he began to experience dramatic mood swings and memory lapses. As Desi later explained, "I was raised in the sixties, when we thought that drugs were not only the answer to a lot of our seeking, but also better than alcohol. My father and I had a lot in common."

CHILDREN OF BABYLON

90

DESI ARNAZ, JR.'S 1980 MARRIAGE TO ACTRESS LINDA PURL LASTED ONLY A FEW MONTHS. *RALPH DOMINGUEZ/GLOBE PHOTOS*

DESI ARNAZ JR.:
LITTLE RICKY GROWS
UP

L̲ucille Ball brought Lucie and Desi Arnaz, Jr., onto her sitcom "Here's Lucy" in order to keep them out of trouble. *GLOBE PHOTOS*

Another affinity he shared with his father was a passion for women. When he was seventeen, he became romantically involved with Patty Duke, then twenty-four, and in the process of getting a divorce. Lucille was enraged by Desi's affair and carried on a verbal war with Patty through the tabloids. Lucy told *Look* magazine writer Laura Berquist, "She's living in some fantastic dream world, and we're the victims of it." Enraged with intrusions by the press, Lucy went on, "I worked for years for a quiet personal life, and now I can thank her for useless notoriety."

When Patty Duke became pregnant by John Astin, who was married at the time, she allowed people to assume the baby was Desi's. Patty later wrote in her own autobiography, "I took no active part in disclaiming Desi as the father, which when you get right down to it was just as bad." In February of 1971, Patty Duke gave birth to Sean Patrick Duke (later Astin), although she did not initially admit the child's true paternity.

With limited talents and a growing drug habit, Desi continued to find acting roles. He made his motion picture debut in the coming-of-age drama *Red Sky at Morning* (1971), and had featured roles in *Marco* (1972) and *Billy Two Hats* (1974), an offbeat western filmed in Israel and starring Gregory Peck. He also appeared on TV in *Mr. and Mrs. Bo Jo Jones* (1971) and guest starred on several series, including "Night Gallery" and "Mod Squad."

During this period, Desi's love life continued to make headlines when, after a brief relationship with Kim Darby, he took up with Liza Minelli in 1972. Liza shared many similarities to her predecessor Patty Duke: a successful entertainer, she had come from an unstable childhood, was divorced, and at twenty-six was several years older than Desi. Although Liza and Desi discussed the possibility of marriage, their relationship was also short-lived.

In 1973, Lucille realized that her son's addictions were out of control and checked her son into a detoxification hospital. Although he managed to reduce his drug consumption, he was still hooked. In 1978, at age twenty-five, he sought medical help for a second time but still could not kick his habit.

Years of drug and alcohol addiction were quietly taking their toll both personally and professionally. In feature films, he appeared in *Joyride* (1977), notable only for his steamy shower scene with Melanie Griffith, and Robert Altman's *A Wedding* (1978). On television, he starred in several inane TV movies: *Having Babies* (1976), *Black Market Baby* (1977), and *The Great American Traffic Jam* (1980). In 1980, the twenty-seven-year-old Desi married actress Linda Purl, but the union ended after several months.

By 1982, Desi was unemployed and a hard-core addict. It was then that Gary Morton recommended that he enter Scripps Hospital (later called the

McDonald Center for Alcoholism and Drug Addiction) in La Jolla, California. Desi started their two-year program and, with the support of his parents, his stepfather, and his sister, learned how to put his life back together. He later said, "For the first time in my life, I realized drugs interfered with everything I'd ever cared about—work, marriage, family, peace of mind. I was killing myself—and I couldn't stop."

Unfortunately, he was not able to revive his acting career and continued to appear in such forgettable TV fare as *The Night the Bridge Fell Down* (1983) and the short-lived series "Automan" (1983). His film credits also include the Pia Zadora starer *Fake-Out* (1982) and *The House of the Long Shadows* (1983). In 1991, Desi portrayed his famous father on film in *Mambo Kings*, a comeback of somewhat dubious merit.

Today Desi lives in Boulder City, Colorado, with his wife, Amy, and adopted daughter Haley. In control of his life, he makes frequent personal appearances to discuss his triumph over chemical dependency. He and Lucie co-own their own production company, DesiLu II, which develops television specials and series.

At the Wheel with Griffin O'Neal

Griffin O'Neal is a member of one of Hollywood's most unruly families. Equally recognized for their acting ability and explosive tempers, Ryan and his two offspring, Tatum and Griffin, have all generated their share of headlines.

Patrick Ryan O'Neal, the son of screenwriter Charles O'Neal and actress Patricia O'Neal, was a lifeguard and amateur boxer before he entered the world of acting. While his short list of film credits include *What's Up Doc* (1972) and *A Bridge Too Far* (1977), he is best remembered for his Oscar-nominated performance in *Love Story* (1970).

During his youth, he was known as a Hollywood womanizer who scored with Ursula Andress, Bianca Jagger, Peggy Lipton, and Anjelica Huston, among others. He also earned the reputation as a brawler. In 1961, Ryan served fifty-one days in jail for slugging a guest at a party. He punched out an entertainment reporter in 1964 and another one in 1978. In 1976, Ryan was arrested when police found five ounces of marijuana in his home.

Just one day after his divorce from actress Joanna Moore in 1967, Ryan married his "Peyton Place" co-star, Leigh Taylor Young. (The marriage, which lasted until 1971, produced one son, Patrick.) Tatum, two, and Griffin, one, remained with their mother. After Joanna developed a dependency on Methedrine from taking diet pills, Ryan attempted to gain custody of the children but failed when Joanna subpoenaed a list of Ryan's former lovers. When Joanna entered an L.A. hospital for drug treatment, Tatum moved in with her father, while Griffin remained with his mom until the age of twelve.

At age ten, Tatum became an instant celebrity, when she outshone her father with her portrayal of a tough-talking, cigarette-smoking con artist in her first movie, *Paper Moon* (1973). Her performance won her an Oscar as Best Supporting Actress and led to several other roles, including *Bad News Bears* (1976), *Nickelodeon* (176), *International Velvet* (1978), and *Little Darlings* (1980). Griffin had a difficult time handling his sister's success. "I was resentful of her success. She had all the recognition, and I had something. I knew I had something and I wanted to work." Griffin finally found work when he landed the title role of *The Escape Artist* in 1979.

Pursuing his own career, Ryan would often leave Griffin alone for long stretches of time. Left to his own devices, Griffin became an angry troublemaker. By 1982, his erratic behavior nearly cost him a second role, in *Hadley's Rebellion*. In 1983, Ryan banished his seventeen-year-old son from his beach house and rented Griffin a cabana in Malibu.

In May of 1983, after a violent altercation, Ryan punched his drugged-out son in the face, knocking out his two front teeth. "He couldn't believe what he'd done," Griffin later said. Ryan grabbed the teeth and said, "Put 'em back in, maybe they'll stick."

Two weeks later, police were called to a Malibu beach house after another tenant complained of a loud disturbance. Inside the trashed apartment, police found Griffin and booked him on suspicion of receiving stolen property after discovering an L.A. parking meter lying on the table. Griffin remained in jail for three days when no one posted his bail. Because it could not be proven that the meter was stolen, the charges were eventually dropped.

Ryan arranged to send Griffin to Habilitat, a private drug and delinquency rehabilitation center located in Oahu, Hawaii. The program, which costs $800 per month, provides an eighteen- to twenty-four-month regime for serious drug addicts. Commenting on her brother's troubles, Tatum told *People* magazine, "My brother has the blues. This path of destructiveness is just his way of begging for affection."

Griffin's "path of destructiveness" would unhappily cross that of the offspring of one Hollywood's greatest movie directors, Francis Ford Cop-

AFTER MANY TURBULENT YEARS, GRIFFIN O'NEAL AND HIS SISTER TATUM REMAIN CLOSE. *RALPH DOMINGUEZ/GLOBE PHOTOS*

pola. Gio Coppola aspired to follow his father's footsteps. At age sixteen, Gio was allowed to leave school by his father in order to become his full-time apprentice. Gio had served as an associate producer on *The Outsiders* and *Rumble Fish*. He had also been second unit director on *The Cotton Club* and the Michael Jackson short, *Captain Eo*. In 1986, Gio, along with brother Roman, served as supervisor of the electronic cinema staff for Coppola's latest epic, *Gardens of Stone*. After the film was completed, Gio was scheduled to intern on Steven Spielberg's television series "Amazing Stories" before taking on his first non-Coppola assignment of second unit director for the Whoopi Goldberg project, *Jumpin' Jack Flash*.

Griffin O'Neal, twenty-one, arrived on location in Virginia ready for double duty. First, he would take on the appropriately named role of Wildman, a sloppy soldier. Second, he would assist his friend Gio in shooting video for the production.

On May 23, 1986, at one-thirty in the morning, Arlington County police caught O'Neal speeding through the suburbs. Griffin was arrested for reckless driving, driving without a license, and carrying a concealed weapon, a high-tech switchblade, in his pocket. Griffin swore to police that the jacket was borrowed and that the knife wasn't his. A few hours later, a production assistant posted the $750 bail and told police that the jacket belonged to Griffin but that the $60,000 Lotus Esprit he was driving was borrowed from Gio. (While the weapons charge would later be dismissed, Griffin received a $500 fine after pleading guilty to reckless driving.)

Three days later, during the Memorial Day break, Griffin, Gio, and Gio's pregnant girlfriend Jacqueline went to a restaurant where they had several glasses of wine with their lunch. After lunch they picked up a six-pack of beer and rented a fourteen-foot motorboat on the South River near Annapolis. Jacqueline, disturbed by the antics of her male companions, was taken back to the dock soon after, while Griffin and Gio continued their afternoon joyride. About 5:15 p.m., the boat sped on a fast course between two larger boats connected by a tow line. As the small boat struck the barely visible line, Gio was thrown headfirst toward the boat's stern, while Griffin received a blow to his shoulder. Griffin, slightly bruised, turned off the engine and leapt to the floor to check on his friend who was suffering from severe head trauma.

Griffin steered the boat to shore, where paramedics hooked the dying youth up to life support equipment and rushed him by ambulance to Anne Arundel General Hospital, where he died of massive cranial injuries at 6:20 p.m. Although Griffin's blood level was never tested, an autopsy revealed that Gio's blood alcohol level was well above the legal driving limit.

When asked what happened, Griffin told authorities that Gio had been driving the boat. When eyewitnesses to the incident came forward and testified that blonde Griffin, not dark-haired Gio, was driving the boat, Griffin was forced to admit that he had lied about the incident.

On May 28, a memorial service was held in a small chapel at Fort Myer. Sam Bottoms, Larry Fishburne, and August Coppola delivered the eulogies. Filming on *Gardens* was suspended for five days, before the grieving father returned to work. In his sorrow he said, "The gods gave me Gio and the gods have taken him away."

During December of 1986, Jacqueline gave birth to Gio's daughter, Gian Carla Coppola. Coincidentally, Griffin O'Neal's trial began. Judge Martin Wolff, who referred to Griffin as an "accident waiting to happen," told the court that he had a "history of lying, little respect for others, and basically an immature personality."

Although he was acquitted of a manslaughter charge, Griffin was found guilty of reckless boat handling. His sentence included 416 hours of community service, eighteen months of probation with drug testing, compulsory school or work, and a $200 fine.

In April of 1987, Griffin began serving his community service sentence by manning a toll-free safety line for the Boat Owners Association of the United States. A month later, Francis Coppola sued Griffin for damages on behalf of his granddaughter and her mother. The suit suggested that because Griffin had left Gio's child fatherless, he ought to take on the financial responsibility.

Since then, Griffin has faced more legal problems. In 1987, he was arrested in Beverly Hills for speeding, probation violation, and possession of marijuana and was sentenced to two more years' probation. In 1989, he was sentenced to eighteen days in jail for fulfilling less than sixty hours of his community service, a violation of his probation. In 1992, Griffin pleaded no contest to a felony charge of shooting at the unoccupied car of his estranged girlfriend. As part of the plea bargain agreement, charges of battery and making terrorist threats were dropped. He was subsequently placed on probation for five years and ordered to submit to bi-weekly drug testing.

Efforts to revive his stagnant acting career have failed. His most recent credits include the direct-to-video films *Assault of the Killer Bimbos* (1988) and *Night Children* (1990).

Griffin's sister Tatum, while managing to stay away from the drug scene, has faced similar career woes. In 1984, Tatum retired from acting to live with (and later marry) tennis brat John McEnroe. Seven years and three children later, she attempted a comeback, appearing in the low budget film *Little Noises* (1991), which had a brief theatrical run. She made her New York stage debut the following year in *A Terrible Beauty*, a play which closed after its first week.

PART III

THE RISE AND FALL OF THE BRAT PACK

I n 1985, *New York* magazine writer David Blum coined the phrase Brat Pack while writing an article on Hollywood's then-current crop of hot young actors. Blum described the bratpackers as attractive young studs from show business families who had found fame and fortune before the age of twenty-five. They had top agents, throngs of fans, and commanded high salaries. They wore trendy clothes, drove expensive cars, and loved to party. Their most distinguishing characteristic was their lack of education: none had graduated from college; none had spent years studying their craft; in short, none had paid his dues.

Blum identified the Brat Pack's charter members as Emilio Estevez, Rob Lowe, Judd Nelson, Timothy Hutton, Matt Dillon, Tom Cruise, and Sean Penn. Over the years, their ranks have seen the additions of Robert Downey, Jr.; Charlie Sheen; Kiefer Sutherland; Demi Moore; Ally Sheedy; and Julia Roberts.

Only Tom Cruise managed to break away from the Pack. He entered

CHILDREN OF BABYLON

Of its members, only Tom Cruise (here with second wife Nicole Kidman) was able to break away from the Brat Pack to become a major box-office talent. RALPH DOMINGUEZ/GLOBE PHOTOS

the big league when he scored at the box office (*Top Gun* and *Cocktail*), proved that he was more than a pretty face (*Rain Man, Born on the Fourth of July*, and *Far and Away*), and found new friends in the feel-good cult of Scientology.

Sean Penn, after years of alternately punching out photographers, movie extras, and then-wife Madonna, left acting to pursue a writing and directing career. Likewise, Emilio Estevez moved behind the camera as a writer and director and found his career taking a cinematic free-fall after such forgettable efforts as *Wisdom, That was Then . . . This is Now,* and *Men at Work.*

The acting careers of Judd (*From the Hip*) Nelson and Rob (*Bad Influence*) Lowe have wound up down the toilet. In 1991, they combined their nontalents in the abysmal comedy *Dark Backward.* The film's plot centered on a nerdy garbageman (Nelson) who becomes a successful stand-up comic after a third arm grows out of his back. According to Judd, "Part of what it says about show business is the idea of a lot of people succeed and it has nothing to do with talent." Truer words have rarely have spoken. The film, which took in a pathetic $17,000 at the box office, succeeded in making *Men at Work* look like a high-concept art film.

Timothy Hutton, despite an Academy Award for his role in *Ordinary People,* has slipped into relative obscurity. (Does anyone remember *A Time of Destiny* or *Torrents of Spring*?) After receiving dismal reviews for his performance in *Q & A,* Timothy began acquiring book rights in an effort to branch out into the directing arena. "I don't like waiting around for something that may or may not come along," he said to *The New York Times.* "Planning for a career as actor, director, and producer just makes more sense to me." It does make more sense, especially when acting assignments begin to dry up.

All of these actors had a big advantage in launching their careers; namely, high-powered family connections. Emilio Estevez and Charlie Sheen are sons of Martin Sheen; Sean Penn is the son of Leo Penn, a television director, and Eileen Ryan, a veteran stage actress; Kiefer Sutherland is the son of actor Donald Sutherland; Timothy Hutton is the son of the late actor Jim Hutton; and Ally Sheedy, a published author at age twelve, is the daughter of literary agent, editor, and writer Charlotte Sheedy. Uneducated, unappreciative, and for the most part untalented, the Brat Packers have earned the critics contempt for their extreme arrogance, tremendous egos, and juvenile behavior.

The Brat Packers love a good fad. Several have recently latched onto the Hollywood tattoo craze. Pretty boy Rob Lowe has permanently marked up his body, as have Nicholas Cage and Charlie Sheen. Kiefer

CHILDREN
OF
BABYLON

In 1987, Judd Nelson pleaded no contest to a disorderly intoxication charge after a brawl in a Florida bar.
ADAM SCULL/GLOBE PHOTOS

Sutherland and Julia Roberts, as a symbol of their undying love, were marked with identical Chinese symbols on their left shoulders. (Given the short term of their engagement, perhaps it would have been wiser to use erasable ink.) Johnny Depp has emblazoned himself in several places, including a tattoo on his left shoulder that reads Winona Forever, in honor of his third fiancée, Winona Ryder. Said the lucky lady, "I was thrilled when he got the tattoo. Wouldn't any woman be?"

The Brat Packers love the sound of their own words. Charlie Sheen, Julia Roberts, and Ally Sheedy are just a few of the brats who spend endless hours churning out inane verse.

Julia Roberts becomes somewhat reticent when talking about her book *All the Makings of Insanity*—"Insanity being the best and worst of chaos as we know it." She has described her unpublished collection of poetry as moments in her life "that had an effect on me, one way or the other, that were funny or that were wicked."

Charlie Sheen modestly told one reporter, "I have a certain amount of Hemingway in me that needs to get out." You would never be able to tell that from his collection of a hundred caustic poems that he describes as a "twisted, inspirational, dark journey" that will "surprise" a lot of people. (Readers of this work will probably be impressed by his prolific use of obscenities and vivid descriptions of vomit.)

Ally Sheedy has described her work *Yesterday I Saw the Sun* (1991) as "a journey I am apparently still on." One can obviously tell that her "journey" has been no picnic from this collection of fifty-three depressing odes that recount her experiences with sex, abortion, bulimia, abusive relationships, and drug addiction.

The Brat Packers also love to spend money, whether on real estate, cars, or clothes. In 1991, Robert Downey, Jr., confessed to one reporter, "I used to just carry around all my money on me all the time. I bought stuff for friends. Now I look back and go, 'I've made *that* much money and I don't have any saved?' What the f __k is going on? I have a car, a house, a bunch of nice clothes, tons of music equipment, toys, and guns." Charlie Sheen, the paragon of bad taste, recently installed a fireman's pole in his $5 million Malibu home so that he can slide from his bedroom into his living room.

Audiences have watched the Brat Pack grow up together in a series of very successful ensemble teen flicks, including *Taps, The Outsiders, The Breakfast Club, Rumblefish, St. Elmo's Fire,* and, later, *Red Dawn* and *Young Guns*. But the public is very fickle and constantly seeks out fresh faces. What else can explain the instant careers of Billy Baldwin, Keanu Reeves, Richard Grieco, and Johnny Depp?

Still, a key question remains: Just how talented are these young actors?

Sean Penn, the most gifted actor of the group, discussed this subject with *American Film* writer Martha Frankel in 1991.

> You see tons of actors who look at their job as just taking all those cute smiles and tactics that they used to help them get laid in high school, and they transfer that into a movie career. And they do whatever the material dictates and whatever people will pay the most attention to. And it just adds up to sh __ .

Since the mid eighties, each member of the Brat Pack has suffered personal as well as professional falls from grace. Their reckless lifestyles have now earned them reputations for drug and alcohol abuse, arrests, sexual indiscretions, and illegitimate children. Now when they are interviewed, their language is filled with the "rehab speak" associated with various twelve-step recovery programs. Some of them are visibly angry over losing the fame and fortune that had come too easily and without merit.

In 1985, in what would turn out to be the peak year for all of the Brat Packers, Emilio Estevez, then twenty-three, was asked of his long-range plans. He confidently responded: "Longevity is in the stars for me. I'm not the kind of guy who's going to be in there for a couple of shots; I don't want to be on one of those shows 'Whatever Happened To . . . ?'"

WHATEVER HAPPENED TO EMILIO ESTEVEZ?

Emilio Estevez (born on May 12, 1962), along with siblings Carlos (Charlie), Ramon, and Rene, grew up in the long shadow cast by his father Martin Sheen. Considered by many to be one of the finest American actors of his generation, Sheen is equally famous for his support of various political causes, which has led to his arrest on several occasions.

Martin Sheen, born Ramon Estevez, was one of ten children born to a Spanish father and Irish mother. After dropping out of high school in 1959, Sheen moved from his home in Dayton, Ohio, to New York City, where he began a new life as a actor. Along the way, he became friends with other struggling unknowns, including Barbra Streisand and Al Pacino. Since acting jobs were scarce and generally low-paying, Sheen supported his wife, Janet, and growing family through low—paying jobs, which included janitor, car washer, and office messenger.

He first gained recognition in 1964 for his leading role in the Broadway

CHILDREN
OF
BABYLON

108

ONE MOVIE, *ST. ELMO'S FIRE*, MANAGED TO SEND THE CAREERS OF (*LEFT TO RIGHT*) EMILIO ESTEVEZ, DEMI MOORE, AND ALLY SHEEDY INTO ORBIT.
RALPH DOMINGUEZ/GLOBE PHOTOS

play, *The Subject Was Roses*—a role he would repeat in the 1968 screen version. During the past three decades, Sheen has demonstrated his considerable talents on film (*Badlands, Apocalypse Now,* and *Wall Street*) and television (*Kennedy* and *The Missiles of October*).

Sheen, who considers himself to be a family man as well as a devout Catholic, insisted that his wife and children accompany him on location while he worked. Hence, the Sheen children travelled extensively during their youth. Sheen brought his family to Ireland (for a film called *The Catholics*), Rome (for *The Cassandra Crossing*), and Mexico (for *Catch-22*). During the periods he was at home in Malibu, Emilio spent his after-school hours shooting home movies with his neighborhood pals Chris and Sean Penn, Rob and Chad Lowe, and his brother Charlie.

In 1976, Sheen brought his family to the Philippines, during the filming of *Apocalypse Now*. Emilio later admitted to *Seventeen*: "My brothers and sister were there, but I hung out with an actor who worked in the movie. Every night, we'd go and drink beer in the red-light district. My folks had no idea. I grew up very fast in the Philippines."

During high school, Emilio excelled in sports, theater, and creative writing ("It was always important for me to excel in either athletics or the theater, very important to be on top."). A popular student, Emilio was voted prom king in what he calls the most embarrassing moment of his life. (Critics would argue that Emilio's most embarrassing moments can be found on screen.)

Possessing a streak of his father's political rebelliousness, Emilio refused to register for the draft when he turned eighteen. He simply threw away the first reminders sent by the Selective Service. It would take years, and the threat of a prison sentence and a $10,000 fine, to convince Emilio to sign up. He told *Washington Post* reporter Paula Span, "Finally I said, 'I must do this.' Four years of passive resistance was statement enough." When he eventually registered, he scrawled underneath his signature, "I am signing this under duress."

After graduation, against his parents' wishes, Emilio decided to pursue an acting career rather than attend college. Said Emilio, "You can be taught within certain parameters, but I don't think anyone can really teach you creative writing or acting." Losing any sense of humility he later said, "Nobody really taught Mozart how to compose at age five, or any of the world's great artists."

Emilio made his stage debut in Florida alongside his father in a small production of *Mister Roberts*. "That was the only job Dad ever placed me in. We were well into production by the time I acquitted myself of the sin of casting nepotism." He even adopted his father's moniker, but decided that

Emilio Sheen sounded "stupid" and returned to Estevez, which he says sounded "more romantic."

Emilio expanded his acting career in television with supporting roles in *To Climb a Mountain* (1981), *17 and Going Nowhere* (1981), and, notably, *In the Custody of Strangers* (1982), starring his father. He slowly broke into feature films with roles in *Tex* (1982), *The Outsiders* (1983), and the cult classic, *Repo Man* (1984).

Emilio's best notices came with his performance as an uptight jock in the John Hughes film *The Breakfast Club* (1985). Janet Maslin of *The New York Times* wrote: "As an athlete, Emilio Estevez has an edgy physical intensity very reminiscent of his father." His performance in *St. Elmo's Fire* that same year, however, did not fare as well with the press. *New York* magazine wrote: "It's a measure of how badly the movie misses that Estevez, whose character is meant to be a youthful romantic, comes off instead as a close equivalent to John Hinckley."

Emilio gained and enjoyed a reputation as a ladies' man. He even went so far as to boast, "I don't eat fatburgers. But I've scarfed some furburgers." His success with women did not come without a price. His on-and-off romance with model Carey Salley produced two illegitimate children and a $3 million paternity suit. Many believe that his involvement with Carey and the children destroyed whatever chances he had for a long-term relationship with *St. Elmo's* co-star and Hollywood party girl, Demi Moore.

As his career began to grow so did his ego. He began to spend lavishly, purchasing land in Montana and later a $2.2 million custom-designed condo on Malibu beach, complete with four bedrooms, four and a half bathrooms, a spa, and a fireplace.

He also began to fancy himself as a screenwriter and director. He told *Los Angeles Times* reporter Deborah Caulfield, "I'm not a power-hungry human being, but I feel that I'm somewhat creative and that I have something to say. I want to bring that into the films that I choose to make, so I think that if I'm able to write and act and someday direct, that it's the best way to get my message across." Judging from his later work, it might have been simpler for Emilio to take out ads for higher education. His father, however, encouraged these high aspirations by saying: "I think eventually Emilio will have to direct to feel the full extent of his talents; his spirits are that big. He's an officer, not a soldier."

Than Was Then . . . This is Now (1985) marked Emilio's screenwriting debut. *People* magazine wrote, "He's more impressive as an actor than as a writer," noting that "the dialogue is full of clunkers."

Emilio has the distinction of appearing in two of the worst films of 1986. While first-time director Stephen King was left holding the bag for *Maximum Overdrive, the commercial and critical failure of *Wisdom* lay solely at the feet of its writer/director/star Estevez. The film is the story of John Wisdom (Emilio) and his girlfriend (Demi), a bank robbing duo who become public heroes for destroying mortgage records.

Demi, proving that love really is blind, said at the time, "I really admire and respect his talent. We've always wanted to work together. I was there from the beginning of *Wisdom,* the day the first page was written—he wrote the role for me absolutely." It might have been better for everyone if Emilio had just sent flowers to impress his love-struck fiancée.

New York Times film critic Vincent Canby referred to the movie as "Bonnie and Clunk." He wrote, "Mr. Estevez is far more at ease as an actor than as a writer or director, though he's certainly as competent as most people making television movies. The problem is that *Wisdom* is aggressively boring, either because one can predict everything that's going to happen and exactly how it will look on the screen or because the concept of the film eventually seems even more confused than the title character." Emilio later admitted that the critical reaction to *Wisdom* was "devastating." Like many viewers, he admits, "If I'm watching TV now and the movie comes on, the first thing I do is change the channel to CNN."

After Emilio put aside his writing and directing aspirations, his career began a noticeable rebound. His role as second banana to former druggie Richard Dreyfuss in the buddy cop film *Stakeout* (1987) garnered good reviews and over $65 million at the box office.

Although Martin Sheen had been supportive of Emilio's relationship with Demi, brother Charlie was less positive. "I think he's crazy to give her a diamond ring; he's too young to get married." The wedding, scheduled for December 7, 1986, never happened, although invitations to the ceremony had already been mailed when the bride-to-be called off the event. Demi, who had doubts about her impending marriage, found comfort in the arms of TV superstar Bruce Willis, whom she met at the premiere of *Stakeout*. During November of 1987, she became Mrs. Bruce Willis. Emilio was reportedly crushed by her decision.

Emilio, along with his brother Charlie, Kiefer Sutherland, and Lou Diamond Phillips, donned cowboy hats and holsters to tell the story of young Billy the Kid in the film *Young Guns* (1988). The film, which substituted bathroom humor for historical fact, while its stars mugged for close-ups, became a commercial hit despite generally mediocre reviews. The box office take of over $44 million convinced its producers to make a sequel two years later. Emilio's strength as a character actor, as opposed to leading man, was duly recognized by *New York Times* critic Janet Maslin, who wrote,

Emilio and Demi's on-and-off engagement officially ended after she was introduced to Bruce Willis at the premiere of Stakeout.
Ralph Dominguez/Globe Photos

WHATEVER HAPPENED TO EMILIO ESTEVEZ?

EMILIO AND THE MOTHER OF HIS TWO ILLEGITIMATE CHILDREN, MODEL CAREY SALLEY. *DARLENE HAMMOND/GLOBE PHOTOS*

"Mr. Estevez . . . is a sturdy if unspectacular presence, best when he's not asked to take center stage."

Buoyed by this success, Emilio returned to ego stroking by scripting another vanity project. *Men at Work* (1990) is a virtually unwatchable comedy in which he and his brother Charlie co-star as a pair of despicable garbage men (roles they were *born to play*) who tackle a murder investigation. *People* magazine wrote, "Finding things to like in this film resembles—what else?—garbage picking." The reviewer even commented that "Sheen especially should be ashamed of himself for stooping to be conquered by such lousy writing."

Since being labeled a brat in 1985, Emilio has maintained a relatively low profile. In July of 1990, Emilio made international headlines when he was detained in Bolivia in connection with a cocaine and marijuana smuggling investigation. The incident began in June when Emilio chartered a Lear jet to fly him and several companions to Bolivia to research a screenplay set in the Amazon jungle. The pilots and the Estevez party were held at the police station overnight when investigators found minute traces of marijuana and cocaine in the plane. The Bolivian police and DEA later cleared the group of all charges. Said Emilio, "It would be ludicrous to bring drugs into a place that exports them."

In 1992, Emilio returned to the screen with a resounding thud in the film, *Freejack*. During the promotional tour for the film, Emilio bragged, "This is a great opportunity for me to show that I can carry a movie without having any of my buddies appearing alongside me." What it proved, actually, was that Emilio's presence can actually sink a film.

The film's plot centered on Alex Furlong (Emilio), a race car driver who is transported from a fatal car crash to the year 2009 by a ruthless bounty hunter (Mick Jagger) who wants to use Furlong's body as a vessel for another man's mind (Anthony Hopkins). Hopkins, despite his third billing, was strictly slumming in a rather minor role, while Mick Jagger, in his film debut, stole the movie away from Emilio with his campy performance. In its review, *The Washington Post* commented that "you know you're in trouble when the cars in a science-fiction movie look like those golf carts with football helmets on them. That's if the presence of Emilio Estevez wasn't already enough of a tip-off."

What can one do when a career begins to slide? Why not marry someone with a higher profile? Just ask Annette Benning, Nicole Kidman, and former fiancée Demi Moore-Willis. Although he once proclaimed that he would not marry someone involved in show business, on April 29, 1992, Emilio did just that. During the Los Angeles riots that erupted after the Rodney King verdict, Emilio and former cheerleader/pop megastar Paula

Abdul said "I do" in a civil ceremony at the Santa Monica courthouse. After the secret ceremony, the newlyweds were led to a holding pen until a limo arrived to safely take them away from the burning city.

Paula, a former cheerleader for the L. A. Lakers, began her career as a music video choreographer. She received her first critical recognition for her association with George Michael, Steve Winwood, and, notably, Janet Jackson, which produced several creative videos (which include "Nasty" and "What Have You Done for Me Lately").

She became a music and video sensation in her own right with her debut album "Forever Your Girl" (1988) and its followup album "Spellbound" (1991). Paula's success has not come without its share of scandal.

In 1991, a former backup singer filed suit against Virgin Records, charging that the vocal tracks she had laid down on three of the album's songs were electronically blended with Paula's vocals, producing a stronger sound. Although Paula has vehemently denied the accusations, the lawsuit, combined with rumors that her romantic involvement with Michael Jackson's brother, Jackie, was responsible for his divorce, sent Paula's public relations staff into overtime to repair any damage to her reputation.

Paula has never hidden her long-term ambition to become an actress. ("I'd like to direct and star in a Broadway musical and act in a couple of films.") Perhaps being married to an actor will help her reach that goal.

Despite the negative critical reaction to his acting, directing, and writing, Emilio is obviously not concerned. In speaking with *US* magazine in 1992, Emilio proclaimed, "I now realize that critics' opinions don't mean sh __ to me. I'm going to direct more movies, I'm going to act in more movies, and there's nothing they can do to stop me."

GOOD TIME CHARLIE SHEEN

Charlie Sheen (born Carlos Irwin Estevez on September 3, 1965) is probably the most notorious member of the Sheen/Estevez clan. His notoriety stems not from the quality of his work, but from his wild exploits, which include stormy relationships, temper tantrums, drugs, and alcohol.

The first of his legal troubles began on his sixteenth birthday, when his parents presented him with a silver BMW. Frustrated by older brother Emilio's success and feeling that his life was in a rut, he became "what you'd call a handful." With a new car and all of Los Angeles at his feet, his school attendance dropped to about 33 percent. One morning he was found asleep at the wheel in Malibu in possession of marijuana and a knife in an ankle sheath. Charlie's mom, Janet, who has spent years bailing out her activist husband, intervened. Charlie later admitted, "The judge was a friend of my mom's and nothing ever came of it." Six years later, Martin Sheen conceded, "If he'd been black, he'd still be in jail."

CHARLIE, SEEN HERE WITH FATHER MARTIN, ADOPTED THE NAME SHEEN BECAUSE HE THOUGHT IT "MIGHT OPEN A DOOR A LITTLE WIDER THAN IT WOULD BE COMING IN AS AN ESTEVEZ." *GLOBE PHOTOS*

The following year, Charlie and a friend pulled off a four-day credit card scam. After telling the manager of the Beverly Hills Hotel that he left a term paper in the lobby, he was allowed to look through the trash. After collecting several credit card receipts, he and his friend began making telephone orders for televisions, jewelry, and Walkmans. "So we'd go in and collect the loot and they'd say 'You want your sh __ gift-wrapped?'" He was arrested at school and charged with credit card forgery. Without any remorse he admitted to *Movieline,* "It was totally despicable and highly illegal, but hell, we gave it a shot." After paying for all of the items, his family once again used its influence to save him from a jail term.

In his senior year, Charlie spent ten dollars on the answers to a biology exam. "I got a hundred on the final. I really f__ked up." The school promptly failed him in the course.

On the brink of flunking out, Charlie needed a C- in English in order to graduate and accept a college baseball scholarship. When his teacher would not allow him to take the test because of an unexplained absence on the preceding day, he "pretty much melted down in front of the whole class." He angrily wadded up a paper ball and threw it at his teacher, knocking off her glasses. That, along with a 1.35 grade point average, put an end to his education and his baseball career.

At age nineteen, Charlie fathered a daughter, Cassandra, with his high school sweetheart. Of her decision to have the baby he said, "I wasn't in favor of it at the time, but it hasn't proven to be a disastrous situation."

While Emilio stuck with his given name, saying he "wanted to break the way people identify with me," Charlie made no such pretense: "I thought I'd get a little more attention at first. I thought it would create a little more curiosity that might open a door a little wider than it would be coming in as an Estevez."

In 1984, Charlie made an inauspicious acting debut in the low-budget horror flick *Grisly 2.* ("I had a few scenes and I was eaten by a bear.") He later found supporting roles on television in *Silence of the Heart* and a string of teen movies: *Red Dawn* (1984), *The Boys Next Door* (1985), *Ferris Bueller's Day Off* (1986), *The Wraith* (1986) and Emilio's film *Wisdom* (1986). While his roles in these films were not particularly noteworthy, they made him financially secure with a $2 million bank account.

Money is very important to Charlie Sheen. ("Money is energy, man! It moves things.") He told *People* magazine how he enjoyed carrying a roll of $100 bills. "I love going into a shopping area just knowing I have the option to buy anything I want."

Charlie got his major break when he was cast in *Platoon* (1986), director Oliver Stone's personal account of his Vietnam War experiences. When the film was initially in development, Charlie was turned down for the lead role because of his mannered audition. ("I was doing all this Tony Danza sh __ .") Emilio was chosen for the part, but just as shooting was about to begin, the film's financing fell through and *Platoon* was shelved for two years. By the time the script resurfaced, Emilio was on to other projects and Charlie was cast. He almost lost the part again, however, when someone from the production company warned Stone of his drinking problem. Said Charlie, "I caught wind of this and I took a baseball bat and destroyed my hotel room, about $3,100 worth of damages. It was do the hotel room or do this guy, and I didn't want to go to jail because I probably would have killed him."

Favorably compared with *Apocalypse Now,* the film was a critical and commercial hit that earned eight Oscar nominations, including Best Supporting Actor nods for Willem Dafoe and Tom Berenger. The film eventually won four Oscars, including Best Picture, Director, Editing, and Sound.

Although Charlie's name was notably absent from the nominee list, he was less interested in accolades than with having a good time. His appreciation of money, booze, fast cars, and fast women became the material of a new tabloid icon. He frequently attended wild parties ("to drink beer and check out butts") and kept a list of women that ranked them according to their attributes ("breasts," "Jacuzzi," etc.).

In between all-night drinking binges, Charlie managed to crank out *No Man's Land* (1987) and *Three for the Road* (1987); films ruined by the lifeless performance of their hungover star. By the time he made *Wall Street* (1987), his life was circling the drain. The film should have belonged to Charlie's ambitious Bud Fox, but Michael Douglas walked away with all of the praise and an Academy Award for his performance as the sinister Gordon Gekko. Vincent Canby noted: "When Mr. Douglas is not at the center of the screen, the movie loses its grit. . . . Mr. Sheen lacks the necessary, nervy intelligence and Miss (Daryl) Hannah has the screen presence of a giant throw pillow." Charlie later confessed that during filming, "I'd be drinking away, doing blow, popping pills, and telling myself I wasn't an addict because there wasn't a needle stuck in my arm."

In 1987, Martin Sheen said of his son, "He's got the world's biggest heart, but he's got a lot of anger—*a lot of anger.*" No kidding! That same year Charlie bragged to one reporter, "I killed a neighbor's peacock a few years ago. It kept sh __ ting all over my basketball court, so I beat it to death with a broomstick. Nobody knew what happened to it."

Martin Sheen was also distressed by the size of Charlie's growing entourage. "There's a lot of strange people hanging around him now, hangers on—a lot of them. Pisses me off." One of those hanging on was Charlie's fiancée Kelly (*Twins*) Preston. Charlie gifted the former Mrs. Kevin (*Spacecamp*) Gage with a $20,000 pink diamond engagement ring and unwanted headlines when she was slightly injured in a gun accident in his bathroom. The romance ended and Kelly now wears a six-carat diamond ring, courtesy of her second husband, John Travolta.

His high cost of living drove Charlie to take any role that came his way—each performance progressively smaller and weaker. In the ensemble films *Eight Men Out* and *Young Guns* he was completely overshadowed by his more talented co-stars. During 1989 and 1990, he appeared in what must be a record-breaking number of critical and/or commercial duds—ten in total. In 1989, he lensed *Beverly Hills Brats* (co-starring his father and

WHEN CHARLIE SHEEN MADE *WALL STREET*, HE WAS "DRINKING AWAY, DOING BLOW, POPPING PILLS, AND TELLING MYSELF I WASN'T AN ADDICT."
GLOBE PHOTOS

D URING THEIR ENGAGEMENT, KELLY PRESTON WAS SLIGHTLY INJURED AFTER ONE OF CHARLIE'S GUNS ACCIDENTLY DISCHARGED.
RALPH DOMINGUEZ/GLOBE PHOTOS

brother Ramon), *Courage Mountain, Major League, Never on Tuesday,* and *A Tale of Two Sisters.* The following year saw Charlie take on five more doomed projects, including *Backtrack,* a Jodie Foster vehicle that was never theatrically released but made its way to cable television in 1992. He probably would have been better off if his other efforts (*Cadence, Men at Work, Navy SEALs,* and *The Rookie*) had remained on the shelves.

On the troubled set of *Navy SEALs,* Charlie kept the crew laughing when he stuck a Post-It on the back of co-star/Sean Young reading, "I Am the Biggest C_ _ t in the World." A frustrated director, Lewis Teague, said of his cast, "They drink all night, get three hours' sleep, and then come to work, and they're temperamental to begin with. It makes things difficult."

CHILDREN
OF
BABYLON

122

A WRITER OF POETRY, CHARLIE ONCE PROCLAIMED, "I HAVE A CERTAIN
AMOUNT OF HEMINGWAY IN ME THAT NEEDS TO GET OUT."
NIGEL HINKES/GLOBE PHOTOS

Charlie has increased his income substantially over the past few years by doing television commercial voice-overs. "It's good cash and it's easy. You get three accounts and you're set. I'm not selling out. I don't appear on camera." He did, however, appear on camera for two Japanese ads for a reported $2 million, which he promptly invested in a Malibu restaurant.

In the summer of 1990, his concerned parents called Charlie home for a family meeting. They convinced him that he was an alcoholic and pleaded with him to seek help. But it was Emilio who knew how to stroke his brother's immense ego. Emilio told him, "If you kill yourself with drugs and alcohol you're robbing the rest of the world of a very valuable talent." Said Charlie, "When I heard what my brother really thought of me, I felt, well . . . wow!"

After a whole month in rehab, spent with girlfriend/porn actress Ginger Lynn Allen, a repentant Charlie Sheen says he's now clean and sober. (Ginger Lynn, however, wound up in police custody in 1992 when she reportedly failed a drug test. The star of such X-rated fare as *Panty Lust,* she was on probation for income tax evasion.) Despite his own problems with substance abuse, Charlie contends that drugs should be legalized. Speaking with one astounded TV reporter, Charlie calmly declared, "Take the money out of drugs and the gangs have nothing—there's no value in the stuff they're killing themselves over. Just legalize drugs across the board."

In 1991, Charlie revived his acting career by using his stiff acting abilities to advantage in playing straight man in the military spoof *Hot Shots.* Although Charlie has said that "*Hot Shots* didn't represent me as an actor," he was one of the first signed up for the film's sequel. In the future, Charlie has expressed an interest in working with Nicholas Cage, Tom Cruise, Kevin Costner, and Julia Roberts.

Charlie, like his brother, has directing and writing ambitions. He has already written a screenplay called *How to Eat and Drive.* Says Charlie, "It's stupid, really, but look at *Porky's* and *Revenge of the Nerds.* If those films can get made and make millions, I can put something on paper and film it."

MOORE OR LESS

In August of 1991, a very pregnant Demi Moore made national headlines by posing nude for the cover of *Vanity Fair*. The actress, then eight months pregnant, was posed cradling her large belly with one hand while covering her breasts with the other. Tina Brown, the magazine's editor, rationalized this cheap exploitation by stating, "There is nothing more glorious than the sight of a woman carrying a child." This, of course, explains the cheesy photo inside the magazine, which shows Demi wearing hookerish lingerie and high heels below the lewd caption "Demi's Big Moment."

One year later, Demi repeated her tawdry stunt for a follow-up article with the magazine. This time around, Demi waited patiently for fourteen hours while body paint was applied to her body to make it appear she was wearing a man's suit. While readers may have been titillated by such exhibitionism, it really wasn't such a long stretch for the actress, who began her career as a covergirl for *Oui* magazine. Topless photos of Demi have also

At age sixteen, Demi dropped out of school and began dating thirty-year-old rocker Freddy Moore.
RALPH DOMINGUEZ/GLOBE PHOTOS

graced the pages of *Celebrity Sleuth* and *High Society* magazines. In 1986, she appeared nude in her stage debut, *The Early Girl*. She has also disrobed on film in *About Last Night* and *The Seventh Sign*.

Demetria Gene Guynes was born in November of 1962 to teenage parents in Roswell, New Mexico. Her mother, Virginia King, a troubled young lady who had twice divorced her first husband, was a pregnant teenager when she married Danny Guynes, a newspaper adman. (Demi has only met her biological father once and to this day shares no relationship with him.)

Young Demi spent a nomadic childhood, as her family followed her father as he moved from town to town in search of a job. At age thirteen, after settling in West Hollywood, Demi's parents divorced. (Danny committed suicide four years later.)

During her teens, Demi has described herself as "pitiful-looking,"—a skinny girl who wore an eye-patch to cover up her crossed eyes. Her first husband, Freddy Moore, disclosed to *Redbook* reporter Audrey Lavin, "Demi told me she grew up with people telling her how stupid and ugly she looked cross-eyed." The problem was eventually corrected after two surgical procedures.

An insecure youth, Demi began to experiment with drugs. Speaking of her troubled teens, Demi admitted, "When I was in school, doing Quaaludes and smoking pot and drinking and ditching was what a majority of kids did."

In her new home, Demi became friends with an young actress who lived in her building. That woman, who happened to be a still unknown Nastassia Kinski, inspired Demi to become an actress: "I saw someone close enough to my age that I realized acting could be a reality." Demi started to attend acting class only to drop out after a few sessions. "I didn't want to have to go to an acting class, because I didn't want to be told that I couldn't do it. I was so afraid that I wasn't good enough, I avoided that."

At age sixteen, Demi dropped out of school and began dating thirty-year-old guitarist Freddy Moore, whom she met after attending several performances of his band, the New Kats. Demi was neither fazed by his age nor the fact that he was already married. "As anybody who's had a relationship with a married man knows, there's a great adrenaline rush with it. I didn't think about the consequences." After Freddy's divorce, Demi Guynes became Demi Moore.

Being a high school dropout with no formal training did not seem to be a hindrance in her plan to become an actress. While working as a part-time file clerk, Demi did some modeling (posing topless for *Oui*) and managed to find bit roles in several B movies: *Choices* (1981), *Parasite* (1982), and *Young Doctors in Love* (1982).

Her first break came in 1982 when "General Hospital" producer Gloria Monty cast her to play reporter Jackie Templeton, the replacement for the show's leading lady Genie Francis of "Luke and Laura" fame. Shortly after she began appearing on the ABC soap, she became the subject of rumors, most of which involved sex and drugs. Freddy later recalled, "The incidents the camera didn't catch were better than those on the actual soap opera. It really shocked me. Demi didn't belong in that kind of environment." Series co-star Brian Patrick Clarke was sympathetic to Demi's plight. "Demi came into 'General Hospital' with great press and great expectations thrust upon her. She was young and inexperienced, she had to sink or swim on her own. . . . I liked her. I thought there was a lot more to Demi than the class clown."

Although her character and story plot never caught on with viewers, Demi was able to take time off from the soap to take supporting roles in *Blame It on Rio* (1984) and *No Small Affair* (1984). With these few acting credits, she decided to dive head first into the movies, but first she had to ditch her excess baggage, including Freddy. "He didn't make any money," she later said. "All along I made more money than he did."

By the time the Moores divorced, Demi had developed some bad habits and a party-girl reputation. Said Freddy: "Toward the end of our relationship, Demi started having a problem with drinking. She would have just one beer and turn into a completely different person." Demi's addictions included more than just beer. By age twenty-two, she was known to have a voracious appetite for both booze and drugs.

Demi went on to be cast in *St. Elmo's Fire* as a coke-addicted yuppie whose life is spinning out of control. Life imitated art as Demi stepped wholeheartedly into the party circuit. "I look at what I did as a healthy outlet, appropriate for the time," Demi later reflected. "There was a moment in this town when drugs and alcohol were very socially acceptable. I got to live, explore, try."

After *St. Elmo's* director Joel Schumacher threatened to fire Demi when her off-camera antics disrupted the production, Demi immediately went into rehab. By that time, she was dating the film's co-star, Emilio Estevez, who proved to be a calming influence in her life. She later said, "I think I had at least some sense of what I wanted to achieve, which I knew might go away if I didn't stop hurting myself."

During the publicity tour that accompanied the release of *St. Elmo's*, Demi proved that she was an amiable if not overly intellectual subject. She naively admitted to *Rolling Stone*, "I love Q-tips. I put them in my ears and my eyes start rolling. I call it eargasms. I must have the cleanest ears I know." All in all, Demi garnered more press from her turbulent engagement to Emilio than she did for any of her subsequent movies, which included *About Last Night* (1986), *One Crazy Summer* (1986), and *Wisdom* (1986).

At the premiere of Emilio's film *Stakeout* (1987), Demi was introduced to Bruce Willis. Bruce, who had become a overnight superstar on television with the ABC series "Moonlighting" had just completed his first motion picture, *Blind Date,* and was obviously on the Hollywood fast track.

Bruce, a known rabble-rouser and womanizer, has had more than a few

CHILDREN OF BABYLON

128

MARRIAGE TO BRUCE WILLIS HAS DONE NOTHING TO LESSEN DEMI'S CLOUT, STATUS . . . OR EGO. *MICHAEL FERGUSON/GLOBE PHOTOS* scrapes with the law. In fact, during the 1987 Memorial Day weekend, Bruce was arrested after an altercation with a police officer who was called to quiet a loud party at his home. The charges, which included assaulting an officer and disturbing the peace, were later dropped after Bruce agreed to apologize to his neighbors. Speaking to *Movieline* in 1989, Bruce remained unrepentant, saying, "I still don't think I did anything wrong. I don't think there's a law against enjoying yourself. The only mistake I made was moving into a neighborhood where the houses were three feet apart."

Four months after they met, Demi and Bruce Willis were wed in a secret ceremony in Las Vegas. The circumstances were unusual to say the least. After returning from a brief vacation in London, Bruce and Demi flew to Vegas to see a boxing match. On the spur of the moment they decided to get married. Demi was so anxious to become Mrs. Bruce Willis (and who wouldn't?) that when she filled out the marriage license, she stated that she'd never been married before. She later explained, "I thought it was going to take longer if I put it on there. I wasn't hiding it—it's been in print—but I wanted to be married before midnight because I wanted *that day* (November 21, 1987) to be the day." As it turned out, Nevada required no proof of divorce before issuing a license for a second marriage.

The twenty-five-year-old Demi and the thirty-two-year-old Bruce were wed at the Golden Nugget Hotel in a private civil service with only Bruce's bodyguard as a witness. The ceremony was repeated one month later when Little Richard married them in front of five hundred friends on a soundstage in Burbank. Demi's brother Morgan, a Marine, was an usher, and Ally Sheedy served as a bridesmaid.

While Demi maintains that being Mrs. Bruce Willis hasn't helped her career, there is little doubt that marrying well in Hollywood certainly can't hurt it. Demi gained a major boost in status after Bruce's success in *Die Hard* (1988) caused his salary to soar: He was paid a reported $5 million for *Die Hard* and $7 million for the movie's sequel. For lending his voice to a smart-aleck baby in *Look Who's Talking,* Bruce pocketed $10 million, while earning $3 million for a few weeks' work on the immortal stinker, *Bonfire of the Vanities* (1990). This newly acquired wealth and status created tremendous egos for both husband and wife.

During 1987, Demi took a hiatus from acting long enough to give birth to her daughter, Rumer Glenn Willis. She may have been out of the spotlight but she was certainly not far from the cameras, since Demi had hired a video operator to film the blessed event. Also present during the fifteen hours of labor were six of the couple's friends, which included her massage therapist and her personal assistant. At one point during the birth, Demi, concerned that the camera be in focus, reportedly turned to the video operator and asked, "Are you getting all this?"

The child was born on August 16, 1987, in Paducah, Kentucky (where Willis was filming *In Country*). Demi, who became very attached to her child, did not return to work until five months after Rumer's birth. In the meantime, Bruce continued to be the major bread winner with roles in *Die Hard 2* (1990) and *Look Who's Talking 2* (1990).

Despite her forgettable performances in the films *The Seventh Sign* (1988) and *We're No Angels* (1989), Demi's ego, along with her entourage, continued to grow. During the filming of her next movie, *Ghost*, Demi's "staff" included a personal assistant, a dialogue coach, a masseuse, a psychic consultant, a bodyguard, and Rumer's nanny. Demi was escorted to and from the set in a limo and insisted on flying between locations on private planes. (Not to be outdone by his wife, Bruce also surrounds himself with a large entourage. During the filming of *The Bonfire of the Vanities*, *Wall Street Journal* reporter Julie Salomon couldn't help but notice the man whose job it was to spray brown powder on Bruce's balding head.)

Aside from all the perks, Demi proved that she could be a difficult actress. Admitting that she's a "perfectionist" who likes to have "a lot of input," Demi would have the set cleared during the middle of the day when she wanted to discuss a scene with *Ghost*'s director Jerry Zucker. Zucker later revealed to *Premiere* that her questioning got "difficult and frustrating," not to mention expensive. Screenwriter Bruce Joel Rubin added, "Demi is truly a movie star in the sense that she perceives herself as a star."

Indeed, being a "star" is very important to Demi. She admitted to *The New York Times* in 1991: "To me, being a movie star without being respected as an actress would be nothing. But to get the kinds of roles you want, it sure helps to be a movie star. I certainly don't think there's anything wrong with being a movie star. If we wanted to be actors, we'd be doing theater and making no money."

After the film's release in 1990, *Ghost* became a blockbuster, grossing more than $200 million at the box office and giving much-needed career boosts to its three stars: Demi, Patrick Swayze, and Whoopi Goldberg. Demi's overwrought performance, however, had *People* magazine suggesting that she must have set "an all-time record for most scenes of tears welling up in the eyes." In their review, *Rolling Stone* noted that "Swayze and Moore are attractive but mannered and self-involved in a way that works against installing a sense of mutual loss."

Fame is very fleeting and Demi was acutely aware of how close she was to the edge. "It won't last long. I'm certainly enjoying it, but I know that it's just one movie, and as quickly as it comes, it goes just as fast." Indeed, it did.

Supporting the idea that the success of *Ghost* was merely a fluke, in 1991, Demi next starred in a trio of commercial failures. The first (and most horrendous) came in Dan Aykroyd's dreadful comedy *Nothing But Trouble*. Despite the universal pans of the movie, Demi explained, "I found it liberating. I got to be goofy, like Lucille Ball." The end result did not have audiences rolling in the aisles, but probably had Lucille Ball turning in her grave.

In *Mortal Thoughts*, Demi portrayed a beautician who helps her best friend (Glenne Headley) cover up the murder of her obnoxious husband (Bruce Willis). The film, with a budget of $7 million, was a chance for Demi to prove herself a more serious actress, while allowing her the honorary credit of co-producer.

After the first week of filming, Demi fired her director Claude Kerven because, she says, "what he was getting was not what I was wanting." (Kerven, who was eventually replaced by Alan Rudolph, has refused to comment on his dismissal.)

Her third movie of 1991 was *The Butcher's Wife*. Demi won the role after the producers first choice, Meg Ryan, walked away from the part. Riding the crest of her *Ghost* fame, the producers reportedly paid Demi $2.5 million to take the role of Marina, a beautiful Southern clairvoyant who, after mistakenly marrying a vacationing butcher (George Dzundza), injects herself into the lives of his customers, including the local psychiatrist (Jeff Daniels), with whom she eventually falls in love.

Jeff Daniels admitted that his co-star was "more into rewriting her character than I was," while director Terry Hughes described her as "very opinionated, very strong." During filming, Hughes found that he had to coax a performance from his star. "She always has another idea, but she'll move toward your way if she agrees with you. She does not respond to directing; you persuade her to let it become her idea." Demi, angered by these remarks, responded, "His statement that I find it difficult to take direction was very offensive. I was fighting to make the movie good, not crying for orange juice on the set."

So what does an actress do when her career begins to slide? Well, how about an outrageous publicity stunt? The photographs, taken by Annie Leibowitz, graced the cover of *Vanity Fair* just one month prior to the release of *The Butcher's Wife*. Demi firmly denies that the photos were for self-promotion. Speaking with Roger Ebert in 1991, Demi admitted, "I think pregnant women are beautiful. When I was pregnant with Rumer, my first child, Annie Leibowitz . . . photographed me naked just for our family, and we have these photographs up in our home."

Demi's second child, Scout Larue, was born on July 20, 1991. Scout (named for the child narrator of the novel *To Kill a Mockingbird*) and her older sister Rumer (named after British novelist Rumer Godden) are evidence of the couple's literary pretensions. Bruce likes to portray himself as an avid reader and even confided to one interviewer that he once spent $1,500 on one visit to a local bookstore. Demi, however, makes no such literary pretense. "I don't have books I could say that really supported me, stirred me up," she confided to Nancy Collins. "My insecurity is almost to the point that I'm afraid to actually go and buy a book because I don't want to buy the wrong book."

Despite Demi's popularity slippage, Bruce was having a much harder time. While the blame for *The Bonfire of the Vanities* (1990) was shared equally by his co-stars Tom Hanks, Melanie Griffith, and director Brian DePalma, the abysmal failure of *Hudson Hawk* (1991) was pinned squarely on Bruce. The box office success of *The Last Boy Scout* (1991) helped repair some of the damage but the washout of *Death Becomes Her* (1992) only reinforced the perception that his days as a leading man were coming to a close.

With huge egos, both Bruce and Demi have become easy targets for the tabloid press. In 1990, the *National Enquirer* reported that Marushka Detmers was dropped from the film *Hudson Hawk* on orders from Demi, who was concerned that the Dutch-born actress and her husband were acting very friendly on the set. Bruce vehemently denies the rumors of any involvement with Marushka or with any problems in his high-profile marriage.

Demi did not endear herself to the cast and crew of her next movie, *A Few Good Men* (1992). Crew members reportedly began calling her "Gimme" Moore after the star complained about the color of the car used to transport her to and from the set.

There is little doubt that Demi intends to remain a power player in Hollywood. "I love this a lot and I plan to be doing it a long time," she declared to writer Jennette Conant. "I just want the end result of things to be the highest quality they can be. I want good work. I want things to be the best they can be. I want greatness."

CHILDREN OF BABYLON

ALLY SHEEDY: POETRY FROM THE EDGE

Ally Sheedy has never been far from the spotlight. A dancer with the American Ballet Theater at age seven, a published author at age thirteen, and a major box office star by age twenty-one, Ally is probably the most talented and intelligent of her Brat Pack peers—which might not be such a great compliment, given the competition. But despite her all-American girl-next-door image, Ally has only recently come to terms with some of the more sordid events in her past.

Born on June 13, 1962, Ally is the eldest daughter of John Sheedy, a successful advertising executive, and Charlotte Sheedy, a high-powered feminist, literary agent, and writer. Ally spent her early years with her parents in their apartment on Central Park West. After they divorced when she was nine, Ally divided her time and spent half of every week with each of her parents. An active child, Ally spent her after-school and weekend hours in dance and acting classes. Charlotte later said, "It was a way for me to make sure the children were occupied during the hours when I was working."

Although she began her film career portraying a wholesome all-American teen in Wargames *(1983),* Ally Sheedy *had already had an abortion and a bout of substance abuse.*
Darlene Hammond/Globe Photos

She first gained public attention at age thirteen, when she and a school chum published a short novel based on the life of Queen Elizabeth I, *She Was Nice to Mice*. Ally wrote the text, while Jessica Levy, also age thirteen, provided the illustrations. Her mother became her agent and made the deal with McGraw-Hill. The book sold over 125,000 copies and made Ally the toast of the celebrity talk show circuit and the subject of articles in *Ms.*, the *Village Voice*, and *The New York Times*.

It could have been a combination of factors—an unstable home environment, fame at an early age, and so on—but Ally found herself pregnant at age sixteen. After she had an abortion, she became addicted to amphetamines. She later told *People*, "I took tranquilizers to escape from my emotional problems."

Ally moved to Los Angeles straight out of high school, settled into an apartment, and found a job as a waitress at a local health food restaurant. She did commercials for several fast-food chains, and made guest appearances on a few network shows, including "Hill Street Blues" and an afterschool special ironically titled "I Want to Have My Baby." She later said, "It was hard to do those minor roles and to accept the fact that it was not my movie. But I did learn a lot watching more experienced actors, like Melissa Gilbert and Jennifer Jason Leigh."

Ally's wholesome looks soon caught the eye of motion picture casting executives. She was cast as Sean Penn's pure girlfriend in her film debut *Bad Boys* (1983), but her first claim to fame was for her performance as Matthew Broderick's toothy girlfriend in *War Games* (1983).

With her newfound fame and fortune, she set up house with boyfriend Eric Stoltz and enrolled in the University of Southern California, where she majored in anthropology and theater. Stoltz describes the time he spent with Ally: "We were just kids in college. We lived together in a commune on Hollywood Boulevard . . . and there were four or five rooms filled with expatriots from England, a handful of homeless people, lots of young, aspiring actors. It was cheap and the atmosphere was exciting. It was a wonderful, messy, fervent time filled with crazy people starting their careers and very excited about what might happen."

Exciting things did begin to happen. Although *Oxford Blues* and *Twice in a Lifetime* failed to ignite any box office flames, in 1985 Ally hit her stride in two very successful films: *The Breakfast Club* and *St. Elmo's Fire*. In *The Breakfast Club,* Ally held her own against several high-profile young actors, including Molly Ringwald and Anthony Michael Hall. Indeed, Ally's star power has certainly outlasted these once famous, now obscure, actors. Molly has been recently seen playing suffering women on made-for-TV

CHILDREN
OF
BABYLON

136

BLUE CITY (1986) DID LITTLE TO ENHANCE THE REPUTATIONS OF ITS STARS, JUDD NELSON AND ALLY. *RALPH DOMINGUEZ/GLOBE PHOTOS*

movies, while Anthony emerged from his boozy teens only to find that no one is really interested in his comeback.

St. Elmo's Fire drew its strength from the ensemble of hot young Brat Pack actors in the cast: Rob Lowe, Demi Moore, Emilio Estevez, and Judd Nelson. Ally, however, was the only actor to survive the film's scathing reviews. *New York* magazine wrote: "The picture is pretty nearly a graveyard for the acting ambitions of its 'hot' young cast. The sole survivor of the general disaster is Ally Sheedy, who manages to make something charming out of the yup petulance. But then Sheedy could probably be charming while eating an artichoke. The other actors will have to settle for lesser vegetables."

Despite her talent, Ally's later films were uneven in terms of script and acting quality. *New York* magazine wrote that *Blue City* (1986) set "new standards of ineptitude. It's poorly written, poorly acted, poorly directed, poorly edited." While most of the critics placed the blame for this debacle squarely on the shoulders of Ally's contemptuous co-star Judd Nelson, the writer went so far as to warn the young starlet: "If her presence grows any smaller, she'll be too slight an actress for a sitcom."

Her performance fared better in the romantic comedy *Short Circuit* (1986). Of course, she found herself playing opposite Steve Guttenberg and a talking robot—make that two talking robots! She also received good notices for her role as a spoiled heiress who learns the error of her ways in the lighthearted comedy *Maid to Order* (1987).

Despite its good intentions, *Heart of Dixie* (1989) was another commercial failure. Ally believes that poor handling by Orion Pictures, the film's distributor, ultimately hurt the film. Even Vincent Canby agreed: "Miss Sheedy is so good as Maggie that the character's liberation, and the rise of her social consciousness, appear to be genuine triumphs."

Ally's personal downfall coincided with her involvement with rocker Richie Samborra of Bon Jovi. She told *Newsday,* "I was involved with someone who had a bad drinking problem, I wasn't sleeping and I got some tranquilizers from a doctor." Samborra responded to *US* magazine, "It didn't really last long—a couple of months. I was going through a bout with alcohol at the time. And she was going through a drug period that I had no idea about. I was on tour, and she was breaking up with me all the time. I dealt with this for a few weeks and finally I just went, 'Fine then f __ k it.' I didn't take any calls anymore."

In 1989, several of her friends, including Demi Moore, handed her an airplane ticket to the famous Hazelden Foundation clinic in Minnesota. She later told *Movieline,* "When I got to Minnesota I felt completely alienated and isolated from everybody, but Rebecca De Mornay visited me, and Alec

CHILDREN OF BABYLON

138

Ally's involvement with Richie Samborra (of the rock group Bon Jovi) contributed to the destructive lifestyle that eventually landed her in rehab. *MICHAEL FERGUSON/GLOBE PHOTOS*

Baldwin, who's probably my best friend in the whole world, called me every single day. Everybody I know has been through something."

During her stay she returned to her poetry and wrote a series of confessional poems called *Yesterday I Saw the Sun*. The book (which includes a dedication to Eric Stoltz, Demi Moore, and Jane Fonda) is a collection of poems, that recount her experiences with drugs, alcohol, bulimia, depression, loneliness, and her teenage abortion. Although the book came under sharp critical scrutiny from the press, she remained unperturbed: "Writing was a big part of my rehab. Pain and turbulence motivate me at the moment. I'd rather write about the pain you have when healing from a relationship." She has completely severed her ties with Samborra, who recently said, "I wish she was able to come to terms with talking to me, because I really did care about her."

Since her return from Hazelden, her work has generally improved but her film choices have been a mixed bag. Ally, along with co-star Anthony LaPaglia, outshone the lead performers of *Betsy's Wedding* (1990), not a difficult task considering the film starred Alan Alda and Molly Ringwald. *The Lost Capone,* a made-for-cable flick starring Eric Roberts, was a complete disaster, leaving one critic to write, "Even if you've misplaced your zapper, be sure to get up and tune out before the abysmal final scene." Vestron Films went bankrupt before it could release *Fear,* an effective chiller in which Ally gives a credible performance as crime-solving psychic.

Ally's most sincere performance to date was the role of John Candy's love interest in the likeable but largely ignored comedy *Only the Lonely*. After the film's release she returned to New York to appear in the off-Broadway play *Advice from a Caterpillar*. Although the play was not well received, Ally walked away with the admiration of her co-star David Lansbury (nephew of actress Angela Lansbury). The couple were wed in October of 1992.

Ally's only addictions these days are cigarettes, writing, and work. She recently said, "When you're in Hollywood there's no escaping that movies are the purpose of existence. That's what the whole town is about. Being a success in Hollywood means your movie made money. It has nothing to do with being a good actor or a good person."

BORN AGAIN CHRISTIAN SLATER

Christian Slater has made his mark as an actor known for his intense portrayals of volatile, dangerous young men and outlaws. That devilishness, however, earned him outlaw status in real life after two drunk driving arrests landed him in jail.

Christian, born on August 19, 1969, in New York City, is the son of stage and TV soap actor Michael Hawkins (the original Frank Ryan on "Ryan's Hope") and casting director Mary Jo Slater. Five years later, his parents divorced and his father relocated to Los Angeles and became a theater director.

Christian's first professional work, at age six, was as a model for Pierre Cardin. He soon eased into television commercials and, at age seven, his mother cast him in a small role on "One Life to Live." Christian had five lines as a tough kid who limps into a clinic after falling off a skateboard. Of the experience, he later said, "My mom gave me the part as a joke. But it

BORN AGAIN
CHRISTIAN SLATER

WITHIN A YEAR OF HIS TWENTIETH BIRTHDAY, CHRISTIAN SLATER WOULD BE CHARGED WITH DRUNK DRIVING, RESISTING ARREST, AND ASSAULT WITH A DEADLY WEAPON. *GREG VIE/GLOBE PHOTOS*

completely backfired in her face because after I did my scene . . . I was hooked."

Christian attended private school until director Michael Kidd spotted him with his mother on the "Joe Franklin Show." The following year Christian spent nine months touring in Kidd's revival of *The Music Man,* appearing with Dick Van Dyke. "I was terrible," he says of his first role. "I kept waving at people in the audience." After leaving the show, Christian continued to find theater work, playing in off-Broadway productions of John Guare's *Landscape of the Body, Oliver, Macbeth,* and *David Copperfield.*

In an interview with *Rolling Stone*'s Bill Flanagan, Christian bragged, "I've done some ballsy sh __ , man." He was, of course, referring to his first film efforts: *The Invisible Boy* (in which, at age twelve, he was required to take off his clothes), the unreleased *Twisted* (in which his pants were pulled off him), and *The Legend of Billie Jean* (in which he appears in drag). Ballsy—yes. Memorable—not really.

It was not until he was cast as Sean Connery's sidekick in *The Name of the Rose* that Christian would begin to show promise as an actor. It took two days to film his first nude scene, having sex with a peasant girl (played by Valentina Vargas) in the abbey kitchen amid piles of dead fish. Christian later told reporter Chris Heath, "It was not the most erotic and exciting situation. It was a good thing I'd lost my virginity. I knew how it worked. I knew where to put it."

Christian attended classes at New York's Professional Children's School, which is noted for its correspondence courses for actors who go off on location. A daydreamer and troublemaker, Christian once lit a cigarette during class "just to get kicked out." He dropped out just a few months shy of graduation. Even Mary Jo agrees. "He concentrates on anything to do with show business and having fun. He's not an intellectual by any stretch of the imagination—he's just a good person."

In 1987, the Slaters relocated to Los Angeles, where with his mother's connections, Christian made his entry into feature films with roles in *Gleaming the Cube* (1988), *Personal Choice* (1988), *Tucker: The Man and His Dreams* (1988), *The Wizard* (1989), and *Tales from the Darkside: The Movie* (1990).

Along the way, Christian earned a bad boy reputation and developed more than a few bad habits. Christian later told *Movieline*'s Stephen Rebello, "I was on a real self-destructive course, staying up all night, partying or sometimes just staying up all the night—like the time I had to loop *Tucker,* with Francis Ford Coppola, do a wardrobe fitting for *Heathers,* finish an episode of "L.A. Law," and missed two out of three."

Christian's notoriety and bad reputation grew during the filming of the satirical comedy *Heathers* (1989). Critics were, for the most part, impressed with Christian's impersonation of Jack Nicholson as the devil in *The Witches of Eastwick*. Christian later admitted that his imitation was actually a tribute "to the best actor around." For those people who were less than appreciative of this he said, "The hell with 'em. I don't care. I did it. F __ k it. I had fun doing it."

Fun is not a word co-star Winona Ryder would use to describe Christian's off-camera antics. "He freaked me out during some of those scenes," she acknowledged. "I got so scared of him, I fled back into my trailer and locked the door." Despite his sometimes chilling performance, he and Winona became good friends off the set. Although he has told reporters, "I fell in love with the girl," Winona has repeatedly shrugged away the idea that the feeling was mutual. Referring to their relationship as a joke, she told *Rolling Stone* in 1989, "We talked about how we were going to do all the Hollywood marriage things, like stage fights in restaurants, be really reclusive but then leak out everything; he'd cover my face when photographers came, like Sean and Madonna."

Christian definitely enjoys playing the role of ladies' man. He blatantly discusses his romantic conquests, as well as his childhood relationship with a pillow. ("My pillow and I got along extremely well") He has been quick to dispel those rumors that label his sexual preferences as anything less than straight. "Anybody that knows me personally pretty much knows that I'm *very* into women," Christian once declared. "I do love women."

The critical success of *Heathers* awakened Christian to the need to personally manage his career. He asserts, "Money's important, let's not bullsh __ , but I want to stay in this business for the rest of my life, and the only way I can do that is to make the right decisions." One of those decisions is to work through each script thoroughly. To do this, Christian goes over his parts with close friend Dan Lauria (known for his role as the father on "The Wonder Years"). Christian revealed, "He and I have worked on, I guess, every film I've ever done, um, we really . . . we sit down and just try and break down the character and just really work on it—just try to make it as natural as possible for me."

In 1989, Christian starred as Mark Hunter, a shy high school student by day, who takes over the radio air waves at night as Hard Harry, a pirate radio deejay in *Pump Up the Volume*. Hard Harry speaks out for all the disenchanted neighborhood teens and rallies his fellow students to rebel against their oppressive school system. He regularly amuses his listeners by pretending to masturbate on the air. "Here it comes, another gusher." The role earned critical praise but received a lukewarm response from audiences.

When Christian told reporter Arthel Nevill in 1991 that he spent "five or

The on-set scuffling among the stars of Mobsters (1991) made tabloid headlines and left Christian (left) with bruised ribs and Patrick Dempsey (right) with a broken nose.
MICHAEL FERGUSON/GLOBE PHOTOS

six years in a coma," he's not kidding. During the filming of *Pump Up the Volume,* director Michael Lehmann had to have someone break in to Christian's house because he was in such a deep sleep. TV actor Phill ("Teech") Lewis, one of Christian's good friends, disclosed to *Rolling Stone,* "I sleep on his couch a lot, and if he's got to wake up early to shoot or rehearse, he sets his alarm and—I swear—it'll wake up the whole building, and Christian will sleep through it. I'm in the other room, I hear the alarm, I get up and go turn it off and wake him up. He can sleep all day."

Christian's fast-paced lifestyle came to a climax of sorts on the morning of December 29, 1989. After an evening of club-hopping, a police car pulled behind Christian on Santa Monica Boulevard and signaled him to stop for doing 50 mph in a 35-mph zone. Driving under the influence and with a suspended license (for a previous drunk driving incident), Christian roared away, leading to a high-speed chase that ended when he crashed his Saab 900 into a telephone pole. Slater fled the scene and was subsequently caught trying to scale a chain-link fence. He was arrested after kicking a police officer, who later complained of pain in his arm, wrist, and leg. Christian was charged with drunken driving, driving with a suspended license, evading arrest, resisting arrest, and assault with a deadly weapon (his cowboy boot). The last two charges were dropped in exchange for no-contest pleas on the other charges. At his sentencing on April 2, 1990, Christian was given five years' probation, suspended from driving for eighteen months, ordered to pay $1,400 in fines, and sentenced to jail for ten days.

When Christian resurfaced months later, he took to the road, doing acts of public contrition and giving explanations. "I did what a lot of people do at a certain age," he says. "I went through a wild period, although I think I took it to an extreme, and I know I could have been smarter."

Christian and his handlers have done extensive damage control and more recently the actor is hard pressed when asked embarrassing questions about his "dark years." He told the *New York Daily News,* "I'd love to go into all of that with you, but I can't remember a thing. I've got a bad case of amnesia about all of that stuff." When pressed on the issue by *Movieline,* he said, "I got treated, and I retired from drinking. I've been to a couple of AA meetings and it's pretty good."

Since claiming to be fully rehabbed, Christian has worked nonstop in several high-profile, if not altogether successful, films, including *Tales from the Darkside, Young Guns II,* and *Mobsters.* Still, Christian has had some difficulty controlling his temper.

When the horse that had been assigned to him for *Young Guns II* became temperamental, he controlled the animal by whacking him on the back of the neck. Unapologetic, he later bragged, "He didn't f __ k with me for the rest of the movie. . . . I'm not going to be beaten by a f __ king horse or by anybody else who gets in my way."

During the filming of *Mobsters* (1991), rumors spread like wildfire about the off-camera clashes and bad blood among the films rowdy stars: Christian, Patrick Dempsey, Richard Grieco, and former soccer player Costas Mandylor. The film, dubbed Young Buns with Tommy Guns, told a fictionalized story of the rise of Lucky Luciano, Meyer Lansky, Bugsy Siegel, and Frank Costello. Faced with a series of preproduction difficulties, director Michael Karbelnikoff was forced to act like a referee during his first feature film job.

Early into the filming, Christian and method actor Patrick Dempsey got into a shoving match. Christian later griped, "It really pissed me off that I had to get an X-ray for my chest after doing that scene with him. It pissed me off that there were no apologies." Karbelnikoff commented, "Patrick and Christian have definitely had their ego battles on this movie. At times, it's been really helpful for the film, at other times detrimental." Christian disagreed, "Patrick did all sorts of useless things that didn't add much of anything but pain and drama. And I'm not one for drama on the set."

Despite its cast of teen idols and heavy promotion, the film earned tepid reviews and was largely ignored by the public during the summer of 1991.

From the start, Christian's second film that year, *Robin Hood: Prince of Thieves,* was destined to be a box-office bonanza. Although the film was rushed into production, which translated into general confusion on the set, Christian would later receive the best notices of the high-profile cast, which included Kevin Costner, Morgan Freeman, and Mary Elizabeth Mastrantonio.

He did not fare as well in the 1992 release *Kuffs,* co-staring Tony Goldwyn and Milla Jovovich. His smirky performance as an irresponsible man who inherits a private police company caused one reviewer to ask, "Don't you think the Jack Nicholson impersonation is wearing a little thin? . . . in *Kuffs* it has all the charm of an abscessed boil."

For the past few years, Christian has moved from one project to the next. "I used to concentrate on one f __ king project at a time. Now, at the advice of people—good advice—I've done one movie after another that will really get seen by the public. . . . I try and stay in the moment as much as possible, because, if I project too far, I f __ k myself up completely." He then added, "This f __ king business is brutal, pressured, so full of abuse. You could be destroyed."

THE POISON PENNS

When *New York* writer David Blum described Sean Penn as a "natural heir to Robert De Niro's throne," he was not alone in singling out this young actor as being the most talented member of the Brat Pack. Unfortunately, Sean is better known as a rude, sometimes violent, young man whose off-screen antics (which included drinking and brawling) led the New York *Daily News* to label him one of "the most offensive people on the planet." An *extremely* private person, in 1985 he married a very public pop superstar. As Mr. Madonna, he then proceeded to wage and lose a fierce battle with the tabloid press, which not only landed him in jail but completely overshadowed a once promising acting career.

It is not surprising that Sean became an actor, considering his family heritage. Sean was born on August 17, 1960, to Leo Penn, a television and film director, and Eileen Ryan, a former actress who retired to raise her three sons, Michael, Sean, and Christopher. Sean and his brothers were raised in California's San Fernando Valley until 1970, when the Penns moved

CHILDREN OF BABYLON

IN 1987, SEAN PENN SPENT THIRTY-TWO DAYS IN THE L.A. COUNTY JAIL FOR PUNCHING OUT A MOVIE EXTRA. *ALPHA/GLOBE PHOTOS*

to Malibu. It was there that Sean became friends with neighborhood kids Emilio Estevez, Charlie Sheen, and Rob and Chad Lowe.

In an interview in 1991, with *Playboy*'s David Rensin, Sean expressed very negative feelings about his own education. "I had a terrible school experience," said Sean. "I regret having gone to school. I think I missed a lot of opportunities to see life during that period." An avid surfer, Sean spent many school days ditching classes to indulge in his true passion, "the beautiful waves."

Despite being raised in a theatrical environment, Sean did not seriously consider becoming an actor until his late teens, when his friends Emilio and Rob began to pursue their own careers. After graduating from Santa Monica High in 1978, Sean found work with the Los Angeles Repertory Group Theater and studied with the famous acting coach Peggy Feury. His first TV role was a one-line walk-on in an episode of "Barnaby Jones," which was followed by sporadic work on network television.

At age nineteen, Sean moved to New York to do stage work. A role in the play *Heartland* resulted in an audition for the film *Taps,* and suddenly he was taken seriously. The film, which co-stared Timothy Hutton and a still unknown Tom Cruise, told the story of military cadets who take over their school when the land is sold to real estate developers. Sean's performance as the sane, moral voice of the group caught the attention of film critics and audiences alike.

Sean's ability to absorb himself into any role was readily apparent in his next film, *Fast Times at Ridgemont High* (1982). His portrayal of a perpetually stoned surfer name Jeff Spicoli literally stole the movie away from co-stars Judge Reinhold, Phoebe Cates, and Jennifer Jason Leigh. His performances in his next two films, *Bad Boys* (1983) and *Crackers* (1984), confirmed expectations that Sean had a wide range of talent, quite often exceeding the mediocre scripts he was given.

Sean's first public troubles took place in 1984, when he refused to do publicity interviews for *Racing with the Moon,* a coming of age film set during World War II. Sean claims that it was not a dislike of the film but other work that restricted his time. "I wasn't even a famous actor at the time, but it became this thing. 'Ah, now we've got a label for him. He's the guy who doesn't support his movies.'" When Sean's co-star (and then girlfriend) Elizabeth McGovern also refused to do interviews, both actors were branded as troublemakers. According to Sean, "*Racing with the Moon* turned into one of the most boring melodramas of the Eighties: The Pugnacious Asshole Story, starring Senn Penn. It was my biggest hit. It was all over the place."

Despite all the upheaval in his life, Sean continued to do exceptional work. In *The Falcon and the Snowman* (1985), Sean reteamed with Timothy Hutton in the true story of Christopher Boyce and Daulton Lee, two childhood friends who were convicted of selling classified government information to the Soviet Union in the seventies. Although he was impressed by both actors, Vincent Canby noted that "It's Mr. Penn who dominates the screen with a performance that, like the film, is arresting in its bizarre details and as cold as ice."

Despite the critical accolades, the conflict between Sean and the tabloid press continued to escalate. During a trip to Nashville in June of 1985, Sean reportedly hurled a rock at a photographer, and then punched out a reporter. At another event, he threatened photographer Janet Gough. "He told me he had a water pistol and if I didn't leave he was going into the men's room, fill the pistol with urine, and come out and squirt me," she later recalled.

The adverse publicity he managed to generate for himself was only a prelude for a maelstrom of bad press that would come from his turbulent romance (and later marriage) with Madonna.

Madonna Louise Ciccone was born on August 16, 1958, in Bay City, Michigan. The oldest girl in a family of six children, she learned to accept responsibility at the age of six, when her mother died of breast cancer. Her father proceeded to move his family to Pontiac, Michigan, and later married the family housekeeper—events which were equally traumatic to young Madonna.

A unruly child, she rebelled against her traditional Catholic upbringing by becoming an outrageous flirt who liked to draw attention to herself. At age seventeen, Madonna left home and moved to New York with plans of becoming a professional dancer. "I sort of got tired of that after a while," she said, "because it was very difficult and there was no money in it." She supported herself by modeling while taking acting classes, but by 1980 she decided to become a singer.

In 1983, Sire records released her first record, the self-titled "Madonna," a collection of disco tracks that included the pop hits "Lucky Star" and "Borderline." Madonna began a fashion trend with her own style of dress, which included bustiers, fingerless gloves, and crucifixes ("Crucifixes are sexy because there's a naked man on them," she once said.)

Although her cameo appearance in the film *Vision Quest* (1984) generated some publicity, it was her second album, "Like a Virgin," that launched her toward superstar status with songs such as "Material Girl" and the title track. Coinciding with the album's success was the release of *Desperately Seeking Susan* (1985), a screwball farce shot on a budget of $5 million, which

At his wedding to pop megastar Madonna, Sean greeted his guests by saying, "Welcome to the remaking of *Apocalypse Now*."
Richard Corkery/Globe Photos

wound up taking in over $27 million domestically and proved that Madonna was a viable box office draw.

Sean was introduced to Madonna on the set of her "Material Girl" video and a stormy romance was born. Madonna's enormous success took Sean completely by surprise. "You have to understand," he explained to *Playboy* in 1991, "when Madonna and I got together, she was an up-and-coming star. She was not a superstar; she was not an icon. She hadn't even gone on tour yet. And that tour, before we got married, didn't indicate to me the enormity of what was coming."

If Madonna's growing popularity didn't indicate the direction her life was taking, the media frenzy surrounding their Malibu wedding surely must have been a tip-off. Although the couple carefully prepared for a "secret" ceremony on August 16, 1985, the press eventually were tipped off to the party's location. When Sean noticed dogged reporters hovering over the site in helicopters, he quickly ran onto the beach and scrawled in twenty-foot letters, F __ K OFF. One tabloid reported that Sean fired a pistol at the choppers and said, "I would have been very excited to see one of those helicopters burn and the bodies inside melt."

Sean and Madonna exchanged their vows in a five-minute ceremony standing, appropriately enough, on the edge of a cliff. Sean then proceeded to greet his guests by saying, "Welcome to the remaking of *Apocalypse Now*." In retrospect, it is not certain whether he was referring to the day's event or predicting his own self-destructive future.

By all accounts, the marriage was stormy from its first days. A heavy drinker, Sean could be easily provoked into a verbal argument, which usually culminated in a fistfight. In April of 1986, he lost his temper in an L.A. nightclub after he spotted songwriter David Wolinski giving Madonna a friendly kiss. Sean attacked Wolinski with punches, kicks, and a chair. He was later fined $1,000 and given a year's probation. Four months later, two photographers approached the couple leaving their New York apartment and found themselves in a shoving match with the belligerent actor.

With the constant barrage of bad press, lawsuits, and court appearances, it is no wonder that his film career began to slide precipitously. *At Close Range* (1986), the story of two brothers (played by Sean and his brother Chris) who are corrupted by their dangerous father (Christopher Walken), was a commercial failure, taking in less than $3 million at the box office.

His second film that year, *Shanghai Surprise*, was a project doomed from the start. The film, produced by ex-Beatle George Harrison, told the story of a shady con artist (Sean) who assists a missionary (Madonna), if you

*S*EAN AND LONG-TIME STEADY ROBIN WRIGHT BECAME PARENTS OF A DAUGHTER, DYLAN FRANCES, IN APRIL OF 1991.
JOHN BARRETT/GLOBE PHOTOS

can believe it, in her quest to find 1,000 pounds of opium to use for medicinal purposes.

With a terrible script, shoddy direction, and stars who had become tabloid targets, it was no surprise the film was universally lambasted. Critic Roxanne Mueller in the Cleveland *Plain Dealer* wrote that the film was "awesome in its awfulness, momentous in its ineptness, and shattering in its stupidity." Peter Travers in *People* magazine commented that "What this movie needs isn't criticism, but a stake through the heart."

Of this disastrous project, Sean later admitted that he "was so pissed off and preoccupied with other things that it's the one time I took a movie entirely for the paycheck. . . . I just said, 'I don't give a f __ k.' I just stayed drunk the whole f __ king time."

At home, Sean continued to menace the obtrusive paparazzi who followed the couple's every movement. Looking back on these altercations, Madonna told *Vanity Fair,* "I liked his public demonstrations of protecting me. In retrospect, I understand why he dealt with the press the way he did, but you have to realize it's a losing battle. It's not going to get you anywhere." By 1987, it appeared that Sean's life was speeding out of control and would eventually land him in jail.

In April of 1987, Sean violated his parole for the Wolinski attack when he assaulted Jeffrie Klein, a scrap metal dealer moonlighting as an extra in the movie *Colors,* a film that had Sean portraying a tough cop. When Klein attempted to snap a souvenir photo of Sean walking around the set with Robert Duvall, he found himself taking blows from the angry actor's fast fists.

The following month, police picked Sean up for speeding and running a red light. A blood test revealed an alcohol content of .11 percent, slightly above the legal limit. Although the charge was later reduced to reckless driving, it represented still another probation violation.

In June of 1987, Sean was sentenced to sixty days in the L.A. County Jail and ordered to undergo counselling for his violent conduct. In protective custody at the L.A. County Jail, Sean's other cellmates included Richard Ramirez (the infamous "night stalker") and Raymond Buckey (of McMartin preschool fame). "This was not a f __ king garden party," Sean later conceded. While her husband was incarcerated, Madonna was quoted as saying, "I think Sean will emerge from jail as a better person and as an even greater actor."

While Sean managed to stay out of trouble for several months after his release, his marriage began to fall apart. In December of 1987, the couple jointly announced that they were seeking a divorce. Madonna had reportedly tired of her husband's temper tantrums and heavy drinking, while Sean had grown wary of his wife's growing entourage, which included close friend Sandra Bernhard. The couple reconciled two weeks later.

Things finally came to a head in 1988 when, after a bitter argument, Sean moved out of their Malibu home. According to published reports, on December 28th, Sean, drunk and irrational, burst into their house and physically abused Madonna for nine hours, at one point tying her to a chair. Although she initially filed a complaint with the police that Sean had assaulted her, twelve days later she dropped the charges.

Instead, Madonna formally filed for divorce. Fearing for her own safety, she requested that the police escort her to her home when she returned to retrieve her possessions. "A SWAT team surrounded my house and came in every door," Sean recalled. "But it happened because on the day that we split up, she developed a concern that if she were to return to the house, she would get a severe haircut."

In 1991, Sean reflected on his marriage to *Newsday*'s Lynn Darling: "The Madonna stuff just made it clear. After it was over, I could see what was left that I was in control of." He continued, "I'm very fond of my ex-wife, but at twenty-four, I didn't realize the difference between a great first date and a lifetime commitment."

Madonna by all accounts was truly smitten with Sean. She told *Vanity Fair*'s Lynn Hirschberg: "Sean was very protective of me. He was like my father in a way. He patrolled what I wore. He'd say, 'You're not wearing that dress. You can see everything in that.' But at least he was paying attention to me. At least he had the balls."

After the union dissolved, Sean continued to turn in good performances in a series of commercially disappointing films. Despite his chilling performance of a ruthless squad leader in *Casualties of War* (1989), the film took in less than $20 million at the box office. The lighthearted caper *We're No Angels* (1989), co-starring Robert De Niro and Demi Moore, brought in only $11 million, while *State of Grace* (1990), which may be Sean's acting finale, brought in a paltry $2 million.

Despite a faltering career, Sean did manage to find some stability in his personal life. During the filming of *State of Grace,* Sean became romantically involved with his co-star, Robin (*The Princess Bride*) Wright. The couple became parents of a daughter, Dylan Frances Penn, on April 13, 1991.

In 1991, Sean decided to quit acting to pursue a career in writing and directing. His first effort, *The Indian Runner,* is the dark, violent story of two brothers; one a local cop and family man, the other an angry Vietnam vet. While the film received generally good notices, it remained virtually ignored by the moviegoing public—a fact which does not faze the novice director. "I'm not worried about being able to get money together. I'm a scrapper. I'll come up with it. I'll sell lemonade on Santa Monica Boulevard to make movies."

PART IV

SEX, PHOTOS, AND VIDEOTAPE

T he odds of successfully making the transition from child star to working adult actor are not especially promising. For some child actors, particularly ones who have grown up in front of television audiences, entering adolescence can be the prelude to the long road to oblivion. Typecast as "cute kids," many juvenile TV actors find themselves permanently unemployed when their series are cancelled. This may explain why so many former child actresses are willing to take drastic (and desperate) steps to resuscitate their waning careers.

The list of former child actresses who have graced the pages of *Playboy* magazine is considerable. According to Judy Norton Taylor ("The Waltons"), the reasons why she posed for *Playboy* (August 1985) were fairly obvious: "Everybody, casting people included, saw me as Mary Ellen, a not particularly attractive farm girl. At the time, remember, it was the glitz and glamour of "Dynasty" that people were looking for. I realized I needed a sexier image. And posing in *Playboy* seemed the easiest way to accomplish

CHILDREN
OF
BABYLON

In 1992 Christina Applegate complained that her TV character, Kelly Bundy, keeps on getting "dumber and dumber."
BOB V. NOBLE/GLOBE PHOTOS

it." Judy later admitted that posing in the magazine "had no effect on my career, whatsoever."

Pamela Sue Martin, who began her career as a model before moving on to television as the lead in "Nancy Drew" (1977–1978) had slightly better luck in making the transition to adult star. After posing in *Playboy* (July 1978) and appearing topless in the 1979 film *The Lady in Red,* Pamela Sue spent three years on "Dynasty," playing the sexy and glamourous Fallon Carrington-Colby.

For an unemployed Dana Plato, the decision to appear in the June, 1989 issue of *Playboy* was rather simple. "Actually, taking my clothes off was the easiest part," said Dana at the time. "The hardest part? It was sitting on my butt for the last two years." Her photo layout, however, did not open a floodgate of film or TV offers and two years later she stood accused of robbing $164 from a Las Vegas video store.

For those who are desperate to prove they are mature actors but are unwilling to bare all their assets, there is always work available at the bottom end of the film industry; namely, horror/teen exploitation flicks. Mary McDonough, who played Erin Walton from 1971 to 1981, appeared topless in her screen debut *Mortuary* (1981), while Donna Wilkes (of "Hello, Larry" fame) wandered her way through *Schizoid* (1980), *Angel* (1983), and *Grotesque* (1987). Danielle Brisebois, who gained recognition as the littlest orphan in the Broadway production of *Annie* and who later appeared on "All in the Family," made futile attempts to cross over into adult roles with *Big Bad Mama II* (1987) and *Kill Crazy* (1989).

Audiences have watched Melissa Gilbert grow up on television, principally as little Half-Pint on the long-running "Little House on the Prairie" (1974–1983). After the series ended, Melissa gave herself a nose job and attempted to take on more mature roles in films such as *Sylvester* (1985) and *Ice House* (1988). Having failed to cross over into motion pictures, Melissa's subsequent roles have been limited to television.

For the most part, attempts by young actors to use their sexuality to propel their careers have backfired. Lisa Bonet is probably the most blatant example of how a sudden image transformation can destroy a career. Appearing nude in magazines and in the film *Angel Heart,* combined with her "don't give a sh __ " attitude, alienated not only her loyal fans but Bill Cosby, the man responsible for launching her career.

Young actresses who promote themselves with their sexual qualities can find themselves typecast as bimbos or sluts. Christina Applegate, who made her name portraying teen tramp Kelly Bundy on the Fox sitcom "Married with Children," is just one example of how one role can create a stereotype.

The daughter of actress Nancy Priddy, Christina made her television debut at only three months old, in a cameo spot on her mother's show, "Days of Our Lives." Acting regularly in commercials and TV movies, Christina purchased her first home at age eleven. Her performance as a rebellious teen on the short-lived police drama "Heart of the City" brought her to the attention of casting executives who were searching for someone to portray the dumbest Bundy. While the public exposure and financial rewards were significant, Christina was well aware of the risks. "When you're on a television show," she said, "people start thinking that's your personality in real life. They can't see you as anything different, and they don't respect you as an actress."

Despite her fear of being typecast in sexy roles, Christina has done little to break away from the mold. In 1987 she was photographed for a poster wearing nothing but ripped cut-offs and a leather vest, while in her feature film debut, *Streets* (1988), she portrayed a homeless prostitute. "I don't blame anybody for typecasting me," she says. "But I am surprised at how few people in this business have any imagination."

Traci Lords's difficulty in earning respect as a serious actress has met with resistance from the industry and audiences alike. Of course, the three years she spent making sex films might have hurt her chances to play the young ingenue. Says Traci, "For so long, I was so worried about what people would think about me, but now I just say, 'What the hell.'"

All of this is not to say that a wholesome, all-American image works. Teri Shields, for example, launched her daughter's acting career by exploiting the child's sexuality in the controversial film *Pretty Baby* (1978). Middle America may have been shocked to see Brooke's buns on film, but film critics were generally impressed with her performance, and predictions of a successful acting career did not seem all that farfetched. Looking back on her career, Brooke commented to one reporter in 1991, "You know, sometimes I look at Jodie Foster and think, 'Gee, what's happening with me?'" What happened was that instead of cutting her teeth with a variety of roles that would improve her skills as an actress, Mother Shields selected insipid scripts (such as *Endless Love* and *Sahara*) that should have been tossed. Brooke's image, that of an overgrown Girl Scout controlled by an insufferable den mother, has virtually removed her from contention for more serious roles.

For some actresses, successful development from child to adult actor stems from a natural independence. Melanie Griffith, for example, left home to live with Don Johnson when she was only fifteen years old. Melanie has successfully parlayed breast implants, along with a Chatty Cathy voice, into

Arrested at age fifteen, Juliette Lewis's Oscar-nominated portrayal of an innocent teenage girl in *Cape Fear* (1991) was a far cry from her own reality. *GLOBE PHOTOS*

SEX, PHOTOS, & VIDEOTAPE

163

a thriving film career. She is, however, aging rapidly, and her days of playing a sex bomb are rapidly drawing to a close.

Juliette Lewis, who at age eighteen earned an Oscar nomination for her sexually-charged performance of an awkward teen in *Cape Fear* (1991), is another actress who has matured beyond her years. At age fourteen, she was legally emancipated from her parents, Glennis Batley and actor Geoffrey ("Flo") Lewis, to avoid the working restrictions of child labor laws. By age sixteen, Juliette had dropped out of school and had been arrested (for being a minor in an underground club). Featured in *Husbands and Wives* (1992), and highly touted as a future leading lady, Juliette's youthful looks and worldly image have helped her launch what appears to be an interesting career.

While many agree that the notion of becoming an overnight success is basically a Hollywood myth, for Julia Roberts wealth and fame appeared to come instantaneously. During her brief career, Julia has gained as much attention for her romantic involvements as her acting accomplishments. Julia's stormy personal life has kept tongues wagging through several high-profile relationships and one very public dis-engagement.

No discussion on sexuality would be complete without mentioning Rob Lowe. A Brat Packer of marginal talents, Rob's most successful film to date turned out to be a home video taken during the 1988 Democratic National Convention in Atlanta.

LISA BONET'S DOUBLE IMAGE

Probably no other young television actress of the eighties has made as many bad personal and professional decisions as Lisa Bonet. At age fifteen, she came out of nowhere to become one of the most popular characters on one of the most successful television series of all time, "The Cosby Show." In less than seven years she had virtually thrown away her career, and faced a failing marriage and several lawsuits.

Lisa is the biracial daughter of a black Cherokee Indian father and a white Jewish mother. Born on November 16, 1967, her parents were divorced when Lisa was only thirteen months old. To this day, Lisa does not have a relationship with her father of whom she says, "My father pretty much pushed me aside for another family when I was really young. So I grew up without him."

Her unusual heritage made her feel uncomfortable growing up in a middle-class California suburb. Reflecting on these early years, Lisa commented to *Washington Post* reporter Trustman Senger, "It was really weird because, like, you know, the black kids would call me Oreo, and I just didn't feel totally accepted with all those, you know, white rich people. . . . I had absolutely no idea where I belonged in life; I mean, position and in school. . . . I don't know, growing up is so hard."

Lisa's mom, Arlene Bonet, an elementary schoolteacher, became her daughter's stage mother, taking her to television auditions. Lisa was a commercial actress by the time she was eleven, hawking everything from burgers to Barbie dolls.

Despite her initial success on TV, Lisa remained unhappy at home. "I didn't have one date in high school," she says. It's a very sad story. . . . I wasn't into anything. I just had a lot of acquaintances. I hung out at home a lot." Lisa decided to take the proficiency test in eleventh grade, drop out of high school, and move to New York.

After a string of commercials and an episode of "St. Elsewhere," she auditioned for "The Cosby Show." As fate would have it, she would be cast over hundreds of aspiring actresses to play Denise, the second eldest daughter of the Huxtable clan. She later confessed, "I didn't even know I really wanted to act when I got the show. It was just something I did after school."

The success of "The Cosby Show" inspired the show's producers to create a spin-off series. In 1987, college-bound Denise Huxtable entered "A Different World" when she moved away from home to study at Hillman College, a predominantly black university.

Despite the money and fame, Lisa found the role of her clean-cut character a bit confining. Before the series began, Lisa shocked her family, friends, and co-workers by accepting the female lead in the highly controversial *Angel Heart*. Set in the fifties, the story centers around Harry Angel (Mickey Rourke), a small-time detective hired by a sinister gentleman (Robert De Niro) to find a famous prewar singer. The search takes him into the dark culture of New Orleans, where he meets Epiphany Proudfoot (Lisa), a bayou fieldworker who happens to be a voodoo priestess. A storm of controversy erupted prior to the film's release over an erotic sex scene between Epiphany and Harry, during which blood pours from above onto their naked bodies. Originally rated X by the Motion Picture Association of America, that scene was eventually trimmed by ten seconds in order to earn an R rating.

Lisa described filming the controversial scene to *The Washington Post*: "Mickey, Mickey was nervous. He was so cute, he was funny. We had a good time. It was just, it was just like a wild, you know, party. That's what it was like, because it's ridiculous. It's the most ridiculous thing. You know, here you are, two people who don't really know too much about each other except for what you've seen them do on camera, you know, hop into bed together and try and make this as passionate as possible and then, you know, and keep it up for three or four hours."

Lisa found that meditating before filming the steamy scene helped calm her down and remove her inhibitions. "I sat there on the bed while Mickey was in the other room undressing, and I had some ice. It felt good. I realized that I didn't care what anyone around the set felt, because people were going to see me on-screen and judge me anyway. So f __ k everyone else and . . . go to town. I felt confident, that's all."

Despite the negative reviews and lukewarm box office reception, Lisa expressed no regrets on her choosing the role. She articulated her sentiments in 1987. "I'm glad that I did this film this year, because no matter how much you do for television, like, actors in this business, they just look at you and it's like, that TV, that TV person, you know. Like they can act and I can't, you know. And it really blows my mind."

Lisa's deliberate attempt to break free of her wholesome image included posing nude for *Interview* and *Rolling Stone* magazines. On "Entertainment Tonight" she defended her sudden transformation from sweet teen to sex symbol. "I don't feel the need to prove anything to anyone as Denise or as Lisa and I feel I just know the difference well, you know, enough that I don't need to prove it to anyone else 'cause I don't need to prove it to myself."

On November 16, 1987, twenty-year-old Lisa married rocker Lenny Kravitz in a secret ceremony in Las Vegas. Having met at a 1985 New Edition concert, Lisa discovered that she and Lenny shared many similarities, including biracial parentage. Lenny is the son of actress Roxie Roker (who, ironically, portrayed Helen Willis, a black woman married to a white man, on "The Jeffersons") and Sy Kravitz, a Jewish businessman. As Lisa later recalled, "It was interesting when we were first finding out about each other, that our backgrounds were so similar. When I first told him my mom was Jewish, and he said 'So's my dad,' I thought that was both unusual and enchanting."

Shortly after they wed, Lisa became pregnant and had to be written off her own show. "A Different World," which had a difficult time establishing itself, later became a hit series and a star-making vehicle for several of its performers, notably Jasmine Guy, Kadeem Hardison, and Marisa (*My Cousin Vinny*) Tomei.

On December 1, 1988, Lisa gave birth at home to a seven-pound, four-ounce girl named Zoe. Said proud papa Lenny, "You know babies sleep a lot, but it's great to look at. I'm sure we will have a lot of fun with her."

In 1989, Lisa's character was written back into "The Cosby Show." Her

CHILDREN
OF
BABYLON

A SERIES OF BAD DECISIONS, BOTH PERSONAL AND PROFESSIONAL, HAS NEARLY ENDED THE ONCE PROMISING CAREER OF LISA BONET.
NBC/GLOBE PHOTOS

$\mathcal{J}$N NOVEMBER OF 1987, LISA ELOPED WITH ROCKER LENNY KRAVITZ IN A SECRET LAS VEGAS CEREMONY. *RALPH DOMINGUEZ/GLOBE PHOTOS*

absence was explained as a year-long sojourn in Africa as a photographer's assistant. Denise surprised the Huxtables by announcing that she was now married to a Navy lieutenant and had adopted his four-year-old daughter (played by the overly precocious Raven Simone). From all appearances, it seemed that Lisa was back on track, working on a successful TV series and living a happy married life.

This illusion came apart that year after two highly publicized incidents. During the summer of 1989, Lisa filed suit against American Drug Stores for $5 million, after a picture of Zoe appeared in the *National Enquirer*. Lisa alleged that the negative for the picture was stolen by a drug store clerk from the local pharmacy that had developed her photographs.

LISA BONET'S DOUBLE IMAGE

Photographs became another source of embarrassment later that year when she reportedly attacked a twenty-three-year-old college student, Michael Wehrman, at New York's Kennedy Airport. Wehrman, who markets celebrity autographs and photos, claimed in his police report that Lisa kicked him in the groin. He filed a complaint with police, charging third-degree assault.

These legal conflicts, along with widely circulated rumors of on-set discord with Cosby, made Lisa and Lenny targets for the ever-vigilant press, who began to speculate on the stability of their marriage. In December of 1990, the couple decided to address rumors that their marriage was on the skids. "I love being married," Lisa declared to *Essence* magazine. "I love having a life partner to help you through everything—who's always on your side and who wants nothing but the best from you. It's not always magic, but the moments that are make all the work that marriage takes worthwhile." Three months later, Lenny announced through his publicist that he and Lisa had filed for a legal separation after three years of marriage. Lenny told *Jet* magazine that his busy work schedule contributed to his marital woes. He said, "I lost my woman, my friend. We didn't talk about some things. . . . We could have dealt with the problems if I was at home."

One month after her separation, NBC announced that Lisa was being dropped from "The Cosby Show." In Cosby's official statement he said that Lisa's time on the show "will be taken up by the new kids on the show who are working hard, studying so hard, and really deserve a shot during what will be our final year." Cosby continued, "There was nothing challenging for her. I blame myself for that—creating a character who simply never developed. Denise never grew up—and it's not funny to have someone twenty-one acting like she's still about twelve."

In early 1987, during the height of her popularity, Lisa speculated on her future: "I don't plan to work in the business more than ten years. I have every intention of marrying young and having kids, and finding a castle in Spain and just disappearing." It would appear that Lisa was partly correct about her future. Since her departure from "Cosby," Lisa has directed a music video and written for *Interview* magazine.

Lisa's post-Cosby career stands in stark contrast to her former TV siblings, Malcolm-Jamal Warner and Tempestt Bledsoe. After the sitcom ended its eight-year run in 1992, Tempestt, a full-time student at New York University, returned to finish college, while embarking on a stage career. Malcolm, who was able to develop his skills as a director while on the sitcom, went on to direct several music videos and a short film, *This Old Man.*

The Taming of Melanie Griffith

Melanie Griffith once said, "There is a bit of a stripper in every woman." Well, maybe not as much as in this hot young actress who has built her career portraying sex-starved women. Now, after three marriages (two with Don Johnson) and two children (one with Johnson), Melanie has spent the past several years trying to put her party girl past behind her.

Melanie was born in New York City on August 9, 1957, and lived there until she was three, when her parents, Peter Griffith, a businessman, and Nathalie "Tippi" Hedren, were divorced. A year later her mother, then a model, moved her to Hollywood.

Tippi Hedren's acting career was launched in the early sixties by Alfred Hitchcock. In a tradition set by Grace Kelly and Janet Leigh, Hedren achieved fame as Hitchcock's icy blonde leading lady in *The Birds* (1963) and *Marnie* (1964). After a falling out with the director, Tippi's career lost its momentum and she found herself taking bit parts in B movies. Tippi

CHILDREN
OF
BABYLON

172

AFTER HER DIVORCE, MELANIE (HERE WITH SON ALEXANDER) BEGAN TO
DRINK AGAIN: "SOMEBODY TOLD ME THAT TAKING BEER WHILE YOU'RE
NURSING IS REALLY GOOD FOR THE BABY—GOOD FOR THE MILK."
ALAN DEREK/GLOBE PHOTOS

eventually married agent and producer Noel (*The Exorcist*) Marshall and raised Melanie with his four children and an assortment of wild animals on his San Fernando Valley ranch.

In 1972, fourteen-year-old Melanie met Don Wayne Johnson while working as an extra on her mother's film *The Harrad Experiment.* Johnson, twenty-one and twice divorced from the same woman, was then living with rock groupie Pamela Miller. A would-be actor and singer, he had starred in two forgettable films: *The Magic Garden of Stanley Sweetheart* (1970) and *Zachariah* (1971), the first (and thankfully only) rock-and-roll Western. After the movie was completed, Melanie relentlessly pursued Johnson and they began a turbulent four-year affair. She set up a home with him in Laurel Canyon at age fifteen, with her mother's approval. "She's always been a young filly at the gate," said Hedren. "She can't wait to get into the race." Johnson later remarked, "She was a lot more woman than most of the girls I had been going with." Although he also admitted, "I did feel a little strange picking her up after school."

Her acting career began at age seventeen, when she auditioned for a featured role in Arthur Penn's *Night Moves* (1975). Without any training, Melanie landed the role of Delly Grastner, the promiscuous runaway daughter of a has-been actress, whose tragic death is investigated by a burned-out private investigator (Gene Hackman). Melanie followed up with supporting roles as sex-starved teens in *The Drowning Pool*, starring Paul Newman, and the satiric comedy *Smile*. While Melanie's career got off to a noteworthy start, Johnson's remained undistinguished with roles in *Return to Macon County* (1975) and the cult film *A Boy and His Dog* (1976).

In her first three films, as well as a *Playboy* spread in October of 1976, Melanie displayed natural acting instincts as well as relatively little inhibition when it came to disrobing in front of the camera. She said at the time, "I don't mind playing nude scenes as long as they're done tastefully."

During this period, the couple lived the fast life. Said Melanie, "Sure I used to do drugs, I used to drink, I was wild. I could do anything I wanted, and I did."

Despite their rocky relationship and her parents' misgivings, Don and Melanie got engaged on her eighteenth birthday. The couple flew to Las Vegas in 1976 and took their vows in blue jeans at the Silver Bell Chapel. The marriage lasted less than a year, after which Melanie walked away with a tattoo of a pear, her pet name for Don, on her left buttock. After their divorce, they both immersed themselves deeper into the party circuit. She later said, "I did a lot of drinking and cocaine. I thought I was just having a good time."

Near tragedy occurred in 1977 during the filming of the wildlife film *Roar,* a family project starring her mother and directed by her stepfather.

Tippi and Noel put up $2.5 million and their five houses as collateral to buy land and import 110 jungle animals. The production was riddled with serious setbacks, including a major flood that destroyed the compound, setting loose forty lions. Nervous policemen called to the scene shot three of the lions. Most of the cast suffered injuries, including Tippi, whose leg was crushed by an elephant, and Melanie, who suffered deep scratches on her face when she was mauled by a 400-pound lion. The film was not released until 1981.

During the late seventies, Melanie's career began a slow but steady decline. In 1977 she appeared in *Joyride,* a low-budget drama notable only for the four showbiz offspring who had starring roles: Melanie; Desi Arnaz, Jr.; Robert Carradine; and Anne Lockhart. She also appeared in the Robby Benson coming of age drama *One On One* (1977). Melanie eventually wound up on television in mediocre movies, such as *Steel Cowboy* (1978), and short-lived series, including "Once an Eagle" (1976–1977) and "Carter Country" (1978–1979).

In 1980, Melanie suffered another near-fatal accident. While standing drunk in a crosswalk, she was hit by a drunk driver and thrown twenty feet. When she awoke she had a broken leg and arm, assorted fractures, a concussion, and amnesia for several days.

After recovering from the accident, she appeared in several television movies, including *Golden Gate* and *Star Maker.* During the filming of *She's in the Army Now* (1981), Melanie became romantically involved with Cuban-born actor Steven Bauer. Melanie admitted to one interviewer that she and her co-star Kathleen Quinlan "had a bet to see who would go to bed with him first." Melanie won. The couple took their wedding vows in May of 1982 in New York's St. Patrick's Cathedral. During her marriage, Melanie attempted to clean up her lifestyle, study her craft, and revive her faltering movie career.

Both actors began getting noteworthy roles: Steven landed a starring role in the 1983 remake of Brian dePalma's *Scarface,* while Melanie gained notoriety for her sexually charged performances in *Fear City* and *Body Double.* In *Fear City,* a searing portrait of prostitutes who are stalked by a psychopath, Melanie raised eyebrows in a love scene with co-star Rae Dawn Chong. It was in Brian dePalma's *Body Double,* however, that Melanie left a lasting impression on audiences in the role of porno film queen Holly Body. The script for Body Double required Melanie to simulate masturbation and to utter the immortal lines, "I do not do animal acts. I do not do S&M or any variation of that particular bent. I do not do water sports, either. I will not shave my pussy. No fist-f __ king and absolutely no coming in my face." Well, a girl has to set some standards.

THE TAMING OF
MELANIE GRIFFITH

175

MELANIE GRIFFITH MOVED IN WITH TWENTY-ONE-YEAR-OLD, TWICE-DIVORCED DON JOHNSON WHEN SHE WAS ONLY FIFTEEN YEARS OLD.
GLOBE PHOTOS

In 1985, Melanie gave birth to son Alexander but found her marriage in trouble. After divorcing Steven in 1986, Melanie found herself alone, depressed, and drinking again. "Somebody told me that taking beer while you're nursing is really good for the baby—good for the milk. Well, that was a good excuse for me."

By the early eighties, Don Johnson's film career had come to a screeching halt. His film credits included such atrocious turkeys as *Revenge of the Stepford Wives* (1980) and *Melanie* (1982). His TV credits during this period were equally unimpressive, with roles in *The Rebels* (1979), *Amateur Night at the Dixie Bar and Grill* (1979), *Beulah Land* (1980), and *Elvis and the Beauty Queen* (1981). In 1980, he had a featured role as Kim Basinger's love interest in the short-lived drama series "From Here to Eternity." During this period, Johnson is better remembered for his relationships with singer Tanya Tucker and actress Patty D'Arbanville. D'Arbanville, his live-in lover of four years, is the mother of his son Jesse.

In 1983, after five failed television pilots and a stint in rehab, NBC executives reluctantly cast Johnson as Detective James "Sonny" Crockett in their new series "Miami Vice." The show, which placed higher priority on wardrobe and music over the script and acting, became a Nielsen hit and transformed Johnson overnight into a hot property.

In 1986, Melanie's career began to ascend after co-starring opposite Jeff Daniels in Jonathan Demme's *Something Wild*. Their performances received accolades from the critics, including *New York Times* critic Vincent Canby, who wrote, "Mr. Daniels . . . and Miss Griffith, who sometimes sounds eerily like Judy Holliday, play—when allowed—with the sort of earnest intensity that is the basis of comedy at its best." She continued to receive good notices for her roles in *Cherry 2000* (1986), *The Milagro Beanfield War* (1988), and *Stormy Monday* (1988).

In 1989, director Mike Nichols signed her to star in *Working Girl,* the Pygmalion story of an ambitious Staten Island secretary who transforms herself into a polished executive. Her performance as Tess McGill ("with a head for business and a bod for sin") earned her Golden Globe and Academy Award nominations. (She won the Golden Globe, while Jodie Foster took home the Oscar that year for *The Accused*.)

Melanie, however, was still troubled by a persistent drinking habit. Johnson, an admitted alcoholic, came to her aid by persuading her to check into the Hazelden Foundation in Minnesota. She said, "I went to the clinic because I just realized finally that I couldn't stop by myself."

In 1987, after Melanie guest starred as a high-class madame on an episode of "Miami Vice," Don broke off his much-publicized affair with Barbra Streisand and reconciled with Melanie. When Melanie revealed to

REPORTS OF BICKERING BETWEEN MELANIE AND DON ON THE SETS OF *PARADISE* (1991) AND *BORN YESTERDAY* (1993) ADDED FUEL TO THE SPECULATION THAT THEIR MARRIAGE WAS ON THE ROCKS.
MARK STEWART/GLOBE PHOTOS

Don that she was pregnant, he surprised her with caviar, apple juice in a champagne bucket, and a four-carat diamond engagement ring. The couple remarried in June of 1990 on Johnson's ranch in Aspen, Colorado. Four months later, Melanie gave birth to the couple's first daughter, Dakota.

The couple has continued to face disapproving reviews from film critics. Melanie has received poor notices for her roles in *In the Spirit, Pacific Heights* (1988), and *The Bonfire of the Vanities* (1990), while Johnson's film career has once again stalled after a succession of box office flops: *Cease Fire*

THE TAMING OF
MELANIE GRIFFITH

BOTH TIPPI HEDREN AND MELANIE WERE SEVERELY INJURED DURING THE FILMING OF ROAR, PROBABLY THE MOST EXPENSIVE FAMILY FILM EVER MADE.
GLOBE PHOTOS

(1985), *G.I. Joe: The Movie* (1987), *Sweet Hearts Dance* (1988), *Dead Band* (1989), and *The Hot Spot* (1990).

During the filming of *Bonfire* (a turkey that one critic labeled "the biggest disaster movie since *The Towering Inferno*"), Melanie reportedly had her breasts enlarged. According to writer Julie Salamon, Melanie unabashedly walked up to director Brian dePalma and pressed her chest against his face and asked, "How do they feel?" The effect was not lost on Vincent Canby, who later wrote, "Miss Griffith's body appears to be so perfect as to look surgically reconstructed."

In 1991, the couple spent several months apart when Don went to Arizona to work on the ill-fated *Harley Davidson and the Marlboro Man*, while Melanie went to England for her role in *Shining Through*. Based on Susan Isaac's best-selling book, it tells the story of a half-Jewish secretary from Queens who becomes a spy in Germany during World War II. Melanie remarked to one reporter during the press junket for the film, "The whole vibe of World War II permeated the air. Maybe I was in the camps in my past life or something."

The couple's four-month separation added fuel to the rumor that their marriage was in trouble. Tabloid reports linked Melanie with her *Shining Through* co-star Michael Douglas, a charge she vehemently denied. In 1991, Melanie and Don decided to spend more time together by appearing as a married couple in the film *Paradise*. The film, which proved that given the right material both Melanie and Don *can* create believable characters, received generally good notices but failed to score with audiences. Reports of off-camera bickering during the filming, however, did little to dispel the notion of marital discord. Even Melanie admitted, "It's hard to work and be together constantly. At times I know he wanted to get away from me." Melanie vented her frustration over the idle gossip concerning her marriage to reporter Laurie Werner. "We work very well together, our marriage works really well. In any marriage, there are things that you have to work out with the other person. What's important is to feel your feelings."

Melanie eventually returned to New York to shoot the Sidney Lumet mystery *A Stranger Among Us,* a movie that had Melanie improbably cast as a tough cop who goes undercover in the Hasidic community in order to solve a crime. When the film was screened during the 1992 Cannes Film Festival, the audience reacted by booing. The film, which *Variety* dubbed "Vitness," was another critical and commercial failure for Melanie.

For their next assignment, Melanie and Don chose to star in a Disney remake of the 1950 classic *Born Yesterday,* in roles originally played by Judy Holliday and William Holden. In the future, Melanie and Don will not always have the opportunity to work together. When asked what they do the night before one of them has to leave for a shoot, Melanie casually responded, "We f __ k each other's brains out."

TRACI LORDS:
A TEST OF CHARACTER

In 1983, fifteen-year-old Nora Kuzma was a troubled runaway in search of a father figure. After a complete makeover, Nora emerged as Traci Lords and for the next three years reigned as the brightest star of sex films, earning as much as $1,000 a day. At age eighteen, the Feds pulled the plug on her XXX-rated party, and after the dust settled, several of her associates were convicted of child pornography and Traci emerged with a desire to become a legitimate actress. In recent years, she has developed a convenient case of amnesia about her sordid past, claiming, "I was always sh __ faced and stoned out of my mind."

Traci Lords was born as Nora Louise Kuzma on May 7, 1968, in the small city of Steubenville, Ohio. The second of four daughters, she had a rocky upbringing by her alcoholic, abusive, steelworker father and her battered mother. Traci later recalled, "My parents never got along. It was a very ugly scene to be part of."

At age twelve, her parents divorced and Traci's mom took her four

From age fifteen to age eighteen, Traci Lords was the reigning queen of porno flicks. Her legitimate acting career hasn't taken off yet. *Tom Rodriguez/Globe Photos*

daughters and headed out to California. According to Traci, "Mom had a boyfriend who went out to get a job, and we followed." To this day Traci has only bitter memories of her father. "I was twelve when I last saw my father. I have no desire to see him. He's dead to me. I don't have a father."

With remarkable candor, Traci has described her teenage years as "booze and boys," and admits that she experimented with all types of drugs, including speed and freebasing cocaine. "From thirteen to nineteen, I was completely out of control, like a car heading toward a cliff," she says. "I'm disgusted with a lot of things I've done in my life." Her already sour attitude toward men slipped even further when, at age fifteen, she became pregnant and had an abortion. "Men suck," she later said. "Men are the lowest form of creatures."

Nora dropped out of high school after the tenth grade. Using a fake ID, she frequented the local bars and began dating older men. She hooked up with one of these older men and ran away from home. She told *Film Comment* in 1989, "I was so rebellious. I was so angry, I didn't have a dad or any male in my life so I went looking for a father figure."

A short time after she ran away from home, Nora showed up at the World Modeling Agency in Sherman Oaks, California, with a man claiming to be her "stepfather" and a new identity, Kristie Elizabeth Nussman. According to reporter Pat Jordan, the World Modeling Agency happened to specialize in nude modeling (often involving simulated sex acts), and usually steered its models into pornographic films. Armed with a bogus ID and birth certificate, one of Nora's first assignments for the agency was a centerfold in *Penthouse* magazine ("It's the Miss America issue with Vanessa Williams and George Burns—and it blows my mind. There I am at fifteen years old!")

Shortly thereafter, Nora/Kristie slimmed down, dyed her hair platinum blonde, and adopted the name Traci Lords after Jack Lord of the television series "Hawaii 5–0," ("When I was a little girl, he was the first man to make me realize I was sexual," says Traci.).

She first entered the world of pornographic movies with bit parts in such movies as *Joys of Erotica,* earning $20 a day. Along the way, Traci earned a reputation as an actress who wouldn't stop having sex after the cameras stopped rolling. By age seventeen, Traci was the highest paid actress in her field, making up to $1,000 a day in such films as *Flashing, Love Bites, Passion Pit, Lust on the Fast Lane,* and *Beverly Hills Copulator.* After forming Traci Lords Productions, she became the producer, writer, and star of her own projects.

The high life ended abruptly in 1986 when Traci was arrested for carrying a false passport upon her return from Paris, where she had completed her last adult film, *I Love You, Traci.* Although the Attorney General's office had no intention of prosecuting Traci, they forced her to testify against some of the leading figures in the porn film industry. All but one of her films were pulled from the shelves and several former associates found themselves under federal indictment for child pornography. At least one video distributor was sentenced to a prison term for marketing her movies.

After the arrests, Traci dropped out of sight for several months. When she reappeared, it was with ambitions of crossing over into the world of legitimate acting. She supported herself by posing for seminude posters and calendars while taking voice, ballet, and acting lessons.

Her progression into the mainstream has been difficult. The 1988 science-fiction movie *Not of This Earth* enjoyed a brief release before winding up on video shelves. Her first major role came in 1990, in the off-beat comedy *Cry-Baby,* a musical love story in which a juvenile delinquent (Johnny Depp) falls in love with an innocent girl (Amy Locane.) Director John Waters, who is known for his bizarre approach to filmmaking, spiced up the cast with Traci (as the town tramp), Troy Donahue, Joey Heatherton, and celebrity ex-con Patty Hearst. "When I got the part, I cried for two days," Traci recalls. "Every morning I'd wake up, call my agent, and ask him if he was really sure I had the role."

As for finding work as a legitimate actress, Traci told *Gentlemen's Quarterly,* "Just because I'm young and pretty doesn't mean I'm bait. I'm not for sale. I don't believe in f __ king fat, stupid Jewish producers to get a role. There are plenty of starlets ready to pull their pants down for that. The only difference between me and them is I did mine on film. I've done it all. That scene bores the sh __ out of me now."

Despite some relatively kind notices for her work on television, her film career has virtually halted. She lost the female leads in *Car 54, Where Are You?, Return of the Swamp Thing,* and *Cool World.* She was most disappointed by losing the female lead in *Dick Tracy.* "I met Warren, talked to him, and thought I had the role. But when we were put side by side, I looked too young for him. Then Madonna said she wanted the role. You know the rest."

In September of 1990, Traci married Brook Yeaton, a propmaster and John Waters' nephew, who had worked on *Cry-Baby.* When asked how she manages to sustain the romance, Traci told *Prevue,* "We'll take a bubble bath, drink champagne, get a little stoned, make love, and eat at two in the morning."

Her more recent credits include several direct-to-video releases: *A Time to Die, The Nutty Nut, Shock 'Em Dead,* and *Raw Nerve.* On television she has made guest appearances on "Wiseguy," "McGyver," and "Married . . . with Children," along with a cameo on the television film *Murder in High Places.* This collection of work led *Variety* to warn, "Lords needs better roles if she is to make the transition from underage screen slut to adult actress." The actress responds, "I've worked hard not to be in that category of the porn queen. More and more, my work is speaking for itself, and I think I'm hitting my stride in my career."

How Low Is Lowe?

Rob Lowe once said, "If you stay in the public eye long enough they're going to try to find a scandal. Anyone who's lived their life to the fullest extent has a scandal buried somewhere. And anyone who doesn't have a scandal I have no interest in meeting, because they haven't lived their lives. I mean, you show me somebody who's led a perfect life and I'll show you a dullard." Well, given that definition, no one can accuse Rob of being a dullard.

Rob Lowe was born on March 17, 1964 in Charlottesville, where his father was attending law school at the University of Virginia. Soon after, the family moved to Dayton, Ohio, where his parents divorced. His mother eventually married a Dayton city planner only to divorce him several years later.

According to Rob, he always had acting aspirations. By the time he was six, he was modeling in ads. By age eight, he was appearing on local TV shows, in Midwest summer stock, on radio, and in several college stage

CHILDREN OF BABYLON

186

After one of his legendary fights with then-girlfriend Melissa Gilbert, Rob Lowe said, "It's scary when love gets undignified."
GLOBE PHOTOS

productions. "There wasn't a lot of competition for roles," he later recalled. When Rob was twelve, his mother was married for a third time, to a psychiatrist, and the family moved to Malibu, California.

Despite his self-described "geeky" appearance, Rob actively auditioned for every role he could. He, along with his younger brother Chad, spent his weekends shooting home movies with his friends, Charlie Sheen and Emilio Estevez.

After sprucing up his looks with a new haircut and contact lenses, he soon caught the eye of television casting directors. His credits included two after-school specials (*Schoolboy Father* and *A Matter of Time*), two pilots ("Mean Jeans" and "Thrills and Chills") and a short-lived sitcom, "A New Kind of Family" (1979–1980). After portraying an ailing teenager in a disease-of-the-week movie *Thursday's Child*, Rob broke into feature films with Francis Ford Coppola's *The Outsiders* (1983). Although most critics were unimpressed by the film, Rob was more interested in his burgeoning status. "When you work with someone like Coppola, people sit up and take notice." No one seemed to notice his second feature that year, *Class*, a forgettable romp about a naive student who has an affair with an older woman (Jacqueline Bisset).

Rob soon became romantically involved with Melissa Gilbert of "Little House on the Prairie" fame. They met while stopped in their cars at a red light on La Cienega Boulevard. Melissa recognized Rob and started honking her horn to attract his attention, and a stormy romance was born.

Despite a rather unimpressive resume, Rob's ego began to grow. After noting the success of Matthew Broderick, Rob told *Teen* magazine in 1984, "He's getting a lot of money now and I absolutely plan to ask what he asks for. I deserve it. My buddies who act on TV are a lot wealthier than I am."

Rob describes his approach to acting as "casual." A high school dropout, Rob has never had any formal training. "I don't look at the script until rehearsal, unless it is a particularly heavy scene," says Rob. "I never spend my free time being concerned with characters." This approach to acting shows throughout his subsequent roles.

Rob has spent his entire career standing in the shadow of his more talented contemporaries. He gave a completely bland performance in *The Hotel New Hampshire* (1984), leaving Jodie Foster to steal the show, while in *Oxford Blues* (1984), he is overshadowed by co-stars Amanda Pays and Ally Sheedy.

Only Ally Sheedy and Mare Winningham survived the brutal criticism of *St. Elmo's Fire* (1985). Of Rob's performance, *People* magazine commented, "Lowe's preening sabotages his character, although his feminine features aren't making the transition into adult roles any easier." In his first truly adult film, *About Last Night* (1986), both Rob and co-star Demi Moore

Rob's minimalist acting in *The Hotel New Hampshire* allowed bloated co-star Jodie Foster to steal the show.
J. BERSTEIN/GLOBE PHOTOS

were outperformed by supporting players Jim Belushi and Elizabeth Perkins, and not even Patrick Swayze could salvage a terrible script in *Youngblood* (1986).

Rob earned his best notices (along with a Golden Globe nomination) for his sensitive portrayal of a mentally retarded youth in *Square Dance* (1987). Although he won over the critics with this risky role, he returned to his pretty boy roots with his next two films, the immortal stinkers *Illegally Yours* and *Masquerade*.

Rob has always been politically and socially outspoken. In 1988, he and several active members of the Hollywood community hitched on to the Michael Dukakis presidential campaign. When hordes of nonvoting, screaming teenagers showed up at one event to hear Rob speak, Dukakis quipped, "If things keep up this way I'm going to have to call Lloyd Bentsen and tell him we're going to have to make Rob Lowe deputy vice president." To which Rob responded, "I don't care why they come out. As long as they are there, they are going to hear the message."

In July of that year, about three dozen film celebrities followed the candidates to Atlanta for the Democratic National Convention. The most visible members of the group were Ally Sheedy, Alec Baldwin, Judd Nelson, and Rob (who had just returned from a vacation in Paris).

On the night of July 17, after a day of photo opportunities, Rob and his entourage headed to Club Rio. The group included Ally Sheedy, Judd Nelson, Holly Robinson, and Alec Baldwin. Word of their arrival at the club spread like wildfire in a town not used to celebrity appearances. "The place was packed with people," Ally later recalled. "I felt like I was trapped. I left with Judd and Alec."

At about eleven, the club's hostess went into the employee lounge for her break, where she found Rob and two boys. "They were doing blow," she told *Rolling Stone* reporter Mike Sager, "and one of the guys asked Rob if he wanted some ecstasy, and he just took it . . . He didn't say anything. He was really drunk." Rob eventually staggered out of the club with two young women: Tara, a twenty-three-year-old receptionist, and Jan, her sixteen-year-old girlfriend.

Shortly after the convention, duplicated copies of a thirty-nine-minute videotape began to circulate around Atlanta. The video was divided into three segments. During the first segment, shot while Rob was still in Paris, he and a twenty-one-year-old male friend are seen having sex with a woman named Jennifer. For twenty-five minutes, Rob sits on the bed and manually arouses himself while watching his friend and Jennifer have sex. Rob then proceeds to take his turn with the woman. At one point he asks her, "Do you like all this attention?"

The second segment of the tape is a seven-minute look at the day's events. It shows Rob in his hotel and at various publicity events, which included a photo session with Tom Hayden and the Atlanta Braves, as well as a local TV interview.

The final portion of the tape shows Jan and Tara having oral and manual sex while Rob looks on. Although Rob is never seen having sex with either of the girls, sources later reported that Tara said that Rob did have sex with Jan but had a hard time achieving orgasm due to the amount of drugs he

R OB'S RECORDED SEXCAPADES, LENSED DURING THE 1988 DEMOCRATIC CONVENTION, ULTIMATELY BECAME HIS MOST MEMORABLE FILM.
GLOBE PHOTOS

CHILDREN OF BABYLON

190

ingested. In the end, Tara reportedly brought Rob to climax orally, whereupon he passed out and the girls left, taking with them the tape, $200 from his wallet, and a bottle of prescription pills.

After finding the tape in Jan's closet, Jan's mother filed a civil suit against Rob in Fulton County, Georgia, alleging that while attending the Democratic convention in Atlanta, the actor "used his celebrity status as an inducement to females to engage in sexual intercourse, sodomy, and multiple-party sexual activity for his immediate sexual gratification, and for the purpose of making pornographic films of these activities." Shortly thereafter, the Fulton County district attorney began an investigation of the criminal allegation of sexually exploiting a minor to produce pornography.

R OB'S SOCIAL LIFE MAY HAVE BECOME QUIETER ONCE HE MARRIED
MAKEUP ARTIST SHERYL BERKOFF, BUT HIS CAREER HAS NOT REVIVED.
JOHN BARRETT/GLOBE PHOTOS

In 1990, Rob told *Interview* magazine that he felt "betrayed" by the lawsuit: "Half of the anger was at myself, for putting myself in a position where I could get taken advantage of. Then there was, not anger, actually more of a hurt, that people's motives aren't always what they seem."

When he was later asked why he actually made the videotape he explained, "It was just one of those quirky, sort of naughty, sort of wild, sort of, you know, drunken things that people will do from time to time. It's just one of those things."

Rob then turned the controversy into the issue of the right to privacy. "People should be allowed to do whatever they want in the privacy of their own home or their own hotel room. When people consent to do something, they should be able to do whatever they want."

Although he was never formally charged, Rob met with the district attorney and agreed to perform twenty hours of community service in his hometown of Dayton, Ohio. He fulfilled his obligation by making speeches at correctional facilities, halfway houses, and juvenile detention centers. "The basic thing I said is: Just because people will say you have f __ ked up does not mean you are f __ ked up. And whether you're a movie star or doing time in a correctional institute, everybody can have bad judgment, and it's something you have to address."

Since the scandal, Rob has taken on several parts as sleazy characters. He portrayed the *Bad Influence* (1990) in James Spader's life, a vulgar talent agent looking to make money off a freak (Judd Nelson) in *The Dark Backward*, and an evil television producer in *Wayne's World*.

The press still asks about the incident and Rob declines any interviews. During the heady days of the Brat Pack fame, Rob boasted to Gene Shalit on "The Today Show," "I learned to act on the big screen. I was never a spear carrier. I was always the star. Always." Given his most recent performances, it would appear that Rob's spear-carrying days have finally arrived.

JULIA ROBERTS: A PRETTY AVAILABLE WOMAN

Director Garry Marshall once said of Julia Roberts, "She performs best when she's loved." Well, considering her astounding success, it is not surprising that Julia has not only enticed audiences worldwide, but captured the hearts of many of her leading men, including Dylan McDermott, Liam Neeson, and Kiefer Sutherland.

For the most part, details concerning Julia's childhood remain sketchy. Born to a theatrical family in November of 1967, Julia and her older siblings Lisa and Eric have all become actors. Her parents, Walter and Betty Roberts, owned and operated a writers and actors studio in Atlanta, a venture that proved unsuccessful. According to Julia, "My dad ended up selling vacuum cleaners and my mom got a job as a secretary." The Robertses divorced in 1971 and fifteen-year-old Eric remained with his father in Atlanta while four-year-old Julia and six-year-old Lisa moved with their mother to Smyrna, Georgia.

Three days after graduating from Campbell High School, Julia went to

Despite her lack of acting training, the astounding success of *Pretty Woman* propelled Julia Roberts into the million-dollar salary level. *GLOBE PHOTOS*

New York and moved in with her sister, with the hope of becoming an actress. "College wasn't for me," says Julia. "I couldn't see bolting out of bed at eight o'clock to be ten minutes late for some f __ king class with some f __ king guy who's gonna stick it to me again."

Upon her arrival in New York, Julia signed up with the Click modeling agency, but was more interested in becoming an actress than model. She supported herself by selling sneakers, while taking speech lessons to help soften her heavy southern accent. She went to only a few acting lessons before dropping out. "I always quit the classes," she later confessed. "Halfway through I thought, this guy's full of sh __ ." To this day, Julia remains an instinctive actress: "I sort of, um, just wing it, you know, and someone eventually tells me it's alright and we move on."

After a year and a half of unsuccessful auditions, brother Eric, who had just been nominated for his performance in *Runaway Train,* lent her a hand by having her cast as his sister in a low-budget western called *Blood Red.* The film, produced in 1986 but not released until 1989, had a brief theatrical run before taking its rightful place as a bottom-shelf video.

To this day, Julia is reluctant to discuss her relationship with her brother, only describing it as "close but complex." Eric, who once studied at the Royal Academy of Dramatic Arts in London, has spent his career for the most part in small but quirky roles in such films as *Star 80* (1983) and *The Pope of Greenwich Village* (1984). In one article Julia compared Eric's acting style to Picasso and hers to Van Gogh, a comment that undoubtedly sent shudders through the art world.

In 1988, Justine Bateman, star of the long-running NBC sitcom "Family Ties," was desperate to break away from her bimbo image and prove to Hollywood that she was a box office draw. In an effort to pacify their star, NBC Productions developed a script that had Justine playing the leader of an all-girl rock band who falls in love with a burned-out songwriter (Liam Neeson) at a summer resort town.

Still a virtual unknown, Julia had to fight to win the role of the band's oversexed bass guitarist. Her manager reportedly lied to the film's casting director, saying that Julia was a musician and then had her enroll in a crash course to learn how to play the drums. During the filming of *Satisfaction,* nineteen-year-old Julia became Neeson's offscreen love interest and briefly lived with the thirty-five-year-old actor.

Satisfaction was basically teen trash whose limited commercial prospects were ruined by Justine's singing. Caryn James in *The New York Times* noted that "Ms. Bateman's singing is so distant from any human voice that the sound engineers must have been the busiest people on the film." Julia chalks up the film as a learning experience. "It taught me a lot about what I hope to never do again in a movie."

After signing up with the William Morris Agency, acting assignments began to come Julia's way. Small roles on the NBC series "Crime Story" and an HBO movie, *Baja, Oklahoma,* led to a significant part in the film *Mystic Pizza* (1988). Julia's performance as a small-town vamp earned her recognition from the public, the critics, and the industry.

In 1988, Julia got her big break when she stepped in as a last-minute replacement for Meg Ryan to play Shelby, the doomed young bride in *Steel Magnolias*. In her first major studio role, she was paid $90,000 to work alongside Sally Field, Olympia Dukakis, Shirley Maclaine, Dolly Parton, and Daryl Hannah. During the filming of the movie Julia became affianced to Dylan McDermott (her onscreen husband), an engagement that ended when the cameras stopped rolling.

Julia was the only one of the star-studded cast to receive an Academy Award nomination for her performance. "Not long after I got the news," she said, "I learned that back in the sixties, Goldie Hawn was nominated in the same category for her first movie—and won. So I really had my hopes up, but when an older, very experienced, and very talented Irish actress won (Brenda Fricker for *My Left Foot*), I wasn't shaken. If it had been someone closer to my own age, though, I'd have been quite hurt."

A few months later, she was selected for the movie that was to rocket her career skyward, *Pretty Woman*. The film's rather implausible plot centers on coldhearted, corporate raider Edward Lewis (Richard Gere), who pays $3,000 to Hollywood whore Vivian Ward (Julia) to be his companion for one week. During the course of those seven days, Vivian is educated in proper etiquette by the hotel manager (Hector Elizondo) and becomes a presentable escort, while Edward learns how to love. With full lips, an exotic face, and a thick mane of hair, Julia captivated audiences with her sexy but naive performance.

When *Pretty Woman* was released in March of 1990, it became the third-highest grossing movie of the year and turned Julia into a hot property. The film earned Julia her second Oscar nomination, but this time Kathy (*Misery*) Bates took home the award. Of the film's astounding success, Julia later said, "There is no reason in the world this movie should have done what it did." Film critic Richard Schickel agreed. "Without taking anything away from Julia Roberts, there were doubtless twenty-five other actresses who could have played the *Pretty Woman* role and played it fine. It wasn't exactly a stretch."

One of those actresses might have been Shelly Michelle, a model whose body doubled for Julia's during the opening moments of the film.

JULIA ROBERTS: A
PRETTY AVAILABLE
WOMAN

*O*F HER RELATIONSHIP WITH KIEFER SUTHERLAND, JULIA ONCE SAID, "WE WORK TOGETHER, WE'RE IN LOVE WITH EACH OTHER. THAT'S A LIFE. YOU CAN'T ASK FOR MORE." *RALPH DOMINGUEZ/GLOBE PHOTOS*

According to Julia, "Only my wardrobe people know how sick and paranoid I am about this. There are body parts that I have a problem with. Those are the ones we hide." Even in the film's enticing poster (in which Julia leans against Richard Gere wearing a revealing outfit and spike heel boots) Julia's head is superimposed on that of a model.

In 1989, Julia accepted $500,000 to appear in the ensemble film *Flatliners,* the story of daring young medical students who experiment with death and receive some very frightening results. It was during rehearsals for this film that Julia began an ill-fated romance with actor Kiefer Sutherland.

Kiefer, the son of Canadian actors Shirley Douglas and Donald Sutherland, was born in 1967 and raised in Beverly Hills. He and his twin sister Rachel were only four years old when their parents divorced. Shirley, a political activist who was once arrested and accused of buying hand grenades for the Black Panthers, took her eight-year-old children back to Canada after being blacklisted in the U.S. for her political activities. Donald remained in Los Angeles to continue his film career. A leading man during the seventies and early eighties (*M*A*S*H, Klute,* and *Ordinary People*), Donald can now be seen in character parts, most recently giving a chilling performance as a pyromaniac in *Backdraft* (1991).

At age fifteen, Kiefer dropped out of the Catholic boarding school he was attending and began his acting career. Donald was able to get him a bit part in *Max Dugan Returns* (1982), but it would take two years of unsuccessful auditions before he landed his first major role in *Bay Boy.* Kiefer first came to prominence with his portrayal of a town bully in *Stand by Me* (1986) and later as a teen vampire in *The Lost Boys* (1987). Kiefer has never enjoyed the critical or commercial success of his father. In fact, his career is littered with a collection of dull movies, including *Renegades* (1989), *Chicago Joe and the Showgirl* (1990), and *Flashback* (1990). Kiefer's most recent film successes have come in ensemble films *Young Guns I* and *II* and in this year's *A Few Good Men.*

At the time Julia met Kiefer, he was already married and the father of a two-year-old daughter, Sarah. He had met his wife, Camelia Kath, in 1987 during the filming of *The Killing Time.* Camelia had been married once before to guitarist Terry Kath of the band Chicago, who had killed himself in 1978 playing Russian Roulette. When they married, Kiefer was twenty-one and she was thirty-two and the mother of an eleven-year-old daughter.

Despite his marriage, shortly after they finished filming *Flatliners,* Julia and Kiefer became an item. In December of 1989, Kiefer gave Julia a diamond ring, "without questions," she later said, "and without a response." In her acceptance speech for Best Supporting Actress at the Golden Globe ceremonies in January of 1990, Julia confirmed the gossip columnist's rumors by thanking her "beautiful, blue-eyed, green-eyed boy" (Kiefer has

JULIA ROBERTS: A
PRETTY AVAILABLE
WOMAN

*O*N HER PLANNED WEDDING DAY, JULIA BOARDED A PLANE TO IRELAND WITH ACTOR JASON PATRIC. *RALPH DOMINGUEZ/GLOBE PHOTOS*

one blue and one green eye). The following month, Kiefer and Camelia filed for divorce after three years of marriage.

During 1990, Julia continued to take on new projects. When Kim Basinger stepped out of *Sleeping with the Enemy,* Julia was reportedly paid $1 million to take over the part of an abused wife who fakes her own death. The film raked in nearly $100 million at the box office and once again proved Julia's bankability. Although publicly Julia and Kiefer were still very much a couple, the tabloids reported that Julia had made a pass at co-star Kevin Anderson.

During the junket for the movie, Julia's big lips got her into big trouble when, during an interview with *Rolling Stone*'s Steve Pond, she expressed her reaction to Abbeville, South Carolina, the film's location. Describing the people as "horribly racist," she described her boredom. "I mean, the town had no restaurants in it. I would go home and sit in this small room with my dog and say, 'So, there's nothing to eat . . . You wanna go to sleep?' I didn't feel like I was on location anymore. I didn't feel like I had a job. I felt like this hell was where I lived."

She then went on to reflect on her Smyrna, Georgia, hometown: "I go back and see that there's been no movement in time. I'm so easily enraged by the flailing ignorance, which is tossed about as if it's God's words." Needless to say, the folks in Abbeville, South Carolina, and Smyrna, Georgia, were not thrilled. Julia issued an apology through her publicist.

In May of 1991, Julia and Kiefer set the date of their wedding for June 14. Just a few days after the announcement, British tabloids reported that Kiefer was having an affair with a Hollywood stripper named Amanda Rice. Rice, whose stage name is Raven, told one reporter that Kiefer referred to his bride-to-be as an "ice-princess" and that "he was tired of Julia's constant nagging." Kiefer denied any romantic involvement with the woman, but the published reports did not improve his image.

Two days after the story appeared, an underweight Julia walked away from the set of her next project, *Hook,* and checked into Cedars-Sinai Medical Center for five days. After a battery of tests, the doctors concluded that she was suffering from nervous exhaustion. Overly zealous reporters speculated that she might be suffering from a nervous breakdown or drug abuse, or might be pregnant.

When asked by *Entertainment Weekly* reporter Cable Neuhaus about her week-long hospital stay, Julia snapped, "I was tired. I had a fever, a bad fever. That was the worst symptom—it was like 104. That's why I was in the hospital for so long. People should be allowed—to put it in gross terms—allowed the luxury of just being sick. I have the flu, I'm sick, f __ k off."

Meanwhile, preparations for her wedding continued as planned. Julia, wearing an $8,000 designer gown, would wed Kiefer on the 20th Century Fox lot. Fox, which was distributing Julia's second movie of 1991, *Dying Young,* was hoping to cash in on the publicity surrounding the event and spent a reported $300,000 to transform one of its soundstages into a vast garden for the two hundred invited guests. Three days before the wedding, the event was called off. Who made the decision to halt the proceedings? According to Kiefer, "There was a mutual appreciation for the fact that it didn't happen."

On the day of her cancelled wedding, Julia was spotted having lunch with actor Jason Patric, an actor she had met on the set of Kiefer's film *The Lost Boys.* Jason Patric Miller, a *very serious* young man, is the son of actor and Pulitzer Prize-winning author Jason Miller and the grandson of Jackie Gleason. Shortly after their lunch, Julia and Jason boarded a plane and flew to Dublin, Ireland, followed by an inquisitive press, who reported on the couple's every movement.

After returning from Ireland, Julia then returned to work on *Hook.* Although Julia fought for the part of Tinkerbell, the shoot proved to be a difficult one. Since she was supposed to be just seven inches tall, most of her acting was done hanging from a wire against a blue screen. After hours of hanging from a wire, Julia's sense of humor would evaporate. Various members of the crew gave her the nickname Tinkerhell, while rumors spread through the Hollywood grapevine that she was arguing with her director, Steven Spielberg. In order to control the damage, both Spielberg and Julia made public statements denying any bad feeling between them.

In the midst of the media avalanche, *Dying Young* opened to rather mediocre reviews and tepid audience response. It is a credit to Julia's drawing power, however, that the movie grossed over $30 million domestically. Given the downbeat subject matter as well as the intense competition that summer (which included *Terminator 2, Robin Hood,* and *City Slickers*), it is doubtful that any other actress could have produced that level of box office receipts.

After her much-publicized breakup with Kiefer, Julia became a Pretty Obnoxious Woman. When one reporter asked if the cancellation of the nuptials would hurt her reputation, she quickly responded, "I can't give a sh __ about some lady in Boise who thinks I made the biggest mistake of my life or that I'm a bad person because I've done this."

For her testiness, Julia received a nomination from the Hollywood Women's Press Club for their annual Sour Apple Award, given to the person who "most believes their own publicity and/or presents the worst image of Hollywood to the world." Although she didn't win the award (which, incidently was given to Sinead O'Connor, Alec Baldwin, and Kim Basinger),

Julia did order a basket of candied apples delivered to the Golden Apple Awards Christmas party.

During the press junket for *Hook,* Julia's publicist insisted that reporters sign an agreement limiting their questions strictly to the movie. Queries concerning her personal life and previous film work were strictly off limits. When one reporter asked Julia what she had learned since her *Pretty Woman* days, she snapped, "I learned not to answer questions like that from the press. I learned the hard way to be more frugal with words around people like you. I've made plenty of mistakes, and everyone's made sure I've known."

After completing her work on *Hook,* Julia decided to take a year-long break from work, moved into Jason's bungalow, and adopted a potbellied pig. Jason's career is a far cry from the success enjoyed by his former female companion. His list of decidedly unspectacular film credits includes *Solarbabies, The Beast,* and *Frankenstein Unbound.* In recent interviews, both Julia and Jason have refused to discuss their relationship. According to Jason, "I want to bring as little baggage as I can to the theater, to keep my palette as clean as possible, so that roles have the best chance to succeed on their own merit." The results of this approach were apparent at the premiere of his 1991 film *Rush,* when crowds booed his arrival.

In 1990, Julia, speaking with writer Boze Hadleigh, expressed her optimism, "If Hollywood ever forgets about me, I'll just remind everybody—because I'm an actress for the long haul. I'll be making pictures when I'm eighty, so I have all the time in world. I can wait."

BROOKE SHIELDS: MOTHER'S LITTLE GIRL

Brooke Shields' career, or lack thereof, is proof positive that mother doesn't always know best. Teri Shields, however, is quick to take a defensive position when discussing the influence she exerts over her daughter. "I protect Brookie. I've been doing that ever since she was born." Although some might question Teri's methods, there is no doubt that Brookie wouldn't be where she is without her mom's help. But exactly where is she?

When Teri became pregnant, she was thirty-one and Brooke's father, Frank Shields, was only twenty-two. By the time Christa Brooke Camille Shields was born on May 31, 1965, Teri and Frank had divorced. Teri admitted to *Redbook* in 1991, "You see, I never wanted to marry Brooke's father. *Never.* I was five months pregnant, and he asked me to marry him. He then gave me two thousand dollars as a gift. I took the money, bought a table, married him, and got rid of him four months later. But I still have the table."

To this day, Brooke admits that having a relationship with her father

TERI SHIELDS HAS BEEN THE DRIVING FORCE BEHIND HER DAUGHTER'S CAREER EVER SINCE BROOKE WAS A TOT. *J. PARTI/GLOBE PHOTOS*

has been difficult. "He's never been able to say 'I love you.' He thinks what I do is so 'Hollywood,' and much easier than it actually is. He's never been instrumental in my career. But as I get older, I'm more comfortable with him because I realize that it's *his* problem."

A shrewd businesswoman, Teri has been guiding her daughter's career since she was a tot. Brooke began appearing in television commercials and magazine ads when she was only eleven months old. At age nine she made her feature film debut with a small role in *Alice, Sweet Alice* (1979).

Brooke first raised eyebrows in 1978, when at age twelve she took on the role of Violet, a child prostitute in Louise Malle's *Pretty Baby*. Set in a New Orleans bordello, Violet becomes romantically involved with a famous photographer (Keith Carradine) during World War I.

By that time Teri had become a belligerent alcoholic. Her constant interference during filming raised tensions whenever she appeared. After becoming angry with her daughter, she reportedly punched Brooke in the face. Her outrageous behavior culminated when Teri was jailed for driving while intoxicated in New Orleans. Associate Producer Polly Platt made the decision to leave Teri in jail overnight, saying that "it was in Teri's own interests." Ms. Platt later expressed her concern over Brooke's exploitation. "Her mother is supposed to be looking after Brooke, but she's just living vicariously through her. That's the real tragedy." Soon after the incident, Teri removed herself from the set.

According to Brooke, "I hated what Mom was like when she was drinking, and I just had to finally face it and do something about it. So I told her that if she didn't stop, I would go live with my father." Rather than risk losing Brooke, Teri admitted herself into a hospital for six weeks of alcohol rehabilitation.

A major source of controversy during the release of *Pretty Baby* centered on the nude scenes twelve-year-old Brooke was required to perform. Teri astounded *New York* reporter Joan Goodman with her blasé attitude. "When Brook was eight, she was asked to pose nude, and it was no problem." (No problem for Teri, anyway.) She then proceeded to ramble on. "When Louis (Malle) signed her up, she was flat as a board, but when we got to New Orleans she had her first period and he could see these two little knobs popping up."

Despite the controversy, the film was highly regarded by film critics. *Newsweek*'s Jack Kroll was impressed with Brooke's "hair-raising instinctive directness and spontaneity." Frank Rich wrote of her: "A child model of astounding beauty, she is also, at least at twelve, a natural actress."

Teri was quick to capitalize on Brooke's new-found notoriety with a string of commercial ventures, including *The Brooke Book* (an autobiography), a Brooke doll, a Brooke calendar, and a stocking line called The Brooke Look. An inexperienced talent manager, Teri exerted tight control over her Brooke's other acting assignments and chose roles for her daughter that reflected her own poor judgment (such as *Just You and Me, Kid* and *Tilt*).

Although Peter Fonda admits he wasn't very impressed with *Pretty Baby,* he had no doubts about casting her in his film *Wanda Nevada,* a film that thankfully never saw theatrical release. On the set of *Wanda,* Brooke's entourage included her godmother, two tutors, and her unavoidable mother. One crew member, referring to Teri, was quoted as saying, "It's embarrassing. Sometimes she makes terrible scenes."

Her next role, strictly teen fodder, was in the R-rated *Blue Lagoon* (1980) for a salary of $300,000 plus a percentage. During filming, a trench had to be cut in the sand so that nineteen-year-old Christopher Atkins would appear taller than his fifteen-year-old, five-foot, ten-inch co-star. Although she had a double for her nude scenes, Brooke felt uncomfortable with some of the love scenes. "In *Pretty Baby* I was not very developed, and I didn't care much about taking off my clothes. Now I do."

The Shieldses continued to capitalize on Brooke's sexuality in her next film, *Endless Love* (1981). The MPAA originally threatened to give the film an X rating for the sexually explicit scenes between Martin Hewitt and Brooke (or rather her double, Christine Jacobsen). Brooke, however, was unfazed by the experience. "I tried to do it the way I'd seen in the movies. It's always the same—the eyes meet and stuff. It's not something you think about after it's over." During her lovemaking scenes, director Franco Zeffirelli would stand off camera and squeeze her big toe, using her pain to pass for a look of ecstasy.

Brooke soon became a top model, gracing the covers of virtually every fashion magazine. She reported earned a cool half million to appear in six suggestive commercials for Calvin Klein jeans. ("You want to know what comes between me and my Calvins? Nothing.") But an embarrassing episode in her past managed to surface in 1981. In 1975, Teri had allowed her ten-year-old daughter to pose nude for photographer Garry Gross for a Playboy Press publication called *Sugar and Spice*. The photo session, arranged by the Ford Model Agency, earned the Shieldses $450.00.

Brooke and her mother filed a motion to ban the use of the photographs, which Gross was planning to publish. Although the case was initially dismissed by a lower court, a state court of appeals found that Brooke "could lawfully disaffirm" consents signed by her mother allowing Gross the right to "use, reuse, and/or publish" the photos. Justice Sidney Asch wrote, "It is not that the photographs are pornographic which renders their circulation

BROOKE SHIELDS:
MOTHER'S LITTLE
GIRL

207

An eternal optimist, Brooke says, "My mother says I'm going to win an Oscar and I believe her. I will win an Oscar."
RALPH DOMINGUEZ/GLOBE PHOTOS

unconscionable. It is that they violate a quintessential right of privacy." He also added, "Ms. Shields was a hapless child victim of a contract of adhesion to which two grasping adults bound her."

The case was finally overturned by the state's highest court in March of 1983. In a 4-to-3 decision, the court ruled that Gross could continue to market the photos as long as he did not sell them to pornographic publications. Speaking for the minority opinion, Judge Matthew Jasen wrote, "I see no reason why the child must continue to bear the burden imposed by her mother's bad judgment." U.S. District Judge Pierre Laval disagreed. In comparing the Gross photos to her "sexually provocative" film roles Laval found that "claim of harm is thus undermined to a substantial extent."

Despite the negative publicity her early work received, Brooke continued to model (earning as much as $10,000 a day), to act, and to write. She earned a reported $1.5 million for her role in the box office dud *Sahara* (1984), while Teri pocketed $250,000 for her work as executive producer. During the filming, two directors quit while an impatient crew suffered the tantrums thrown by an overbearing stage mom.

In 1983, Brooke took time off from her career to attend Princeton University. While not welcomed with open arms, Teri boasted that Brooke's SATs were 610 verbal, and 610 math, not significantly lower than the class average of 649 and 695, respectively. Arriving at the University with press in tow, Brooke did not endear herself to her classmates. In a 1985 interview with *Washington Post* reporter Lee Michael Katz, Brooke described her lonely first days on campus: "Everybody avoided me; no one talked to me. They wanted to not pay any attention to me because they thought that I get paid attention to everywhere and these people wanted to be different and not make me appear special at all. . . . I can remember talking with groups of people in a courtyard and having them all leave. I did a great deal of studying."

Brooke's isolation during her college days may have been a direct result of her celebrity status, which many of her classmates believed earned her special treatment from the school's faculty. For her senior thesis, Brooke was allowed to write on the treatment of children in the films of Louis Malle—not a real stretch for someone who starred in *Pretty Baby*. Another source of irritation stemmed from her ever-present mother. When Brooke appeared in various student productions, Teri could be found front and center during all rehearsals. Despite all the attention, Brooke graduated with honors from Princeton in 1987 with a B.A. in Romance Languages and Literature.

Since her graduation she has appeared at charity benefits, in foreign commercials, and on several Bob Hope specials. Her acting career, however, has faltered after a string of forgettable box office flops, including *Speed Zone* (1989) and *Backstreet Dreams* (1990).

With a faltering acting career, Brooke pinned her hopes on the long-shelved film *Brenda Starr*. Filmed in 1986, *Brenda Starr* is based on the globe-trotting reporter of comic strip fame. Co-starring Tony Peck and Timothy Dalton, the film eventually became linked with the BCCI banking scandal. According to published reports, it seems that Sheik Abdul Aziz al Ibrahim, brother-in-law of Saudi King Fahd and a fan of Brooke, funneled as much as $22.3 million cash and BCCI loan proceeds into the feature film. One of the strings attached to the money was that Brooke play the lead role.

Before the film could be released in the U.S., it became entangled in a series of business failures, leaving its star to bemoan the loss. "*Brenda* has some of my best work." Not according to the *Entertainment Weekly* reviewer, who, in giving the film a grade F, wrote: "No wonder this has been sitting on the shelf for five years: It's one of the worst movies ever made. . . . Brooke Shields comes off as a giggly—if spectacularly elongated—high school princess. Even taken on its own spoofed-up terms, the film is so flaccid and cheap-looking, so ineptly pieced together, that it verges on the avant-garde. We suspect they won't even like it in France." Of her performance, *People* magazine critic Ralph Novak was somewhat kinder: "Shields, 21 when the film was made, is not the worse actress-who-is-really-just-a transmuted-model of all time. . . . Mostly she raises questions about how so much sheer prettiness can generate so little sensuality."

A millionaire several times over, Brooke is an obviously worried young lady, who expressed her concerns to *Redbook* in 1991: "I'm feeling restless and stressed all the time. I get a feeling that things aren't working right. I'm not sleeping. My system is all messed up—my stomach is often in knots. . . . I get depressed and cry a lot. I worry about everything. And everything feels so heavy. In the past, I used to throw myself into school-work or films, but I don't have those anymore." True enough, Brooke poses no threat to Winona Ryder, Jodie Foster, Laura Dern, or her other contemporaries. She has not appeared on the latest Bob Hope specials. Modeling assignments and commercial endorsements are scarce these days. Brooke now spends her evenings attending celebrity parties and can be seen standing close to brighter stars in numerous paparazzi shots.

But for the future, Brooke remains an eternal optimist. "I consider myself an actress before a model. I don't think I'm good—I know I am. I've always been a survivor. And my time will come. I know it will. Just like I know I'm talented. My mother says I'm going to win an Oscar and I believe her. I will win an Oscar."

PART V

THE COMEBACK KIDS

Contrary to popular belief, there are very few actors or actresses who go unscathed by scandal in their rise to the top. The road to stardom for many of today's most successful film stars has been littered with potholes, dead ends, detours, and dangerous curves. Very few of those who fall from grace actually make their way back to the spotlight. Those who do, tend to have selective memories about their past. They cover their tracks, make the incidents in their life seem unworthy footnotes for discussion; and in essence rewrite their own biographies.

Jodie Foster, who began a tremendously successful career at age three, spent her youth preparing for adult roles by selecting scripts that expanded her range. As she entered her twenties, however, Jodie became an unwilling victim of a deranged fan, who attempted to assassinate the President in an effort to win her love. She also made headlines for her own drug arrest and the provocative photos that made their way to a porn magazine. By 1987 her standing in Hollywood was so low that she had to audition for the role that

CHILDREN
OF
BABYLON

FORMER OSCAR NOMINEE LINDA BLAIR'S MOST RECENT "ACTING" CREDITS INCLUDE *CHAINED HEAT*, *SAVAGE ISLAND*, AND *HELL NIGHT*.
MARK LEINDAL/GLOBE PHOTOS

earned her an Academy Award, *The Accused.* After winning a second Oscar in 1992, for *The Silence of the Lambs,* Jodie has become one of the most powerful women in Hollywood. A woman in complete control, Jodie enjoys her celebrity status, but strictly on *her* own terms.

Matthew Broderick, who received recognition for his work on stage and screen during his early twenties, had to revitalize a fading career after a disastrous automobile accident in 1987, which killed two women and severely injured the young actor. The details of the accident remain a mystery, and Matthew claims amnesia from the accident.

Anjelica Huston lived for many years in relative obscurity under the shadow of her famous father John (the brilliant director) and her lover of seventeen years, Jack Nicholson. In 1977, Anjelica found herself in the middle of one of Hollywood's most infamous sex scandals: the arrest of director Roman Polanski in connection with the statutory rape of a minor. This incident, along with a near-fatal car crash in 1980, caused her to reexamine her goals both personally and professionally. Anjelica's career remained on the fringe until 1985, when she was propelled into stardom with her Oscar-winning performance in *Prizzi's Honor,* a film directed by her father and starring her lover. Anjelica today casts a tall shadow of her own.

Although Jodie, Matthew, and Anjelica were able to overcome their personal adversity, many others have been less fortunate. Linda Blair, the former child model, is just one actress who, after a series of commercial flops and one highly publicized arrest, has spent her entire adult career working on the fringe of the mainstream motion picture industry.

Although Linda received an Oscar nomination for her performance in the controversial horror classic *The Exorcist* (1973), in her subsequent films (*Airport 1975* and *Rollerboogie*) she failed to exhibit any latent talent. For her work in *Exorcist II: The Heretic* (1977), John Simon commented: "Linda Blair, not a very talented or proposing youngster then, is even less interesting now, though considerably more bovine; I doubt whether a postpubertal acting style can be made out of mere chubbiness."

After a well-publicized drug arrest in December of 1977, Linda returned to the big screen, but was only able to find work in the horror/exploitation market. A prolific but unremarkable actress, her credits generally fall into three categories: women-in-prison films (*Chained Heat* and *Savage Island*), cheap horror/adventure flicks (*Hell Night* and *Savage Streets*), and inane comedies (*Up Your Alley* and *Repossessed*). Throughout the years, Linda has managed to keep her perspective. "I have to work," she says. "It's not an easy business."

Jodie Foster: Running from Her Past

Jodie Foster recently told one interviewer, "The thing that everybody finds out about me once they really get to know me is just how terrifically boring I am, and how I aspire to being boring." Regardless of her aspirations, Jodie is anything but boring.

Alicia Christian Foster was born on November 19, 1962, the youngest of four children, to Lucius and Evelyn "Brandy" Foster. Brandy was four months pregnant with Jodie when she divorced Lucius, a real estate agent, after ten years of marriage. Alone and pregnant, Brandy struggled to support her three other children, eight-year-old Lucinda, seven-year-old Constance, and five-year-old Lucius (called Buddy). According to Brandy, Lucius stopped making alimony payments after just a few months. She told reporter Lloyd Shearer, "When I married Lucius Foster, he'd already had three sons by his first wife, and it was I who wondered later how he could shun his responsibility for those three boys. Now I could see he was doing the same thing to me."

JODIE FOSTER:
RUNNING FROM HER
PAST

ℑODIE FOSTER EARNED HER FIRST OSCAR NOMINATION AT AGE FOURTEEN, PLAYING A HOOKER IN *TAXI DRIVER* (1972). AMONG HER MANY ADMIRERS WAS THE OBSESSIVE JOHN HINCKLEY. *BOB NOBLE/GLOBE PHOTOS*

Shortly after she stopped receiving child support, Brandy, with the help of a family friend, began making the rounds of talent agents with Buddy. A blonde, blue-eyed all-American boy, Buddy eventually became the family breadwinner, appearing on television commercials while Brandy managed his career. With the exposure he gained from commercial work, Buddy was able to move onto television series in regular roles on "Green Acres," "Hondo," and "Mayberry, R.F.D."

From the beginning, Jodie demonstrated gifts that distinguished her from her older siblings Lucinda, Constance, and Buddy. Jodie began talking at nine months, was speaking in sentences at one year, and taught herself to read by the time she was three. At age five, Jodie could read and comprehend scripts.

Jodie's acting career was strictly accidental. One day Brandy took Buddy to an audition and brought three-year-old Jodie along. As Jodie remembers it, "My mother didn't want to leave me in the car, because it was hot and it was a really bad neighborhood." One look at Jodie and admen selected her to become the bare-bottomed Coppertone kid.

In only three years, Jodie was a veteran of some forty-five commercials, including Ken-L-Ration, Crest, and Oreo cookies. Jodie later recalled, "I remember being in commercials and doing them over and over again, having to eat sickening things all day, and throwing up. After being in a shampoo ad I couldn't get the sh __ out of my hair for ten days."

In 1969, Jodie made her television acting debut on an episode of her brother's show, "Mayberry R.F.D." Over the next five years she became one of the busiest child actors, appearing on more than a dozen television programs, including "The Courtship of Eddie's Father," "My Three Sons," "The Partridge Family," and "Medical Center." She had featured roles on network series ("Bob & Carol & Ted & Alice," and "Paper Moon") and TV movies (*Smile, Jenny, You're Dead; Rookie of the Year;* and *The Life of T. K. Dearing*).

When she was eight years old, Jodie graduated to feature films, although her first role, in the Disney production *Napoleon and Samantha,* was almost her last. The film is the tale of a girl (Jodie), a boy (Johnny Whitaker), and their pet lion. After an exceedingly long day, the ill-tempered lion decided to take a bite out of Jodie. "His mane sort of reached around my body, took me up by the hip, turned me sideways, and started shaking me. I thought it was an earthquake. He sort of turned me around. I was looking sideways, and everybody was running. Everybody ran away!" Jodie was flown to a Portland hospital, where she remained for several days. To this day, scars on her back and stomach are reminders of this horrifying experience. Always a professional, she returned to the set two weeks later to complete the film.

After working steadily in a string of films (*Kansas City Bomber*, 1972; *One Little Indian*, 1973; and *Tom Sawyer*, 1973), Jodie began to break away from her Disney image with a role as the street-smart youth in *Alice Doesn't Live Here Anymore* (1974), an exceptional film that earned its star, Ellen Burstyn, an Academy Award for Best Actress. Although her role was relatively minor, director Martin Scorsese was so impressed that a year later he decided to cast her as a twelve-year-old hooker in *Taxi Driver*.

An explosive and highly controversial film, *Taxi Driver* told the story of Travis Bickle (Robert De Niro), a psychotic cabby who aspires to kill a presidential candidate in order to impress a girl (Cybill Shepherd) he worships from afar. Unable to complete his task, Travis gains the national spotlight when he saves a twelve-year-old hooker (Jodie) from her pimp.

At first, Jodie was intimidated by the subject matter. She later recalled, "When I first read the script I thought, 'Wow, they've got to be kidding!' It was a great part of a twenty-one-year-old, but I couldn't believe they were offering it to me." Neither could the California Labor Board, which raised objections because of her age and ordered a psychiatric evaluation. Jodie described her examination to Rex Reed: "He asked me what kind of food I ate and would I like to get married. I said not at thirteen." The Board allowed Jodie to take the part only after it was agreed that she would be replaced in the more sexually explicit scenes by a double (who turned out to be her own twenty-year-old sister, Connie).

The filming of *Taxi Driver* would have a dramatic impact on her life, both personally and professionally. "I had never thought of making movies as anything but a nice little hobby that I would probably give up when I was fifteen," she said. Her performance won her an Oscar nomination for Best Supporting Actress, and many admirers (including John Hinkley). Scorsese, who received a threatening letter before the ceremony that read, "If Jodie Foster wins for what you made her do, you will pay for it with your life," may have been somewhat relieved when Beatrice Straight took home the award for her work in *Network*.

During the next three years she proceeded to turn out an amazing number of films, albeit not all of them are truly memorable. In 1976 she was seen in *Bugsy Malone, Echoes of a Summer,* and *Freaky Friday*. In 1977 her credits included *Candleshoe, Foxes,* and *The Little Girl Who Lives Down the Lane*. Some of her best notices were earned for her performance in the 1980 film *Carney*.

In June 1980, Jodie graduated at the top of her class from the prestigious Lycée Francais in Los Angeles. A straight-A student and valedictorian

JODIE FOSTER:

RUNNING FROM HER

PAST

AFTER GRADUATING FROM YALE, JODIE'S REPUTATION IN HOLLYWOOD WAS SO LOW THAT SHE HAD TO READ FOR THE PRODUCERS OF *THE ACCUSED*. IN 1988 SHE WON AN OSCAR FOR HER PERFORMANCE.
RALPH DOMINGUEZ/GLOBE PHOTOS

of her thirty-student class, Jodie was accepted to Yale, Harvard, Princeton, Columbia, Berkeley, and Stanford. A two-day visit to Yale was all she needed to clinch her decision. "It was the first time I've every been around only people my own age," she chirped to *People* magazine. "They were so brilliant, so special, the *creme* of American students. And everyone talks so fast! That's what I want."

In an "off to college" piece for *Esquire* magazine, Jodie wrote: "Yale actually invited me—little smog-ridden me—to sink my blonde teeth into its dusty brick and ivy. Just coat me with some eastern tsuris, grease up my hair for luck, and watch me dive into the depths of academia."

Jodie's dreams for some normalcy were shattered on March 31, 1981, when in Washington, D.C., John Hinkley, Jr., emerged from a crowd and fired six shots into the Presidential party, wounding President Ronald Reagan, press secretary James Brady, and two members of the security team. Her life was abruptly transformed into a nightmare.

Upon hearing the news, Jodie sought refuge with a close friend. She admitted in an *Esquire* article titled "Why Me?" that her tears turned into a convulsive laughter. "My body jerked in painful convulsions. I was hurt. I was no longer thinking of the President, of the assailant, of the crime, of the press. I was crying for myself. Me, the unwilling victim. The one who would pay in the end. The one who paid all along—and, yes, keeps paying."

Despite the tremendous stress of the situation, Jodie managed to keep her cool. She organized her own press conference during which she disclosed that Hinkley had sent her numerous letters. She also declared that she had "never met, spoken to, or associated with [Hinkley]." The following day, however, investigators revealed that among Hinckley's possessions was a tape-recorded conversation between him and the actress.

Just one month after the shooting, federal authorities arrested Edward Michael Richardson, who, after watching Jodie in a campus play, headed to Washington with a loaded gun intent on finishing what Hinckley had left undone. Jodie was forced to leave her dorm for a more secure residence and was assigned plainclothes protection.

In her bitter account of days following the incident, Jodie vented her considerable anger at fellow students (who willingly discussed her with virtually every reporter) and the press. "They were hurting me intentionally . . . they wanted to bring me down to their level from the great silver screen."

During Hinckley's trial, Jodie took a leave of absence from Yale to film *Svengali* (starring Peter O'Toole) and work at *Esquire* magazine. "I just sat around at *Esquire* and read fiction all day," she admitted to the *Washington Post* in 1983. "The editor asked me, 'Is this what you want to do?' I said, 'Yes.' But when I hit a photographer, then I knew it was time to leave."

Hinckley's obsession continued during his post-trial incarceration at St. Elizabeth's Hospital in Washington. When *High Society* magazine published six pages of semi-nude photographs of Jodie in their March 1982 issue, John insisted on getting hold of a copy. When family members refused to buy him one, John sent a formal request to the magazine's editors, who forwarded a copy to John's doctors, allowing them the option of deciding if John should see it.

During her summer vacations and school breaks, Jodie continued to make films. "I wasn't going to make the dumb-ass comedies so my films

CHILDREN
OF
BABYLON

AT THE 1991 ACADEMY AWARDS CEREMONY, JODIE RAISED EYEBROWS WITH HER FASHION STATEMENT. DESIGNER BOB MACKIE NOTED THAT SHE "LOOKED BEAUTIFUL AS LONG AS SHE STOOD UP STRAIGHT."
RALPH DOMINGUEZ/GLOBE PHOTOS

didn't do really well." Her most notable film during her college days was *The Hotel New Hampshire* (1984). Jodie described her affection for the film in *Interview*. "The part where I end up sleeping with my brother, and then say 'That's it, goodbye, here's to the rest of our lives!' always touches me. When we finished the picture, we were all teary-eyed and drunk and knew we would never be like this again."

In 1980, Brandy boasted to *People* magazine that her daughter was "violently opposed to drugs," adding that Jodie's "intelligent enough to see what has happened to other people." That same year Jodie reiterated this to *Working Woman* magazine. "These days it's hard to find anyone who doesn't take drugs. . . . It's very disheartening. I can't be around people on drugs. I can't accept it at all, even if they don't offer me any." Just three years later Jodie was picked up at Boston's Logan Airport and charged with possessing a small amount of cocaine. Apparently, customs officials had stopped Jodie at the airport on December 19, 1982, and discovered a small amount of white powder in her luggage. After Jodie admitted that the powder was cocaine, she paid a $100 fine and received a Notice of Misdemeanor Complaint. In February of 1984, Jodie was sentenced to one year on probation and fined $500 in court costs after pleading guilty to the charges.

Jodie graduated cum laude from Yale in 1985, but by that time Hollywood casting directors had forgotten about her. "My career was at a low point when I graduated, but I couldn't let it go without a real push. Then it struck me that I wasn't going to do dreck." The parts she chose postgraduation ranged from bizarre, moody films (such as *Five Corners* and *Siesta*) to pure dreck (*Mesmerized*). By the time she received a script for *The Accused*, her standing was so low that she had to read for the title role.

In a story taken from the headlines, *The Accused* (1988) is the tale of a frank-talking sexually liberated woman (Jodie) who is gang-raped at a bar while onlookers cheer. Kelly McGillis portrayed the Assistant D.A. who attempts to get indictments against both the rapists and the witnesses.

The emotional impact of the story took its toll on Jodie, who had doubts about her performance. "It almost repulsed me," said Jodie, who, exhausted from the experience, contemplated leaving the country. Her alternate plan was to "never listen to anything emotional ever again. I just wanted to smoke pot and lie in bed."

Despite the harshness of the role, Jodie became fast friends with co-star Kelly McGillis. "Pretty soon after I met her I felt she was my sister. . . . She's completely astute, never haphazard like I tend to be. She's also deeply emotional . . . Kelly doesn't repress anything. She's very real and she doesn't lie. She can't. She doesn't know how to."

Kelly McGillis had an equally high opinion of Jodie, which she voiced to

CHILDREN OF BABYLON

224

THE ROLE OF FBI TRAINEE CLARICE STARLING IN *THE SILENCE OF THE LAMBS* WAS ORIGINALLY OFFERED TO MICHELLE PFEIFFER. AGAIN JODIE HAD TO FIGHT FOR THE ROLE—WHICH WON HER A GOLDEN GLOBE AND ANOTHER OSCAR. *MICHAEL FERGUSON/GLOBE PHOTOS*

Interview in 1987: "We got along fabulously. There were so many things we didn't have to discuss, because we already knew the answers. There was an immediate closeness between us. We didn't have to struggle to achieve it."

Jodie would just as soon forget the choices she made following *The Accused*. Of the baseball movie *Stealing Home* (1989), *People* magazine wrote, "Jodie Foster has a lock on this year's award for best performance by an actress in a howling dog of a movie." *Backtrack,* directed by voyeur Dennis Hopper, displayed Jodie's body in scenes involving steamy showers and black lingerie. The film was never theatrically released but made its way to home video and cable TV in 1992.

Despite winning the Oscar, Jodie had to fight to get the role of FBI trainee Clarice Starling in *The Silence of the Lambs*. Director Jonathan Demme, who initially offered the role to Michelle Pfeiffer, told *Rolling Stone,* "Michelle read it and it became apparent that she was unable to come to terms with the overpowering darkness of the piece." After lobbying Demme and Orion Pictures, Jodie finally got the part." You fight for the ones you have serious personal connections with," she later said.

In 1991, Jodie decided to cash in or her newfound clout and chose the script for *Little Man Tate* as her directorial debut. A hesitant Orion Pictures agreed to let her direct only after signing her on as the film's star. The screenplay is about a child genius, Fred Tate, who is pulled between his warm, blue-collar mother Dede (Jodie) and a cool, highly educated teacher of gifted children, Jane (Diane Wiest).

Despite a string of sexual performances, Jodie has never been called a sex symbol. Her androgenous qualities have been noted by more than one writer. Julia Cameron noted in *American Film,* "Foster contains elements of each sex: the husky voice of a femme fatale and the bravado of a young man on the rise . . . She's more Robin Hood than Maid Marian." Cameron also noted that Jodie has a streak of "machismo lurking just beneath the surface."

Jodie has avoided questions dealing with her sexual preferences. When confronted by reporter Boze Hadleigh with the widely circulated rumors that linked her romantically with Kelly McGillis during the filming of *The Accused,* Jodie responded, "There are always rumors. Um, Kelly has since been married. Nowadays people wonder which side of the fence you're on until you get married." When he reminded Jodie that gay performers, such as Rock Hudson, had married for the sake of their screen images, Jodie replied, "Yeah, and that goes on today. I think marriage should be based on love, but in Hollywood it's really based on what it does for your career. I also think marriage doesn't mean obtaining a contract. The length and quality of the relationship is what matters."

Jodie is skilled at avoiding questions and issues that make her uncomfortable, including Hinckley, her drug arrest, her romantic life, and her artistic failures. In 1992, Jodie addressed the subject of normalcy, "I was not raised like a normal person. I didn't have a normal life, but that didn't mean it wasn't healthy. Normal is not something to aspire to, it's something to get away from. It was tough figuring out how to remain healthy."

Matthew Broderick: The Road Back

In 1980, shortly before his high school graduation, Matthew Broderick decided to pursue an acting career. Within three years, he was on the fast track to stardom both on Broadway, as Neil Simon's protégé, and in motion pictures. But an accident on August 5, 1987, left two people dead and seriously injured Matthew—and left great questions about what career he might yet have.

Born on March 21, 1962, Matthew, the youngest of three children, grew up in a theatrical environment in New York's Greenwich Village. His mother, Patricia, was a playwright before she became an artist, while his father, the late James Broderick, was a star of stage and screen best remembered as Kristy McNichol's father in the series "Family" (1976–1980).

Bitten by the acting bug, Matthew found himself actively studying his craft to the detriment of his schoolwork. Matthew later said of his high

MATTHEW BRODERICK'S FILM AND STAGE CAREER WAS LAUNCHED BY HIS FRIEND NEIL SIMON. *JOHN BARRETT/GLOBE PHOTOS*

school years, "I did badly and weaseled my way out of work. And as I got better at acting, I got worse grades."

Eight months out of high school, Matthew was elated to be cast opposite Sally Field in the motion picture *No Small Affair,* to be directed by Martin Ritt. His joy was short-lived, however, when the film was cancelled two weeks into rehearsals. (The film was later lensed with John Cryer and Demi Moore.) Matthew's only credit that first year out of school was a commercial for anti-itch cream.

Eventually he landed the role of a fifteen-year-old gay boy who is adopted by a homosexual drag queen in Harvey Fierstein's play *Torch Song Trilogy*. With this role, Matthew soon came to the attention of writer Neil Simon.

In 1981, he co-starred opposite Simon's then-wife Marsha Mason in the

BOTH MATTHEW BRODERICK AND JENNIFER GREY WERE UNABLE TO
EXPLAIN THE EVENTS THAT LED TO THE CAR CRASH THAT TOOK TWO LIVES.
GLOBE PHOTOS

film *Max Dugan Returns*. That same year, Matthew landed the part of a computer hacker who nearly starts World War III in the box office smash *WarGames*. Then, he returned to New York to star as fifteen-year-old Eugene Morris Jerome in the first of Simon's autobiographical plays, *Brighton Beach Memoirs*—a role that earned Matthew a Tony Award for Best Actor.

With his youthful looks, slight build, and the ability to look perpetually surprised, Matthew was typecast as a street-smart teenager in a slew of films (*1918, Master Harold and the Boys,* and *Ladyhawke*). His first mature role came in 1985, when he returned to Broadway to star as the eighteen-year-old Eugene in the second installment of Neil Simon's trilogy, *Biloxi Blues*.

In 1986, at age twenty-four, Matthew hit box office pay dirt by playing a

MATTHEW
BRODERICK: THE
ROAD BACK

229

CHILDREN OF BABYLON

The box-office failures of *Family Business* and *Out on a Limb* did little to revive Matthew's acting stature. He has since turned his attention toward a directing career. *Stephen Trupp/Globe Photos*

mischievous seventeen-year-old in *Ferris Bueller's Day Off.* This comedy, directed and scripted by John Hughes, grossed more than $70 million at the box office. The film co-starred several young performers, including Mia Sara, Charlie Sheen, and, notably, Jennifer Grey (daughter of actor Joel Grey), with whom Matthew became romantically involved.

Up to this point, Matthew had avoided the social trappings of his Brat Pack contemporaries. Intelligent and level-headed, he managed to stay away from drugs, alcohol, and the party circuit. He had also kept his live-in relationship with Jennifer, two years his senior, out of the gossip columns. This situation would change, however, in August of 1987.

After completing *Ferris Bueller,* Matthew and Jennifer went on to different projects. Jennifer starred opposite Patrick Swayze in *Dirty Dancing,* while Matthew made *Project X* and the film version of *Biloxi Blues,* earning a reported $2 million for the latter.

Before starting publicity rounds on their respective films, Matthew and Jennifer decided to take a vacation in Northern Ireland, at the Broderick family home in Donegal. On August 5, 1987, Matthew and Jennifer were on an excursion from Irvinestown to Maguiresbridge. While the road they were traveling on was wet from an earlier rainstorm, it had no curves and visibility was good. Tragedy struck when the red BMW Matthew was driving collided head-on with a brown Volvo driven by Anna Gallagher, twenty-eight. Both she and her widowed mother, Margaret Doherty, age sixty-three, were killed, while Matthew was severely injured. The local fire brigade had to cut away Matthew's door in order to give him first aid. According to one witness, Matthew repeatedly asked, "Did I hurt them? Did I hurt them?" Jennifer, covered with Matthew's blood, had only minor bruises.

Margaret Doherty suffered from multiple sclerosis and for five years prior to the accident had been confined to a wheelchair. She lived with her mechanic son, Martin, twenty-four, in the rural town of Enniskillen, eighty miles southwest of Belfast. Anna, who was recovering from a recent miscarriage, frequently took her mother shopping in Martin's car.

All four were rushed to Erne Hospital in Enniskillen, where Margaret and Anna were pronounced dead, while Jennifer was treated for shock and released. Matthew, however, suffered a collapsed lung, a concussion, a severely broken leg, and several broken ribs. He was later transferred to The Royal Victorian Hospital in Belfast, where he spent three weeks recovering. He still bears facial scars as well as a pin in his leg from the accident.

Suffering from amnesia, Matthew has been unable to remember any events of that day. Jennifer, who was adjusting the car's tape deck at the time of the accident cannot explain what happened either. A team of forensic specialists, as well as private investigators hired by the Broderick family, could not determine the cause of the accident. It has been speculated that Matthew may have started to drive on the right side of the road, instead of the left, the proper side in Ireland.

In September, in a temporary courtroom set up in the hospital, Matthew was formally charged with only one count of reckless driving (in causing the death of Anna Gallagher)—a charge that might have led to a ten-year prison sentence. Released on $4,075 bail, Matthew returned home on crutches. In February of 1988, the court fined Matthew $175 for reckless driving, saying that the cause of the accident could not be determined. John Gallagher, Anna's husband, referred to the ruling as a "travesty of justice."

Upon his return home, Matthew underwent intensive physical therapy to correct a limp, as well as psychotherapy for his emotional scars. His star slightly dimmed once he returned to work. His roles after the accident included the film version of *Torch Song Trilogy* (1988) and *Family Business* (1989), starring Sean Connery and Dustin Hoffman, which took in a disappointing $12 million at the box office.

In 1989, his career began a modest comeback with his portrayal of Robert Gould Shaw in the Civil War drama *Glory*. Although most critics were unimpressed with Matthew's performance, two of his co-stars, Denzel Washington and Morgan Freeman, would later receive Oscar nominations (Washington won for Best Supporting Actor).

The following year, Matthew, twenty-seven, starred opposite Marlon Brando as a naive NYU student in *The Freshman*. While the film was critically acclaimed, it was virtually lost in the competitive 1990 summer release schedule and grossed only $21 million. His 1992 film, *Out On a Limb*, fared even worse and took in less than $2 million during the course of its three week run.

Matthew has tried to put the past behind him, stating, "I've had bad things in my life and good things. I don't think about their relationship, really." John Gallagher may have summed it up best after his wife's funeral: "He has to live with this the rest of his life."

Anjelica Huston: Out of the Shadows

For the better part of two decades, Anjelica Huston remained in the shadows of two of Hollywood's most powerful men. The first was her father, the legendary John Huston, who died in 1987, after a film career that spanned sixty years. The second was her lover of seventeen years, Jack Nicholson. With their help, Anjelica became a star in her own right, after giving an Academy Award-winning performance in *Prizzi's Honor* (1985).

The son of Academy Award winner Walter Huston, John was a brilliant, hard-drinking womanizer. He was forty-three when he married his fourth wife, Enrica "Ricki" Soma, a nineteen-year-old ballet dancer and model. Anjelica, the Hustons' second child, was born in Los Angeles on July 8, 1951, while her father was in the Congo directing *The African Queen*. (John congratulated his wife via telegram.)

Five months later, Huston took his family to Ireland, where he had purchased a large Georgian estate in western Galway. The lavish 110-acre

JOHN HUSTON DIRECTED HIS FIFTEEN-YEAR-OLD ANJELICA AND ASSAF DAYAN (SON OF MOSHE DAYAN) IN *A WALK WITH LOVE AND DEATH*.
GLOBE PHOTOS

spread and two homes—one for John and one for Ricki and the children. With his family comfortably settled, John left to travel the world to make movies, which included *Beat the Devil* (1953), *Moby Dick* (1956), and *Heaven Knows, Mr. Allison* (1957).

In a 1989 interview with *New York Times* reporter James Kaplan, Anjelica recalled her father who was not particularly warm and loving: "He had a cruel streak—made him interesting. He liked his fun. It was certainly sometimes at the expense of others. . . . But I think that if there were a sin there, it was that he was very much preoccupied with what he wanted to do, which didn't necessarily coincide with his having a wife or having children."

At first Anjelica and her brother Tony were educated by tutors, but at a certain point they were sent to local Catholic schools, while lonely Ricki remained at home doing needlepoint. After years of isolation, Ricki separated from John and took her eleven-year-old daughter and thirteen-year-old son to London.

In the midst of a turbulent adolescence, John cast fifteen-year-old Anjelica in the lead role in *A Walk with Love and Death,* the story of a doomed love of a student and a young noblewoman during the Hundred Years' War in France. As Anjelica recalled to writer Susan Morgan, she was not eager to do the film: "I was more interested in wearing black fishnet stockings and a lot of makeup. I was playing a medieval maiden, who wasn't supposed to wear a lot of makeup. . . . My basic objective was to run around and smoke cigarettes with my girlfriends." Anjelica had cut her long hair just before the movie started shooting, and played a beleaguered maiden in a heavy wig opposite Assaf Dayan (son of Israeli defense minister Moshe Dayan).

Anjelica also grew to resent her father's strong direction. "Part of his idea to have me in the movie was, I think, to be able to discipline me, both personally and as an actress." Although the film had its supporters, the general critical reaction was very negative. John Simon wrote, "There is a perfectly blank, supremely inept performance . . . by Huston's daughter, Anjelica, who has the face of an exhausted gnu, the voice of an unstrung tennis racket, and a figure of no describable shape." The overall effect of the movie was to give a crushing blow to Anjelica's self-esteem. "I was roundly criticized and made to feel very unattractive."

On January 29, 1969, thirty-nine-year-old Ricki was killed in a car crash in France. The impact on the sixteen-year-old Anjelica was devastating: "It was like losing my best friend, my mother and my sister all in one. Nothing has happened to me before or since to equal the impact of that shock." Shortly thereafter, Anjelica, who had been understudying for Marianne Faithfull in the role of Ophelia in the London production of *Hamlet,* decided to go with the play to New York.

In 1971, she began modeling for *Vogue.* "I loved the clothes, the champagne, the attention," she says. "Everything but my own looks." For the next two years, Anjelica did most of her modeling in Europe, where her dark, unusual looks were more appreciated.

In 1973, Anjelica returned to L.A. and spent several months as the houseguest of John and his fifth wife, Cici. During this time, Anjelica, twenty-two, was taken to a party at Jack Nicholson's house, where she caught more than just the attention of the admiring host.

Born on April 22, 1937, in Neptune, New Jersey, Jack Nicholson was the illegitimate child of a seventeen-year-old girl named June Nicholson. During

ROMAN POLANSKI WAS ARRESTED ON CHARGES OF RAPE, PERVERSION, AND SODOMY WHILE ANJELICA WAS STAYING AT JACK NICHOLSON'S HOUSE.
JERRY WATSON/GLOBE PHOTOS

his teens, he became a rebel and landed in Hollywood during a time when rebels were in vogue. After making several low-budget Roger Corman movies, Jack was launched into superstardom after roles in *Easy Rider* (1969), *Five Easy Pieces* (1970), and *The Last Detail* (1973), portrayals that would earn him Oscar nominations. By the time he met Anjelica, he had divorced his first wife Sandra Knight, the mother of his daughter Jennifer.

Anjelica decided to put her career on hold while she and Jack pursued an on-again/off-again relationship. Abandoning her modeling career, she moved in with Jack and tended house for three years. The bit parts she managed to snare in *The Last Tycoon* and *Swashbuckler* did little to enhance her career. Jack, on the other hand, was widely recognized as a major talent, with his outstanding performances in *Chinatown* (1974) and *One Flew Over the Cuckoo's Nest* (1975), the latter earning him an Academy Award for Best Actor.

Although Anjelica was very much Jack's companion, their relationship ran hot and cold. During one of their cold periods in 1977, director Roman Polanski was invited to stay at his house. Polanski, who had directed Nicholson and John Huston in *Chinatown* (1974), decided to use the location to shoot photographs of a thirteen-year-old actress named Sandra for the French magazine *Vogue Hommes*.

The following day, Polanski was arrested on charges that included rape by use of drugs, perversion, and sodomy. When police returned to the Nicholson house with Polanski to search the premises, they found a visibly annoyed Anjelica at home. "I was present when the police came," she later admitted. "It was not a legal entry." In their search, detectives discovered a large container of hashish in a drawer in Jack's bedroom and a small amount of cocaine in Anjelica's purse.

In her statement to police, Anjelica said that when she had entered the house on the day in question, she found Polanski and Sandra in one of the bedrooms "going at it." Polanski, reportedly naked from the waist down, said, "We'll be out in a few minutes." When the girl emerged twenty minutes later, she appeared disheveled and woozy. Polanski then took the child home.

Anjelica agreed to testify against Polanski if the D.A. would drop the drug charges against her. Polanski later pleaded guilty to unlawful sexual intercourse and spent forty-two days undergoing psychiatric observation at Chino State Prison to determine if he was a habitual sex offender. Released before his formal sentencing, Polanski borrowed $1,000 from film producer Dino De Laurentiis and fled the country.

In 1982, Anjelica, twenty-nine, survived a near-fatal car accident. "A car came into me at sixty miles per hour. Head on. No seat belt. My nose went through the windshield! It was flattened. But I had no cuts. So I was really lucky to have had such a strong nose. Otherwise, who knows?" The accident caused her to revise her own aspirations, both personally and professionally.

Without breaking up with Jack, Anjelica moved into her own house. Anjelica explained her need to assert her own independence to *Washington Post* reporter Cynthia Gorney in 1986: "I needed to draw away. I needed to know that when the phone rang, it rang for me. I needed to know who I saw

Anjelica (here with Jack Nicholson, Kathleen Turner, and John Huston) was the only member of the cast and crew to take home an Oscar for *Prizzi's Honor*. GLOBE PHOTOS

in my life, as opposed to who we-all saw. And it was very good . . . you know, having one's *key,* to one's own *house.*"

She also decided to revive her own acting career. Her first break came when Lee Grant asked her to be in a Strindberg play she was directing, whose cast included Maximillian Schell, Richard Jordan, and Carol Kane. After rehearsals began, Lee took Anjelica aside and said, "You should go to acting school." Those acting classes not only developed Anjelica's latent talent but built up her own self-esteem.

After a while, little acting parts started to come up. Penny Marshall invited Anjelica to make two guest appearances on "Laverne and Shirley."

She took small roles in *The Postman Always Rings Twice* (1981) and *Frances* (1982). She received her best notices in 1984 for her performances of a fiery swordswoman in *Ice Pirates,* and an overbearing publicist in *This Is Spinal Tap.*

In 1985, Anjelica was cast by her father as Mafia princess Maerose Prizzi, in his dark comedy *Prizzi's Honor.* The project was a dual treat for Anjelica; She would be directed by her father and working alongside Jack. Anjelica was well aware that the studio producing the film, Paramount Pictures, was less than thrilled with her involvement. "They only let me be in the movie because he (Huston) was directing and Jack was acting." After asking for more than the scale wages that were offered, a sharp answer came back. "I heard the genius money man saying 'Great, ask for more money, we'd love you to ask for more money. Because you know what? We don't want her in the movie.'"

During the press junket for the movie, the couple's friends gave curious testimonials to their relationship. "He used to be a very big player—not even Warren Beatty has been so successful with women—but now that seems to have subsided," producer Bob Evans chirped to *People* magazine. He also added, "The man is a diamond, and she's given him a beautiful setting." Producer John Foreman gave an equally puzzling quote. "Jack does everything but rise when Anjelica comes into the room." (Well then, what does he do?) John Huston added his own vote of confidence. "Twelve years! That's longer than any of my five marriages lasted."

Despite their protestations of affection, the question of their impending marriage remained doubtful. Jack told *People,* "We've talked about marriage, but it never became a critical issue." As for their separate residences, "It's just evolved out of the kind of people we are. Right now it seems to work better, and what the hell, she's only two minutes away."

Prizzi's Honor became the critical sensation of the year and garnered eight Oscar nominations, including Best Picture, Director, and Actor. Anjelica, however, was the only winner, in the category of Best Supporting Actress. "After the Governor's Ball we went to Dad's hotel room," she recalled to *Film Comment*'s Beverly Walker. Everyone was a bit pissed off that he didn't get it, but I wasn't going to allow that to spoil my parade."

In early 1989, Anjelica described her long-standing relationship with Jack: "Whatever it is Jack wants to do, and whatever it is I want to do, we seem to accommodate each other. He's a soulmate. It goes beyond commitment. It's not as if one has any choice in the matter. Jack's true blue. He doesn't disappoint—he doesn't have it in him."

British actress Karen Mayo-Chandler agreed, in a December, 1989 issue of *Playboy,* in an article titled "The Joker Is Wild." Mayo-Chandler, who had a small part on the CBS soap "The Young and the Restless," recounted her graphic experiences with the "randy" actor. "He's into fun and games in bed—all the really horny things that I get off on, like spankings, handcuffs, whips, and Polaroid pictures. Now that's a man to die for."

Not without scruples, Karen says that she would not have entered into the affair if he had been married. "I knew that Anjelica Huston had been his steady lady for years—you can't miss the one picture of her he keeps in his bathroom—but I rather gathered their relationship had become a friendship thing by that time."

She added, "I do remember that when her father, John Huston, died, Jack was very upset. I knew that the three of them had made *Prizzi's Honor* together and that Jack admired the old man immensely. But on the night before Mr. Huston's funeral, Jack called me up to his house and I had to wonder why he wasn't consoling Anjelica instead of making love to me. My God, he was passionate that night."

A second blow to Anjelica came shortly after, when she learned that Jack was having a child with an actress and waitress named Rebecca Broussard, who had been a bit player in *The Two Jakes*.

In May of 1992, after a brief engagement, Anjelica married Robert Graham at the Bel Air Hotel. *The Associated Press* reported that model Jerry Hall was a member of the wedding party and that the guest list included Mick Jagger, Lauren Bacall, Warren Beatty, Annette Bening, Meryl Streep, Arnold Schwarzenegger, Joe Pesci, Penny Marshall, Carrie Fisher, and Lauren Hutton.

Since her triumph in *Prizzi's Honor,* Anjelica has turned in a number of outstanding performances, both large and small. Her most recent credits include *The Dead* (1987), *Gardens of Stone* (1987), *A Handful of Dust* (1988), *Mr. North* (1988), *Crimes and Misdemeanors* (1989), *Enemies, A Love Story* (1989), and *The Addams Family* (1991). In 1990, Anjelica earned her second Oscar nomination for her icy portrayal of a cunning con artist in *The Grifters* (in a role originally meant for Melanie Griffith).

In 1991, she said, "When everything is so good, I'm apt to wonder what's coming that isn't so good. I feel a little trepidatious. But all in all, I'm glad I'm out from under the dark clouds."

PART VI

FADE TO BLACK

Raised in an environment of wealth, beauty, talent, and fame, the Children of Babylon seem to lead enviable lives. Yet, recent events indicate that even nonfamous children of famous Hollywood couples have trouble bearing under pressure. Hollywood history is full of celebrity offspring who have committed suicide, met tragic deaths, or succumbed to their addictions. The statistics make grim reading.

Michael Boyer, the only child of French actor Charles Boyer, shot and killed himself on the morning of September 23, 1965, at the age of twenty-one.

Diane Linkletter, the twenty-one-year-old daughter of Art Linkletter, after getting high on LSD, plunged to her death from her sixth-floor apartment in October of 1969.

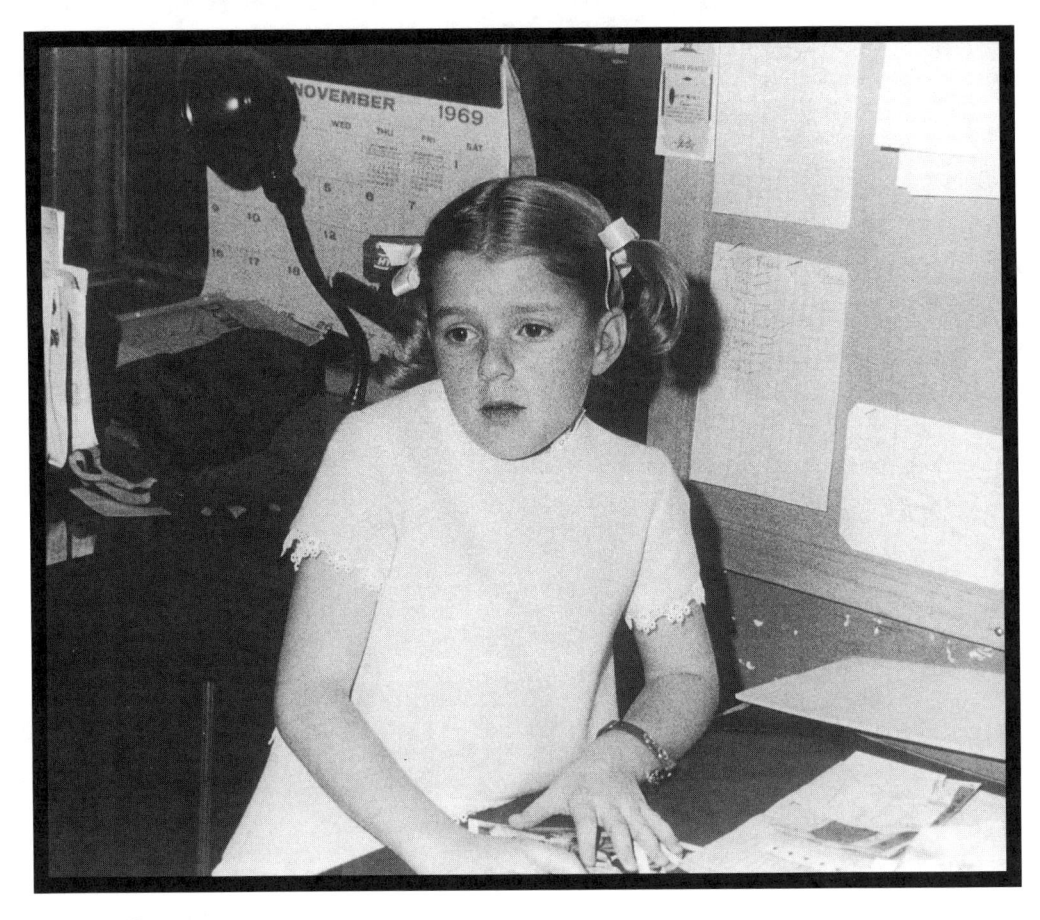

Shortly after coming into her trust fund savings, eighteen-year-old Anissa overdosed on barbiturates. ART ZELIN/GLOBE PHOTOS

Jenny Arness, daughter of James Arness, at age twenty-four, took her own life in May of 1975, leaving behind a twenty-page rambling rationale for her actions. Two years later, her mother Virginia repeated Jenny's actions, leaving twenty pages of notes before swallowing a large quantity of sleeping pills.

Jonathan Peck, the thirty-year-old son of Gregory Peck, was found dead in July of 1975 in his Santa Barbara home. An apparent suicide, Jon left no note.

Allan Scott Newman, the twenty-eight-year-old son of actor Paul Newman, died in November of 1978 after ingesting a lethal combination of rum, Valium and Quaaludes, and cocaine.

Kelly Jean Van Dyke-Nance, the thirty-three-year-old daughter of Jerry Van Dyke, was found hanging from a rope in the bedroom of her home in November of 1991.

Perhaps equally distressing is the high incidence of tragedy that has followed some former child actors. Those who come to an early end, whether after losing a struggle with their own internal demons or by the will of others.

On August 28, 1976, the body of Mary Anissa Jones was discovered on the floor of a friend's home in Oceanside, California. The cause of death was determined to be a lethal combination of barbiturates and alcohol. She had recently turned eighteen. Anissa Jones will always be remembered as the adorable pigtailed blonde Buffy in the long-running sitcom "Family Affair." The show began its successful seven-year run in 1966 and starred Brian Keith. Five years after the show's cancellation in 1971, and shortly after coming into her trust fund earnings, Anissa became just another fatality in Hollywood's growing drug community.

On January 18, 1982, at 1:45 a.m., the body of twenty-year-old Trent Lawson Lehman was found hanging from a school fence, across the street from his home in California's San Fernando Valley. A suicide note was found in his pocket. At the time of his death, Trent Lehman had become a forgotten face in the crowd, but at the age of ten he was known to millions of viewers as Butch Everett, one of the three spirited children of a widowed professor in the television series "Nanny and the Professor." The series, which starred Richard Long and Juliet Mills, ran from 1970 to 1971. Back then he earned $1,200 a week, but by 1982 he had become an unemployed and despondent cocaine addict.

Both of these deaths serve as grim reminders of the inherent problems associated with being a child celebrity. In recent years, several more young performers have sustained the tragedy of an untimely end, due to either murder, accident, or suicide. Dominique Dunne was killed at the hands of her former lover, while Rebecca Schaeffer was murdered by a complete stranger. Brandon de Wilde lost his life in a tragic accident during a heavy rainstorm, while Rusty Hamer decided to end his on his own. These are their stories.

BRANDON DE WILDE

T he year was 1949 and a young novelist, Carson McCullers, had written her first play, *The Member of the Wedding,* which producer Robert Whitehead had decided to bring to Broadway. For Whitehead and his director Harold Clurman, selection of the two female leads for the play had been relatively simple. Julie Harris was cast for the role of Frankie Addams, an emotionally charged adolescent, while Ethel Waters, a veteran of film and stage, was selected for the role of Bernice "Sadie" Brown, the compassionate housekeeper of the Addams's household.

But the producers were having a great deal of difficulty in casting a third key role, that of John Henry, Frankie's cousin. By the time Fay Harris, the show's casting director, had stopped by to have dinner with her stage manager, Frederic "Fritz" de Wilde, and his wife Hilda, more than fifty young boys had auditioned unsuccessfully for the role. Harris was an old friend of the de Wildes, having once appeared in the play *Tobacco Road* with Hilda, an attractive blonde.

BRANDON DE WILDE CELEBRATED HIS SIXTEENTH BIRTHDAY WITH ACTRESS CAROL LYNLEY ON THE SET OF *BLUE DENIM* (1959). THE STAR OF SHANE HAD STARTED TO PUT HIS LIFE BACK TOGETHER WHEN HE DIED IN A CAR ACCIDENT AT AGE THIRTY. *GLOBE PHOTOS*

At dinner, Harris looked at the seven-year-old boy sitting across from her, then asked Hilda, "Why don't you try out Brandon for the role of John Henry?" Hilda replied, "What's the use. He has no experience and besides he's not an actor." The next morning the young boy was brought before Whitehead and Clurman, who nodded approvingly. Whitehead looked at his stage director standing beside his son. "Can he act?" Fritz responded, "I doubt it." "Can he learn his lines?" Clurman asked. "He can't even remember his own address," came the reply. "Take a crack at it anyway, Fritz," Harris pleaded.

Brandon and Fritz did take "a crack at it" and when the play opened at the Empire Theatre in Manhattan on January 5, 1950, to rave notices, the talent of Brandon de Wilde was evident for all to see, including Bosley Crowther of the *New York Times,* who later wrote:

> Everyone is in love with Brandon de Wilde's sober and plump little performance as the boy next door . . . In other hands than those of Master de Wilde it could be unbearably precocious. But he plays it unself-consciously. In addition to that, he plays it with an air of personal indomitability that preserves the independence of the character amid the whirl of the play . . . Small as he is, he has the magnetic personality of a real performer.

Brandon would go on to play 572 performances on Broadway without missing a show—even going on once when he had sprained his ankle, refusing to let his understudy go on. He eventually won the Donaldson Award, for the best debut performance in a play, in August of 1950. After the show's run was concluded, he went on to a succession of roles on Broadway, first appearing in the play *Mrs. McThing,* followed by a serious role in *The Emperor's Clothes.*

In 1953, Hollywood reached out to tap the young boy for a role in a western that would star four big Hollywood stars: Alan Ladd, Jack Palance, Van Heflin, and Jean Arthur. The movie, *Shane,* was a film that later became one of the select few western films that could be truly labelled a classic.

As the young son of a rancher (Heflin), Brandon's plaintive plea to Alan Ladd, "Shane, come back, Shane, Shane," was to echo down through the years long after the film's historic gunfight between Ladd and Palance had faded from memory. For his work in *Shane,* twelve-year-old Brandon was nominated for an Academy Award in the Best Supporting Actor category in 1954.

In the space of five years, the boy from Baldwin, New York, had earned not only the applause of his peers in the acting profession but a five-figure income that had, at his parents insistence, been salted away in a trust account, exclusively for his future use.

But the early fame that cloaked Brandon with acclaim and wealth was to slip away year by year as the teenager grew into manhood. By the time he was in his twenties, Brandon had appeared in a succession of films that, with the exception of *Hud,* starring Paul Newman, were less than noteworthy.

Brandon, who had once dreamed of becoming a director by age twenty-five, found his career floundering in supporting roles in mediocre movies.

Married in December of 1963 to a New York debutante, he was divorced six years later after fathering a son, Jesse. As his career slid, Brandon, bored with marriage and acting, tried a brief stint as a country western singer. He entered the drug scene, where he remained for several years, experiencing the inevitable highs and lows that accompany pills. Speaking of her encounter with Brandon in 1969, Pamela Des Barres wrote, "Sex with Brandon was awe–inspiring. He had the energy of ten men and required very little sleep, so I was always exhausted, stoned, worn out, and in heat."

By 1972, Brandon, age thirty, had begun to pull out of the dive that had brought his career from its high altitude to at or below sea level. He returned to his first love, the stage, and began appearing in plays in the Southern California area. As the blind young man in *Butterflies Are Free,* critics took note once again of his talent. By July of that year, Brandon was off drugs, had remarried, and was traveling with the play. His life was on track once again.

On July 6, 1972, Brandon, alone in his van, was driving in a blinding rainstorm in the Denver suburb of Lakewood when his van smashed into and under a flatbed truck parked alongside the road. Pulled from the wreckage with a broken neck and back, he survived a few hours before succumbing in a nearby hospital in Denver. The tragic death of Brandon de Wilde on that rainy day in July marked with sad finality a career that had soared at its inception but had faltered in mid–flight only to come crashing to earth.

DOMINIQUE DUNNE

Dominique Dunne, a striking beauty with considerable talent, is best remembered for her role in the box office smash *Poltergeist.* At twenty-three, Dominique seemed destined for stardom until the evening of October 30, 1982, when she was brutally strangled by a former boyfriend.

The daughter of a prominent Hollywood family, Dominique was born in 1959 in Santa Monica, California, and was raised, with her two older brothers, in a privileged environment. Indeed, the Dunne family reads from a list of Who's Who in Hollywood. Her father, Dominick, was a movie producer (*The Boys in the Band, Panic in Needle Park,* and *Ash Wednesday* among his credits); her brother Griffin was an actor and producer who had starred in *An American Werewolf in London* (1981); her aunt and uncle were respected authors Joan Didion (*Salvador*) and John Gregory Dunne (*True Confessions*).

Dominique had weathered some difficult moments during her youth:

the divorce of her parents when she was eleven years old, her father's subsequent bouts with drug and alcohol addiction, and the suicide of an uncle. In 1975, her mother Ellen, called Lenny by family and friends, was diagnosed with multiple sclerosis.

Dominique was educated at the Westlake School in Los Angeles, the Taft School in Connecticut, and the Fountain Valley School in Colorado. She later spent a year in Florence, Italy, and attended the British Institute and the Michelangelo schools.

When Dominique decided to become an actress, she had little difficulty in finding work. She appeared in several television films, including *Diary of a Teenage Hitchhiker* (1979); *Valentine Magic on Love Island* (1980); *The Day the Loving Stopped* (1981), co-starring Ally Sheedy; and *The Shadow Riders* (1982). She also made numerous guest appearances on prime-time network series, including "Breaking Away," "Family," "Lou Grant," "CHiPs," "Fame," and "Hill Street Blues."

Poltergeist, released in June of 1982, was Dominique's first motion picture role. The film tells the story of a suburban middle-class family whose lives are turned inside out when the hostile spirits in their home kidnap their five-year-old daughter. The film starred Craig T. Nelson, JoBeth Williams, Oliver Robbins, Heather O'Rourke, and Dominique as the troubled members of the Freeling family. In the film, Dominique portrayed Dana, sixteen, the eldest daughter of Steven and Diana Freeling. Although she had little screen time, the enormous success of the film made her a recognizable star at age twenty-two.

While her parents were pleased at her success, they were, however, concerned over her romantic involvement with John Thomas Sweeny. Sweeny, twenty-five, worked as a chef at fashionable Ma Maison and lived with Dominique in West Hollywood. He came from a poor family in Hazeltown, Pennsylvania. His waitress mother and alcoholic father were divorced when he was fourteen. Ambitious and ashamed of his upbringing, Sweeny had many differences with Dominique during the time they lived together.

In August of 1982, Dominique, wary of Sweeny's increasing possessiveness and jealous rages, became fearful of her obsessed lover. After many arguments, some of which became violent, Dominique tried to end the relationship and persuaded Sweeny to move out.

On the evening of October 30, Dominique was at her home with actor David Packer, twenty-two, rehearsing a scene from the upcoming NBC pilot *V.* Shortly before 9 p.m., Sweeny arrived and began to argue with Dominique on her front porch. Sweeny, athletic and muscular, proceeded to strangle the life from Dominique while Packer frantically called the police for help.

When Dominique arrived at Cedars-Sinai, she was in full cardiac arrest.

The Freeling family in *Poltergeist* may have outwitted their demons, but two of the movie's child actors did not. Dominique Dunne (*front*), at age twenty-three was killed at the hands of her former lover in 1982. *Globe Photos*

She was immediately revived and placed on life support, but, sadly, she was already brain dead. On November 4, after saying goodbye to their comatose daughter, Dominick and Lenny, now confined to a wheelchair, signed her off life support and donated her kidneys and heart. The following morning, Sweeny was arraigned on murder charges and bail was set at $150,000. On November 6, Dominique was buried in the Westwood Cemetery near the grave of her mother's old friend, Natalie Wood.

In August of 1983, the Dunne family relived the tragic events that led to Dominique's murder as the case against John Sweeny came to trial. To their horror, the defense was allowed to slander Dominique's character. Sweeny himself testified that his fatal attack was brought on by her refusal to reconcile with him. Judge Burton S. Katz, the presiding judge, did not allow the prosecution to present the testimony from Sweeny's former girlfriend, who had told investigators that Sweeny had beaten her several times, once sending her to the hospital with a collapsed lung. Judge Katz also ruled that Lenny Dunne could not testify that her daughter came to her, a few months prior to her death, beaten and terrified of Sweeny.

On September 21, Sweeny was convicted of voluntary manslaughter and misdemeanor assault. On November 10, he was sentenced to the maximum term of six and a half years in prison. He was released after serving only three years on June 21, 1986.

In April of 1984, Dominick Dunne vented his anger with the judicial system in an article for *Vanity Fair* titled "Justice," which included excerpts from his personal journal of the court proceedings. That same year, he completed the novel he had begun before his daughter's murder. *The Two Mrs. Grenvilles,* the fictionalized account of the infamous Woodward scandal, became a national best-seller, and later a television miniseries. In recent years, Dominick has authored several best-selling society-based novels, including *People Like Us* and *An Inconvenient Woman.* Collections of his articles written for *Vanity Fair* have been published under the titles *Fatal Charms* and *Mansions of Limbo.* A crusader for the victim's rights movement, Dominick is actively involved with the National Victim Center and Parents of Murdered Children.

HEATHER O'ROURKE

Six years after the death of Dominique Dunne, another *Poltergeist* star would suffer a painful, unnecessary death.

In 1981, Heather O'Rourke was discovered by producer and director Steven Spielberg while eating lunch in the MGM commissary. Spielberg, impressed by her striking looks and charming personality, asked her to audition for a role in his upcoming project *Poltergeist*. Heather landed the role over a hundred other young girls, including young Drew Barrymore.

With long platinum blonde hair, expressive blue eyes, and an angelic face, Heather played the key role of the family's youngest child Carol Ann, five, who could communicate with the ghosts that haunted her home through the family television sets. She eerily delivered the film's catch phrase "They're heeere!," which later became the focal point of the movie's marketing campaign.

Heather soon became a familiar face on network television, appearing on such shows as "Webster" and "Still the Beaver," and regularly on the ABC sitcom "Happy Days" from 1982 to 1983. In that series she portrayed the daughter of a divorcee (Linda Purl) who was the love interest for the show's lead character Fonzie (Henry Winkler). She also appeared in the television movies *Masserati and the Brain* (1982) and *Surviving* (1985).

With the money she earned, Heather's family was able to move from a mobile home to a modest house in Big Bear, California, 120 miles east of L.A. Her parents, Michael, a construction worker, and Kathleen, had divorced in 1981. Three years later, Kathleen married Jim Peele, a truck driver whom Heather grew very fond of.

The success of *Poltergeist* naturally spawned a sequel, which was released in 1986. In *Poltergeist 2,* all of the original cast members (except Dominique Dunne) returned once again to fight the sinister creatures from the other world that had followed them to their new home. In the film, Carol Ann tells her grandmother (Geraldine Fitzgerald) that she "don't want to grow up much." Sadly, no one realized how prophetic this line was. Success, however, did not follow the moviemakers. The film opened to mixed reviews and lukewarm audience reception.

All was well in Heather's home until a series of suspicious events began to unfold in early 1987. In January, Heather began to exhibit flu-like symptoms and swollen feet. After being examined by doctors at the Kaiser Foundation, Heather was diagnosed as having a parasitic infection and treated with medication. Still concerned about a possible recurrence, her family moved from their mountain home, where they were informed that parasites were more common, to a Lakeside, California apartment complex. Also, as a precaution, before the filming of *Poltergeist 3* was to begin, Heather's mother took her back to Kaiser for a follow-up. According to Kathleen, after a series of tests, Heather was diagnosed with Crohn's disease, a bowel inflammation, and was treated with cortisone and sulfa.

From April through June of 1987, Heather filmed the third installment of *Poltergeist*, which starred Tom Skerritt, Nancy Allen, and Lara Flynn Boyle. In this episode, her character, Carol Ann Freeling, moves to Chicago to live with her aunt and uncle to attend a school for gifted children with emotional problems. Once again, a sinister force follows and kidnaps her.

Healthwise, Heather seemed to be doing well and enjoyed the summer by traveling with her family on an extended two-month vacation. But on January 31, 1988, Heather woke up vomiting. Her mother, thinking that she had the flu, was not overly concerned until the following morning when she saw that Heather was having difficulty breathing. As Kathleen prepared to take her to the doctor, Heather collapsed on the floor. When an ambulance arrived Heather was in septic shock but was still conscious. During the

THIRTEEN-YEAR-OLD HEATHER O'ROURKE SUFFERED A PAINFUL DEATH IN FEBRUARY OF 1988. *RALPH DOMINGUEZ/GLOBE PHOTOS*

ambulance ride to American Medical International Hospital in El Cajon, Heather suffered cardiac arrest. She was resuscitated at the hospital and then flown by helicopter to Children's Hospital and Health Center in San Diego, where she was listed in critical condition with possible brain damage.

Doctors at Children's Hospital performed an exploratory operation on her abdomen and discovered what they had suspected since her arrival—an obstructed bowel. They corrected the situation, but it was too late. At 2:43 p.m., Heather was pronounced dead. The cause of death was intestinal stenosis, a severe bowel obstruction, the propensity for which Heather had been born with. The obstruction caused an infection that brought on septic shock. The shock, in turn, induced full cardiac and pulmonary arrest.

Four months later, *Poltergeist 3* was released to universally negative reviews and generated a dismal $14 million at the box office. A few days before the film's release, Heather's mother filed a wrongful death suit against the Kaiser Foundation and Southern California Permanente Medical Group for misdiagnosing her daughter's illness.

RUSTY HAMER

On January 20, 1990, the *Los Angeles Times* reported the suicide death of Rusty Hamer. Audiences in the fifties and sixties had watched Rusty grow up on one of the most successful television series of all time. By the time of his death at age forty-two, Rusty had become a depressed, bitter person who floundered from one low-paying job to the next. Finally giving into his interminable depression, Rusty died of a self-inflicted gunshot wound at his home in De Ridder, Louisiana.

The real-life son of a shirt salesman, Rusty had appeared in several Abbott and Costello films before being selected by Danny Thomas to play his son during the open auditions for his show "Make Room for Daddy."

"Make Room for Daddy" was a show that came about by accident. In 1953, ABC began to form a television network and desperately wanted Ray Bolger to do a weekly variety show for them. The William Morris Agency, which represented Bolger, would agree to the deal only if the network would also do a show for Thomas. ABC reluctantly agreed, figuring that the

After years working as a laborer, messenger, and housepainter, Rusty Hamer (*upper right*) committed suicide in 1991. *GLOBE PHOTOS*

Thomas show would probably fail and that their losses would be minimal. As things turned out, "Make Room for Daddy" lasted eleven years, while the Ray Bolger show lasted only two seasons.

The concept of the show evolved from Danny's hectic schedule. He traveled so frequently that his children referred to him as Uncle Daddy.

The series, which made its debut in the fall of 1953, showed the trials and tribulations of nightclub entertainer Danny Williams, a sometimes loud but ultimately softhearted family man who was constantly upstaged by his precocious children: six-year-old Rusty (Rusty Hamer) and eleven-year-old Terry (Sherry Jackson). After three years, the show was switched from ABC to CBS, where it was reincarnated as "The Danny Thomas Show" and remained on the schedule until September of 1965.

Danny Thomas enjoyed working with both Rusty and Sherry. Between shots, Danny and Rusty could be found outside tossing a football or basketball. Early in the series, Rusty's own father died and Danny did all he could to comfort the boy. Danny later recalled, "One day, he came up, threw his arms around me, and said weepingly, 'You're the only Daddy I have now.'"

After the series ended its eleven-year run, Rusty transferred from a film-lot school to a public one, an adjustment that proved difficult for the seventeen-year-old. Thomas described him as a "fish out of water."

In 1970, the series was again reborn in the form of "Make Room for Granddaddy." Most of the original cast, including Rusty, who was then twenty-three, returned for the show. Despite guest appearances by Frank Sinatra; Milton Berle; Sammy Davis, Jr.; and Diana Ross, the series only lasted one season. Audiences complained that Danny and his TV wife Marjorie Lord looked too young to be grandparents. Their appearance was not the only aspect that hurt the show; part of the difficulty lay with Rusty. According to Danny, "I had always said Rusty was the best boy actor I'd ever worked with, but in "Make Room for Granddaddy" he was an adult and much of the youthful ebullience was gone."

After the series ended, Rusty enjoyed little success for the rest of his life. He worked briefly for a Los Angeles messenger service. After moving to Louisiana, Rusty wandered through a series of jobs, including newspaper delivery, housepainting, and occasional restaurant work.

Rusty's brother John discovered his body in the trailer where he lived near DeRidder, about forty miles north of Lake Charles in southwestern Louisiana. The cause of death was a shot to the head from a .357 revolver.

According to Danny Thomas, "It was one of the saddest days of my life when I read that in the newspapers. He had been my surrogate son, and I *had* loved him the way I loved my own Tony."

Rebecca Schaeffer

Rebecca Schaeffer seemed to have it all. A well-liked young actress, with looks and talent, in 1989 Rebecca was only just beginning what appeared to be a promising career. On the morning of July 18, 1989, Rebecca's life came to a violent end when she opened her front door and stood face-to-face with Robert John Bardo.

Born and raised in Portland, Oregon, Rebecca was the only child of a psychologist and writer couple, Benson and Dana Schaeffer. By the time she had reached her teens, Rebecca had received so many compliments about her looks that she decided to apply for a modeling job with a local agency. Nanette Troutman, owner of the first talent agency that interviewed Rebecca, said later, "I took one look and fell in love with her. She had a fresh, charismatic way about her and was very gorgeous, with big brown eyes, dimples, and a beautiful smile."

Rebecca worked as a model for a year in Portland before deciding, at age sixteen, to move to New York for a modeling career in the Big Apple. She

CHILDREN
OF
BABYLON

On July 18, 1989, twenty-two-year-old Rebecca Schaeffer answered her doorbell and came face-to-face with her biggest fan—and her killer. *Ralph Dominguez/Globe Photos*

found many assignments, made many friends, and attended many parties before deciding that modeling was boring and that her future career path was as an actress.

But there are many aspiring actresses in New York and all too few acting assignments to satisfy all who apply. Money became scarce and she fell behind in her rent payments. "I lost my bank card, and then they took my phone out," she later recalled. "I had no money and I was out looking for a waitress job and a cheaper apartment." But in true Hollywood style, Rebecca would eventually get her break. "I came home and found a note on my door. Warner Brothers wanted me to audition and I had to fly to L.A. that night. I had no phone and I didn't even have enough money for a bus. I ran twenty blocks to find my agent."

The audition was for a new show, a sitcom about two sisters living in San Francisco and their experiences with the people who pass through their lives (and apartment) in a seemingly endless succession of comic and romantic interludes. Rebecca won the role of Patti, the younger sister of Sam, played by Pam Dawber of "Mork & Mindy" fame.

"My Sister Sam" ran for three seasons, from 1986 to 1988. Rebecca then moved on to other roles that began to show her promise as an actress. She appeared in the film *Scenes from a Class Struggle in Beverly Hills* and spent time in Italy, where she had a supporting role in a television miniseries about the hijacking of the *Achille Lauro* cruise liner.

In 1989, she was back in her apartment in the Fairfax district of L.A. She was twenty-one and on the threshold of a promising, exciting, and lucrative career. It all came to an end on the morning of July 18, when Rebecca opened her front door and came face-to-face with a nineteen-year-old named Robert John Bardo.

Robert had grown up in a world completely at variance with that of Rebecca. The youngest of seven children, he is the son of a former noncommissioned officer in the Air Force. Robert's mother, a Korean resident of Japan, had met her husband while he was stationed at Yakota Air Base.

From the time he entered his teens, Robert was, as one teacher said later, a "time bomb waiting to explode." At age thirteen, while the family was living in Tucson, Arizona, he stole $140 from his mother's purse and took a bus to Maine, searching for Samantha Smith, the teenager who had gained fame by sending a letter to the then-Soviet president, Mikhail Gorbachev. Picked up by juvenile authorities, he was returned to his home, but not before he had used a pen to stab himself in the wrist.

Back in Tucson, he was a straight-A student but a loner—a letter writer who would send lengthy notes to one of his teachers telling her that he would have to kill her and signing them as Scarface, James Bond, or Dirty

Harry. Before dropping out of school at age fifteen, he was hospitalized twice as a "severely emotionally handicapped youth, but each time his parents maintained that John was perfectly normal and insisted on his release.

During his trial, psychiatrists suggested that while living at home, Robert suffered from physical abuse. After working as a janitor in a local fast-food restaurant, he would come home to immerse himself in the fantasy world of rock music and television. In the fall of 1986, the sixteen-year-old outcast became a fan of a new TV series called "My Sister Sam," and of the woman who played Patti. He would later recall, "She came into my life at the right time. She was bright, beautiful, spunky—I was impressed with her innocence. She was like a goddess for me—an icon. I was an athcist out there. I worshipped her."

He began writing to her, and Rebecca, trying to be nice to an obviously smitten fan, sent him a handwritten postcard in which she said his letter to her was "the nicest, most real" she had received. She drew a peace symbol and heart on the card and signed it "Love, Rebecca."

After receiving the letter, Robert wrote in his diary, "When I think about her I want to become famous and impress her." With these words, the sixteen-year-old began a dark passage of love and hate for a woman who was probably unaware of his existence up until the final moments of her life.

In June of 1987, Robert traveled to the studios in Burbank where the TV series was being filmed. At the gate, a polite but firm security guard stopped Robert, who was carrying a five-foot-tall teddy bear, a huge bouquet of flowers, and a letter for Rebecca. Incensed by the rebuff, Robert returned one month later. This time he was angry and carried a knife "because I thought she was turning arrogant." Turned away again, he returned to Tucson. His attention turned away temporarily from the young actress until he saw her in a film clip from the comedy *Scenes from a Class Struggle in Beverly Hills*. In the scene, Rebecca appeared in bed with an actor and, to an enraged Robert, the sweet innocent girl he had loved had now become just "another Hollywood whore."

Shortly after, Robert read how Arthur Jackson, a stalker (and attacker) of actress Theresa Saldana, had obtained her address through a private detective agency. Robert retained the services of an agency in Los Angeles and got his older brother, Edward, to purchase a gun in Tucson. (State law in Arizona requires that a person must be twenty-one-years or older in order to purchase a weapon.)

On July 17, 1989, ten days after his brother had given him the gun, Robert boarded an overnight bus terminating at Union Station in L.A. From there he took a local bus to the Fairfax district and found the apartment building on North Sweetzer Avenue, where Rebecca lived.

Early on the following morning, Robert rang the doorbell at the entrance to her apartment, handed her a note, mumbled something under his breath, and then quickly walked away. After his initial brief meeting with Rebecca, he walked a few blocks from her apartment house to a diner, where he ordered what would have struck most observers as a rather odd breakfast combination—onion rings and cheesecake. He also called his older sister in Tennessee, who, upon learning where he was, asked him to leave immediately and to come visit her at her home.

After hanging up, Robert thought for a few minutes and then walked into the diner's men's room, where he removed a .357 magnum from a red-and-white plastic grocery bag. He loaded the weapon and placed the gun back in its bag. He then left the diner and walked back to North Sweetzer Avenue.

"It was close to 10:15 when Rebecca Schaeffer, who had just gotten off the phone, heard her buzzer sound again. Because her intercom was not functioning, she left her apartment and came down to the entrance to personally greet her visitor. She opened the security door and began to scream as the youth pulled the weapon from his bag, pointed it at her chest, and pulled the trigger. The hollow-tipped cartridge exploded as it hit her body.

As the sandal-clad Robert turned and jogged a bit clumsily away from the apartment, Rebecca fell back in the doorway. Her eyes were open, glazing over as her life seeped away in the bright morning sunshine. She was pronounced dead thirty minutes later at Cedars-Sinai Medical Center.

The tragedy of Rebecca's death would lead to an eventual change in California law, which would limit access to drivers license records. Robert had obtained Rebecca's address through the simple expedient of hiring a private detective (for a fee of $300) to obtain her address from the Department of Motor Vehicles.

At his trial two years later, Robert's defense counsel used as his defense that the youth, the victim of an abused, neglected childhood was too mentally ill to premeditate murder. The judge rejected the defense argument and on October 29, 1991, Robert John Bardo was found guilty of first-degree murder and the special circumstance of lying in wait, a conviction that carries a mandatory life sentence without parole.

As he was led away from the courtroom, Rebecca's mother, Dana, leaned against the railing and said to the convicted youth, "Have a nice life. Have a good time in jail." To onlookers she said, "Rebecca is never going to come back. Given that, I'm satisfied that justice is going to be served." With that, she burst into tears. She was led away, still weeping as the door leading to the waiting cell slammed behind Bardo.

PART VII

FROM HERE TO OBSCURITY

When the fledgling Fox television network launched "Beverly Hills 90210" during the fall of 1990, no one had any idea of the commotion that would result. The show, which initially languished in the ratings, remained on the schedule for the simple reason that Fox had nothing to replace it with. As the show continued to air, the audience began to grow, and grow, and grow. After two seasons, the show's popularity with teenage girls catapulted its stars Jason Priestley, Shannon Doherty, and Luke Perry into the realm of the teen idol, a status that to them had very frightening implications. Jason Priestley expressed his concerns to *Interview* in 1992:

> It's like a nightmare. It's turning into a runaway train, and there's nothing that can stop it. What worries me with all this merchandising stuff, all these dolls and paperweights and paper clips and pencil tops, is that that will become the perception of me. And the ramifications of that

LUKE PERRY (*RIGHT*) IS AMAZED OVER THE SUCCESS OF "90210," A SHOW THAT HAS TRANSFORMED HIM AND HIS CO-STARS JASON PRIESTLEY AND SHANNON DOHERTY INTO TEEN IDOLS. SAYS PERRY, "I AIN'T THAT F___ KING SENSITIVE." *ALAN HUNTER/GLOBE PHOTOS*

are absolutely terrifying. All you have to do is look at who it's happened to before and see what's happening to their careers now.

The roster of those who once wore the crown of Teen Idol include Sandra Dee, Bobby Sherman, Davey Jones, Donny Osmond, David Cassidy, Shaun Cassidy, Barry Williams, Jason Bateman, Justine Bateman, River Phoenix, and Kirk Cameron. Over the years, many idols have come and gone, while others have struggled to make their comeback or simply just hold on.

David Cassidy, who spent years trying to shed his squeaky clean

AFTER "90210" BECAME A HIT, JASON PRIESTLEY (*LEFT*), SEEN HERE WITH CHARLIE SHEEN, BEGAN DEMANDING THAT THE SET BE CLEARED WHILE HE WAS WORKING AND REFUSED TO DO INTERVIEWS WITH OTHER CAST MEMBERS.
MICHAEL FERGUSON/GLOBE PHOTOS

FROM HERE TO OBSCURITY

"Partridge" past, knows the feeling: "When I thought of teen idols, I thought of all those kids—those pretty-faced no-talents. I didn't want to be that! I knew as soon as it started to happen to me the credibility was gone and it scared the hell out of me."

It scares the hell out of Luke Perry, too. "I ain't no f __ kin' idol," he has said. Not so, according to the millions of young fans who tune in each week to see bad boy Dylan McKay strut around the halls of West Beverly High in tight jeans. Luke is one of several young actors whose manner and dress have been taken from the James Dean school of style. But, unlike Dean, the question of his acting talent has yet to be proved.

Luke began his acting career straight out of high school, when he left home in Ohio and moved to L.A. After two years of continual rejections, Luke moved to New York, where he found sporadic work on commercials and two soap operas.

After several years, Perry returned to L.A. and supported himself with an odd assortment of jobs, which included laying asphalt and waiting tables. In 1988, Luke made his feature film debut as an obnoxious jerk in *Terminal Bliss,* a movie that was not released until 1992. And then came "Beverly Hills 90210," a series that would transform Luke from construction worker to TV star. He was thrilled to get the job. "I couldn't ask for a better situation. I mean, Aaron Spelling produces this show. I couldn't have grown up without him. "Starsky and Hutch," I lived for that sh __ when I was a kid. It's a dream come true for me."

The success was overwhelming. Prepubescent girls were screaming, and at one mall, Luke had to be escorted from a mob scene in a laundry hamper. "They weren't running at me," Luke later said. "They were running at Dylan McKay. They don't know me. They wouldn't want to run at me. I don't sing or nothing." He then added, "I ain't that f __ kin' sensitive."

What happens after the teen idol glow fades. "It'll pass," Luke told *Details* writer Jeff Giles. "If I do some sh __ ty work, you know? Or if I videotape some dude banging a chick in a hotel room—some sh __ like that. Then it'll blow over. Then they won't want to know about me anymore, and I can concentrate on my work." Maybe, but if you ask some former teen idols, as soon as the loyal legions of fans move on to someone else, so does the industry. Johnny Depp and Richard Grieco are just two examples of former TV heartthrobs who have had trouble continuing their careers after leaving the show that made them stars.

Johnny Depp is the quintessential bad boy from Florida. The fourth child of John and Betty Sue Depp, he claims to have lost his virginity at age thirteen and to have experienced with every type of drug by age fourteen. Two years later, he dropped out of high school and joined a rock band. At

As a teenager, Johnny Depp's vices included sex, drugs, and petty crime. As the star of "21 Jump Street," Johnny (seen here with co-star Peter DeLuise) became famous for his large ego, on-set tantrums, and off-set brawling. *JOHN BARRETT/GLOBE PHOTOS*

On the prospect of returning to TV, Johnny (pictured with fiancee Winona Ryder) says, "I'd rather dig a hole through the center of the earth with my tongue." GLOBE PHOTOS

age twenty, he married the sister of one of his friends and moved to Hollywood, where the marriage dissolved shortly thereafter.

Alone and in debt, Johnny decided to try his hand at acting and, with a little help from buddy Nicholas Cage, made his screen debut in *Nightmare on Elm Street*. Other small roles followed on film (such as *Private Resort,* and *Platoon*) and on television (*Slow Burn* and a guest spot on "Lady Blue").

Launched during the spring of 1987, "21 Jump Street" told the story of youthful-looking cops who go undercover in various high schools. Although the role on the show made him a recognizable name, Johnny has little appreciation for the television medium. "To be honest, I took 'Jump Street' because I thought it would only last a year," he later recalled. To everyone's

In 1987, Richard Grieco brazenly declared his own self-admiration: "I've analyzed everyone around, and I just don't see anyone who has what I do." *DONALD SANDERS/GLOBE PHOTOS*

surprise, the show became a hit and Johnny was locked into a contract. With a large ego and a paycheck to match, Johnny began to generate headlines with his many "engagements" (to Sherilyn Fenn, Jennifer Grey, and Winona Ryder), his on-set tantrums, and off-hours brawling (for which he once spent a night in jail).

With all of the trouble they had controlling a rather impetuous star, the producers of "Jump Street" wrote in a storyline involving rogue cop Dennis Booker, portrayed by Richard Grieco. If Johnny's attitude improved, Booker would be killed off; if not, Richard would take over the lead. As it turned out, Richard proved to be so popular with the show's female audience that the producers scrapped plans to kill him and decided to create a spin-off show for him, called "Booker." Richard enjoyed his new-found celebrity and brazenly declared to *TV Guide* in 1987, "I see myself hot for the next seven years at least. I've analyzed everyone around, and I just don't see anyone who has what I do."

After "Jump Street" and "Booker" were cancelled in 1990, Johnny and Richard decided they were ready to accept some of the many film offers coming their way. Johnny, in a desperate attempt to break away from his *Tiger Beat* status, chose quirky assignments in rather small movies (*Cry-Baby, Edward Scissorhands,* and *Arizona Dream*)—roles that did little to impress audiences, critics, or the industry.

Of Richard's film debut, *If Looks Could Kill, People* magazine wrote, "He's competent, although the main impression he leaves is of having spent too long in makeup—he resembles Prince on a mascara binge." In his second film, *Mobsters* (1991), Richard found himself unfavorably compared to former soccer player Costas Mandylor. In 1992, Richard justified his decision to return to television to Arsenio Hall.

> The bottom line is, I mean, feature films for me, um, for the past ten months . . . I'd rather do great work on television than do a piece of crap in features, you know. The bottom line, I'd rather play great character than just do something just for the sake of doing a movie. And I'm still gonna be doing features but I just want to continue to grow as an actor, and the features that I was reading, hint, hint, were real bad and so I decided to go back and do a little television again.

As for Jason, Shannon, and Luke, only time will tell if their current success is a prelude to much grander achievements or rather just their fifteen minutes of fame. In 1992, Luke declared, "I'm not in this for my ego, and not out to become the biggest, baddest dude on the block. But I will get what's coming to me." Of that, there is no doubt.

From Here to Obscurity

277

A TELEVISION VETERAN, SHANNON DOHERTY (PICTURED WITH "OUR HOUSE" CO-STAR CHAD ALLEN) ONCE SAID, "I WORK JUST AS HARD AS ADULTS DO AND EXPECT THE RESPECT I DESERVE."
GARY NULL/GLOBE PHOTOS

On the set of "90210," Shannon has been described as "difficult" and "a spoiled brat." Her mood swings and temper tantrums are becoming the stuff of Hollywood legend.
MICHAEL FERGUSON/GLOBE PHOTOS

CONCLUSION

The saga of children and adolescents who emerge from obscurity to media stardom is a continuing one. Since the days when Shirley Temple sang and danced her way into America's heart, talented youngsters have parlayed their fresh faces and wholesome smiles into successful, albeit brief, performing careers.

On the surface, these youngsters appear to lead enviable lives. While this may be true to a certain extent, there is no doubt that a successful career in Hollywood also involves a fair share of hard work, self-promotion, rejection and work demands which can be difficult for an adult to handle, much less a child. All the while, the clock ticks for these youngsters, for whom the onset of puberty can relegate them to the category of "has-been."

Those who have survived to become power players in the industry usually credit strong family support for helping them through this transition period. According to Jodie Foster, it was her single mother Brandy who provided constant reassurance and thoughtful advice throughout her accomplished career. Says Jodie: "I really am very lucky to have had somebody who was a real person who was there to protect me and who wasn't enamored with the possibility of a flashy career. Because you *do* live vicariously through your children's successes, so much of it was about her really wanting me to be respected and taken seriously."

Unfortunately, many of the child actors discussed in this text did not have such careful nurturing. A majority have come from broken homes and several (including Patty Duke and Lauren Chapin) claim to have been abused by their guardians either physically, sexually or emotionally. Others pin the blame of their unhappy adult lives squarely on relatives whom they perceive as using them as pint-sized money makers or to complete their own unfulfilled aspirations. Jay North, who portrayed *Dennis The Menace*, blames his aunt and uncle for making his life miserable while he worked in an "evil, vile system." Erin Moran, who spent the ages between 13 and 23 portraying Ron Howard's precocious little sister on *Happy Days*, has recently denounced her relatives as "bloodsuckers." Paul Peterson (*The Donna Reed Show*) declares bitterly; "Parents who put their kids in show business are basically pimps. They've sold their children into show biz."

Considering the extraordinary amounts of money that successful child actors can earn for their parents and business associates, the temptation exists to exploit them for personal gain or use them as pawns in financial power plays. In February 1993, after a four year legal struggle, Gary Coleman was awarded a $1.3 million judgement against his parents and a former business manager who were found to have taken excessive fees from his *Diff'rent Strokes* earnings. In 1992, Universal Pictures filed a $190,000 lawsuit against *Problem Child* star Michael Oliver, alleging that he and his mother held the studio hostage during the production of the film's sequel, by demanding a $420,000 salary increase one week before production was to begin. (Rather than halt the $4 million production, the studio grudgingly acquiesced to what it considered "economic duress").

On a much grander scale, former juvenile actor Kit Culkin has burned many bridges in order to advance the career of his son Macaulay. While Twentieth Century Fox was planning the sequel to their tremendously successful *Home Alone*, Kit Culkin used his leverage with the studio to compel them to cast Mack in the lead of *The Good Son*. After quarreling with the movie's original producer and director (both of whom eventually left the project), Kit also demanded that his daughter Quinn play Macaulay's sister in the picture. Although Kit's actions have created a lot of resentment in Hollywood, he insists that his objective is to build a long-term career for his son. "The best thing you can do for Mack is give him the opportunity to be thought of as an actor, not just a cute kid," says Kit.

In most cases, however, it is a lack of any genuine talent which sounds the death knell for most child actors. Former Oscar nominee Linda Blair, *Time* magazine cover girl Molly Ringwald and disco king John Travolta are just a few of the names that were once touted as the "stars of tomorrow." Although these teen idols of the past are still working in the industry, there is a noticeable lack of regard for their "acting" abilities. The fact that many young actors are uneducated and lacking any theatrical training eventually catches up with them. Hence the continuing popularity and staying power of today's hottest stars including Keanu Reeves, Winona Ryder, Moira Kelly and Juliette Lewis remains in doubt. Liam Neeson says of his former lover Julia Roberts, "She should get acting lessons. She has deep feeling, but you can't rely on that forever."

A select few who market themselves from their past (including Charlie Sheen, Emilio Estevez and Demi Moore) continue to receive high salaries and above-the-line credit for efforts, which most often can be described as mediocre. In an industry with a long memory, respect can not be earned by taking roles in witless comedies (*Hot Shots, Loaded Weapon I,* and *Wayne's World*), by posing nude for national magazines, by baring one's soul on syndicated talk shows. However, given the exorbitant costs involved in the making these films, producers find themselves returning to the same tried and tested pool of talent.

Contrary to popular belief, not all child actors will spend their post puberty years hooked on crack or robbing video stores. The truth of the matter is that most former child stars, like old soldiers, simply fade away. In recent years, however, media attention has focused on those former juvenile performers who have come forward to tell their tales of substance abuse, divorces, arrests, suicides, mishandled careers and bitterness. Many have expressed their anger and frustration at an industry they feel *owes* them.

In fairness to these disgruntled performers, there may be a kernel of truth to their anger and disillusionment. When one contrasts the Hollywood film studios of the '40s and '50s with those of today the differences are striking. In earlier days the major studios took an active interest in their hot properties. While their academic education may have been given short shrift, child actors were provided with lessons in diction, acting, dancing and singing to improve their skills in their chosen profession. While the studios undoubtedly had commercial motivations, many of these children *did* learn how to register the emotions that their scripts and directors called for: quite simply, they eventually learned the true craft of acting.

But to dwell on the past is to ignore the realities of the present. While there may have been some advantages to the studio system, the fact remains that stars of the past were never provided with the financial compensation packages offered to today's young stars. One could successfully argue that these actors have the resources to improve their craft, but tend to use them for immediate gratification: cars, clothes and expensive toys.

In the final analysis, the careers of many these child actors have been, or will be determined not by the actions of exterior forces but by their inner resources—in essence, their character.

As we approach the end of the twentieth century, a new generation of young actors are stepping forward to stake their claim as the celebrities of tomorrow. Those who are fortunate enough to be gifted with the talent and temperament to maintain their sense of proportion and relative worth will most likely enjoy the longest runs in their acting careers. Unfortunately it would appear that these enlightened youngsters have been, are, and will continue to be the minority—the rest will continue to be remembered as the Children of Babylon.

BIBLIOGRAPHY

The Bare Facts Video Guide, 2d ed., Craig Hosoda, The Bare Facts, 1992.
Call Me Anna: The Autobiography of Patty Duke, Patty Duke and Kenneth Turan, Bantam, 1987.
The Celebrity Almanac, Ed Lucaire, Prentice-Hall, 1991.
The Complete Directory to Prime Time Network TV Shows, 1946–Present, 5th ed., Tim Brooks and Earle Marsh, Ballantine, 1992.
The Complete Directory to Prime Time TV Stars, 1964–Present, Tim Brooks, Ballantine, 1987.
Coppola, Peter Cowie, Charles Scribner's Sons, 1989.
Debbie, My Life, Debbie Reynolds and David Patrick Columbia, Simon & Schuster, 1988.
The Devil's Candy: The Bonfire of the Vanities *Goes to Hollywood,* Julie Salamon, Houghton Mifflin, 1991.
The Emmys, Thomas O'Neil, Penguin, 1992.
Encyclopedia of Film, James Monaco and the editors of *Baseline,* Perigee, 1991.
Fallen Angels, Kirk Crivello, Citadel Press, 1988.
Fatal Charms and Other Tales of Today, Dominick Dunne, Crown, 1986.
Father Does Know Best, Lauren Chapin with Andrew Collins, Thomas Nelson, 1989.
The Film Encyclopedia, Ephraim Katz, Harper & Row, 1979.
The Hustons, Lawrence Grobel, Avon, 1990.
I'm with the Band: Confessions of a Groupie, Pamela Des Barres, William Morrow, 1987.
Inside Oscar: The Unofficial History of the Academy Awards, Mason Wiley and Damien Bona, Ballantine, 1987.
Johnny Depp, Randi Reisfeld, St. Martin's Press, 1989.
Leonard Maltin's Movie and Video Guide 1993, Leonard Maltin, ed., Signet, 1992.
Little Girl Lost, Drew Barrymore with Todd Gold, Simon & Schuster, 1990.
Lucy: The Real Life of Lucille Ball, Charles Higham, St. Martin's Press, 1986.
Lucy & Desi: The Legendary Love Story of Television's Most Famous Couple, Warren G. Harris, Simon & Schuster, 1991.
Madonna Unauthorized, Christopher Andersen, Dell, 1991.
Make Room for Danny, Danny Thomas with Bill Davidson, G.P. Putnam's Sons, 1991.
Marilyn Beck's Hollywood, Marilyn Beck, Hawthorn, 1973.
Martin Scorsese: A Journey, Mary Pat Kelly, Thunder's Mouth Press, 1991.
Notes on the Making of Apocalypse Now, Eleanor Coppola, Limelight Editions, 1991.
Polanski: A Biography, Barbara Leaming, Simon & Schuster, 1981.
She Was Nice to Mice, Alexandra Elizabeth Sheedy, McGraw-Hill, 1975.

The Sheens: Martin, Charlie, and Emilio Estevez, Lee Riley and David Shumacher, St. Martin's Press, 1989.
That's Hollywood, Peter Van Gelder, Harper Collins, 1990.
Variety *Movie Guide,* Derek Elley, ed., Prentice-Hall, 1992.
Video Movie Guide 1992, Mick Martin and Marsha Porter, Ballantine, 1991.
Yesterday I Saw the Sun, Ally Sheedy, Summit, 1991.